Unreal Engine Pro: Advanced Development Secrets

Mastering Unreal Engine: From Novice to Pro

Kameron Hussain and Frahaan Hussain

Published by Sonar Publishing, 2023.

UNREAL ENGINE PRO: ADVANCED DEVELOPMENT SECRETS

First edition. December 5, 2023.

ISBN: 979-8223749912

Written by Kameron Hussain and Frahaan Hussain.

Table of Contents

Contributing to Open Source Unreal Projects

Networking and Building Professional Relationships

Respecting Diversity and Inclusiveness

Chapter 1: Mastering the Unreal Engine Ecosystem

1.1. Deep Dive into Engine Architecture

IN THIS SECTION, WE will take an in-depth look at the Unreal Engine's architecture. Understanding the engine's architecture is crucial for developers looking to harness its full potential.

Unreal Engine is built upon a modular architecture that comprises various components and systems designed to work together seamlessly. At its core, Unreal Engine utilizes the Entity-Component-System (ECS) architecture, which is a fundamental concept in modern game development.

Components of Unreal Engine's Architecture

1. **Engine Core**: The engine's core provides the foundation for all functionalities. It manages tasks such as rendering, physics simulation, and input handling.
2. **Editor**: Unreal Engine's editor is a critical tool for developers, allowing them to design levels, create assets, and script game logic. It's also extensible through plugins.
3. **Game Framework**: This framework includes classes and systems for managing game states, actors, and gameplay mechanics. It forms the backbone of any Unreal game.
4. **Rendering System**: Unreal Engine boasts a powerful rendering system capable of delivering stunning visuals. It uses modern rendering techniques such as physically-based rendering (PBR) to achieve realistic graphics.
5. **Physics Engine**: The physics engine is responsible for simulating realistic interactions between objects in the

game world. It calculates forces, collisions, and animations.

Entity-Component-System (ECS)

UNREAL ENGINE'S ADOPTION of the ECS architecture is a significant departure from traditional game development approaches. In ECS, the game world is composed of entities, which are essentially containers for components. Each entity can have multiple components attached, and these components define the entity's behavior and properties.

Here's a simplified example of how ECS works in Unreal Engine:

```
// Define a simple entity with components

class MyEntity : public AActor {

UPROPERTY()

UStaticMeshComponent* MeshComponent;

UPROPERTY()

UHealthComponent* Health;

UPROPERTY()

UWeaponComponent* Weapon;

};
```

In the example above, MyEntity is an actor that has various components, including a MeshComponent for rendering, a HealthComponent to manage its health, and a WeaponComponent for combat functionality.

Advantages of ECS

- **Modularity**: ECS promotes a modular approach to game development. Developers can create reusable components that can be easily combined to create complex behaviors.

- **Performance**: ECS can offer significant performance benefits by allowing for efficient memory layout and parallel processing of entities and components.

- **Flexibility**: It provides flexibility in defining and customizing entities and their behaviors. Game designers and developers can iterate quickly.

UNDERSTANDING UNREAL Engine's architecture, especially the ECS paradigm, is a fundamental step towards becoming proficient with the engine. In the following sections, we'll explore more advanced topics within the Unreal Engine ecosystem, building upon this architectural knowledge.

1.2. Navigating Through Advanced Editor Tools

IN THIS SECTION, WE will delve into the advanced editor tools available in Unreal Engine. These tools are essential for creating, designing, and fine-tuning game environments, levels, and assets.

Unreal Editor Overview

UNREAL EDITOR IS A powerful and versatile tool that provides an integrated environment for all aspects of game development. It's divided into several key areas:

1. **Viewport**: The main area where you can view and interact with your game world. You can have multiple viewports for different perspectives.
2. **Content Browser**: This is where you manage and organize your project's assets, including meshes, textures, materials, and more. You can create, import, and edit assets here.
3. **World Outliner**: The World Outliner displays a hierarchical view of all the actors and objects in your level. It allows you to select and manipulate them easily.
4. **Details Panel**: When you select an asset or object in the editor, the Details Panel provides a user-friendly interface for modifying its properties and settings.
5. **Modes Panel**: The Modes Panel contains various editing modes, such as Geometry Editing, Landscape Editing, and Paint. You can switch between these modes to perform specific tasks.

Advanced Editing Tools

Geometry Editing

UNREAL ENGINE OFFERS advanced geometry editing tools for creating and shaping game environments. You can add, subtract, and modify brushes and static meshes to build your levels. Here are some key features:

- **Boolean Operations**: Use Boolean operations like Union, Subtract, and Intersect to combine or cut through geometry seamlessly.

- **Vertex Editing**: Precisely adjust vertices, edges, and faces of brushes and meshes for fine-tuning.

- **Vertex Snapping**: Snap vertices to a grid or other geometry to ensure precise alignment.

Landscape Editing

FOR OUTDOOR ENVIRONMENTS, Unreal Engine's Landscape system is a powerful tool. You can sculpt, paint, and populate terrains with foliage and assets. Key features include:

- **Sculpting Tools**: Use brushes to sculpt the terrain, creating hills, valleys, and other natural features.

- **Layer Painting**: Paint different materials and textures onto the landscape to define various terrain types.

- **Foliage Painting**: Populate your landscape with trees, grass, and other foliage using the Foliage tool.

Blueprint Editor

UNREAL'S VISUAL SCRIPTING system, Blueprints, allows you to create game logic without writing code. The Blueprint Editor is a critical tool for designing complex interactions, AI behaviors, and gameplay mechanics.

- **Node-Based Scripting**: Connect nodes to define logic and behavior. Blueprints support a wide range of nodes, including conditionals, loops, and custom functions.

- **Custom Events**: Define custom events that trigger specific actions in your game.

- **Animation Blueprint**: Create Animation Blueprints to control character animations and blend them seamlessly.

Material Editor

THE MATERIAL EDITOR is where you create and manipulate materials for your game objects. Unreal Engine's materials support complex shading and visual effects. Key features include:

- **Node-Based Material Graph**: Construct materials by connecting nodes that represent various shading operations.
- **Real-Time Preview**: See how your materials look in real-time on 3D models.
- **Material Instances**: Create instances of materials to vary their parameters at runtime.

Unreal Engine's advanced editor tools empower developers and artists to bring their creative visions to life. Mastering these tools is essential for efficiently designing and building immersive game worlds. In the following sections, we will explore further customization and optimization techniques to enhance your Unreal Engine projects.

1.3. Customizing the Unreal Editor for Efficiency

IN THIS SECTION, WE will explore how you can customize the Unreal Editor to streamline your workflow and improve efficiency. Unreal Engine provides a range of customization options, allowing you to tailor the editor to your specific needs.

Personalizing the User Interface

UNREAL ENGINE'S USER interface (UI) is highly customizable, enabling you to arrange and configure panels, windows, and toolbars according to your preferences. Here's how you can personalize the UI:

- **Layouts**: Save and load custom layout configurations. You can have different layouts for level design, blueprint scripting, and asset management.

- **Docking and Floating**: Easily drag and drop panels to dock or float them as separate windows. This flexibility allows you to create a workspace that suits your workflow.

- **Toolbars**: Customize toolbars by adding, removing, or rearranging buttons for frequently used commands.

Hotkeys and Key Bindings

EFFICIENT NAVIGATION and quick access to functions are crucial for productivity. Unreal Engine lets you create and modify key bindings for various actions and commands. Here's how you can make the most of this feature:

- **Custom Key Bindings**: Assign specific key combinations to actions you use frequently. For example, you can set a custom key binding to toggle grid snapping.

- **Context-Sensitive Actions**: Unreal Engine's context-sensitive actions adapt to the selected tool or mode, allowing you to have different key bindings based on the context.

Editor Preferences

UNREAL ENGINE OFFERS a plethora of editor preferences that you can tweak to match your workflow. These preferences cover various aspects of the editor, from display settings to content creation. Some areas you can customize include:

- **Display Settings**: Adjust visual settings such as grid size, viewport rendering quality, and visual effects to optimize your working environment.
- **Content Creation**: Customize settings related to asset creation, import/export options, and asset browser behavior.
- **Auto-Save and Backup**: Configure auto-save intervals and backup settings to prevent data loss and facilitate version control.

Custom Editor Tools and Plugins

ONE OF THE STRENGTHS of Unreal Engine is its extensibility. You can create custom editor tools and plugins to automate repetitive tasks or add new functionalities to the editor. Here's how you can harness this capability:

- **Blueprint Editor Scripts**: Use Blueprints to create custom editor scripts that automate actions or streamline complex processes. For instance, you can create a script to automatically populate a level with assets.
- **Python Scripts**: Unreal Engine supports Python scripting, allowing you to create custom tools and

automate editor tasks. Python is particularly useful for batch operations.

- **Plugin Development**: For more advanced customizations, consider developing plugins. Plugins can add new features, tools, and asset types to the editor.

Collaborative Workflows

IF YOU'RE WORKING IN a team, customization can also enhance collaboration:

- **Source Control Integration**: Integrate your preferred source control system into the editor to manage versioning and collaborative development effectively.

- **Project Sharing**: Configure project settings and collaborate on projects by managing access permissions and shared resources.

Customizing the Unreal Editor not only boosts your efficiency but also adapts the engine to your unique development needs. Whether you're a level designer, programmer, or artist, tailoring the editor to your workflow can significantly improve your productivity and creativity. In the subsequent sections, we will dive deeper into Unreal Engine's advanced features and techniques.

1.4. Exploring the Marketplace and Community Resources

IN THIS SECTION, WE will delve into the Unreal Engine Marketplace and the wealth of community resources available to Unreal Engine developers. These resources can be invaluable in enhancing your projects, saving time, and learning from the experiences of others.

Unreal Engine Marketplace

THE UNREAL ENGINE MARKETPLACE is a curated store where developers can find a wide range of assets, tools, and plugins created by both Epic Games and third-party developers. Here's what you can discover on the Marketplace:

- **3D Assets**: Browse and purchase 3D models, characters, environments, and props to use in your game projects.

- **Materials and Textures**: Access high-quality materials, textures, and shaders to enhance the visual fidelity of your games.

- **Blueprints and Plugins**: Discover pre-made Blueprints and plugins that can add new gameplay mechanics, systems, or functionality to your projects.

- **Audio Assets**: Find music, sound effects, and audio middleware solutions to enrich your game's audio experience.

- **Animations**: Access animation packs, motion capture data, and character animations to bring your characters and creatures to life.

- **Environments**: Explore complete environments and level kits that can serve as the foundation for your game worlds.

- **Visual Effects**: Get access to particle systems, visual effects, and post-processing materials to add cinematic quality to your games.

Purchasing assets from the Marketplace can save you significant development time and effort, allowing you to focus on other critical aspects of your project.

Community Resources

UNREAL ENGINE BOASTS a vibrant and supportive community of developers, artists, and enthusiasts. Leveraging community resources can be incredibly beneficial:

- **Forums and Discussion Boards**: Unreal Engine's official forums and other online communities are excellent places to seek advice, share your knowledge, and collaborate with others.

- **Tutorials and Documentation**: You'll find a wealth of tutorials, guides, and documentation created by the community that covers a wide range of topics, from beginner to advanced.

- **Sample Projects**: Many community members share sample projects and templates, providing valuable insights into various game mechanics and techniques.

- **Plugins and Tools**: Beyond the Marketplace, the community often develops free plugins and tools that can extend the capabilities of Unreal Engine.

- **Events and Meetups**: Look for local or online Unreal Engine meetups and events to network with fellow developers and stay up-to-date with industry trends.

- **GitHub and Open Source Projects**: Some developers open-source their Unreal Engine projects on platforms like GitHub, enabling collaboration and learning from real-world code.

Contributing to the Community

AS YOU BENEFIT FROM community resources, consider giving back. Share your knowledge, contribute to forums, or release your own assets, tools, or tutorials. Engaging with the community can foster collaboration, expand your network, and enhance your skills.

Staying Informed

UNREAL ENGINE'S ECOSYSTEM is continually evolving. Stay informed about updates, new assets, and community developments by regularly checking official sources, forums, and community websites. Being aware of the latest resources can keep your projects on the cutting edge of Unreal Engine technology.

In the subsequent chapters of this book, we will continue to explore advanced topics and techniques, building upon the foundation of knowledge you've gained in this section.

1.5. Integrating External Tools and Software

IN THIS SECTION, WE will discuss the importance of integrating external tools and software into your Unreal Engine workflow. Unreal Engine's extensibility allows you to seamlessly incorporate third-party tools and software to enhance your development process and achieve specific goals.

Benefits of Integration

INTEGRATING EXTERNAL tools and software can provide several advantages:

- **Specialized Tools**: External tools often specialize in certain tasks, such as 3D modeling, audio editing, or code version control. By integrating them, you can leverage their capabilities without leaving the Unreal Engine environment.

- **Workflow Efficiency**: Streamline your workflow by reducing the need to switch between different applications. This can save time and reduce the risk of errors.

- **Customization**: Tailor your development pipeline to your specific needs. Choose the best tools for each aspect of your project.

Common Integrations

3D Modeling and Animation Software

EXTERNAL SOFTWARE LIKE Autodesk Maya, Blender, or Houdini is commonly used for 3D modeling and animation. Unreal Engine supports various file formats, making it easy to import assets created in these tools. You can also set up round-trip workflows to update assets seamlessly.

// Example of importing a 3D model

```
UStaticMesh* MyMesh = LoadObject<UStaticMesh>(nullptr, TEXT("/Game/Path/To/MyModel.MyModel"));
```

Audio Editing Software

FOR AUDIO EDITING AND sound design, software like Adobe Audition or Pro Tools can be integrated. Unreal Engine supports various audio formats, and you can manage audio assets directly within the engine.

```
// Example of loading and playing a sound cue

USoundCue* MySoundCue = LoadObject<USoundCue>(nullptr, TEXT("/Game/Path/To/MySoundCue.MySoundCue"));

UGameplayStatics::PlaySound2D(this, MySoundCue);
```

Version Control Systems

VERSION CONTROL SYSTEMS like Git, Perforce, or SVN are essential for collaborative development. Unreal Engine has built-in support for version control, allowing you to check in and manage project assets directly from the editor.

Middleware and Plugins

YOU CAN INTEGRATE MIDDLEWARE and plugins for specific functionalities. For example, if you need advanced AI, you can integrate third-party AI frameworks. Unreal Engine's plugin system enables you to extend the engine's capabilities with custom functionality.

Best Practices

WHEN INTEGRATING EXTERNAL tools and software, consider these best practices:

- **Documentation**: Ensure that your team is well-documented on how to use external tools and their integration with Unreal Engine.

- **Version Compatibility**: Keep software versions in check to avoid compatibility issues. Unreal Engine periodically updates its integration with popular software, so stay up to date.

- **Asset Management**: Maintain a structured asset management system to keep track of imported and exported assets.

- **Pipeline Automation**: Whenever possible, automate the import and export processes to minimize manual work.

- **Backup and Version Control**: Implement robust backup and version control practices to safeguard your project's integrity.

- **Performance Considerations**: Be mindful of the performance impact of integrating third-party tools. Some processes may be resource-intensive.

Conclusion

INTEGRATING EXTERNAL tools and software into your Unreal Engine workflow can significantly enhance your project's efficiency and capabilities. By carefully selecting and configuring these tools, you can create a development pipeline that suits your project's specific needs. In the subsequent chapters, we will continue to explore advanced Unreal Engine topics to further empower your game development endeavors.

Chapter 2: Expert-Level Blueprint Scripting

2.1. Advanced Blueprint Concepts and Techniques

IN THIS SECTION, WE will delve into advanced Blueprint scripting concepts and techniques that will enable you to create sophisticated gameplay mechanics and systems within Unreal Engine. Blueprints offer a powerful visual scripting language that can be used to implement complex logic without writing traditional code.

Event Dispatchers

EVENT DISPATCHERS ARE a powerful way to create custom events in Blueprints. They allow you to define and broadcast your own events, which other Blueprints can then listen to and respond to. This is incredibly useful for decoupling different parts of your game logic and creating modular systems.

Here's an example of how you can use Event Dispatchers:

```
// Creating a custom event dispatcher

UPROPERTY(BlueprintAssignable, Category = "Game Events")

FMyCustomEventSignature OnMyCustomEvent;

UFUNCTION(BlueprintCallable, Category = "Game Events")

void MyFunctionThatTriggersEvent()

{
```

```
// Trigger the custom event

OnMyCustomEvent.Broadcast();

}
```

In this example, we define an event dispatcher called OnMyCustomEvent. We can then call Broadcast on this dispatcher to notify any Blueprint that has bound to it.

Interfaces

BLUEPRINT INTERFACES allow you to define a set of functions that Blueprint classes can implement. This is useful for creating common behavior that multiple actors or components should share. By implementing an interface, you ensure that certain functions are available and can be called.

Here's how you can create and use a Blueprint Interface:

```
// Creating a Blueprint Interface

UINTERFACE(BlueprintType)

class UMyInterface : public UInterface

{

GENERATED_BODY()

};

class MYGAME_API IMyInterface

{

GENERATED_BODY()
```

```
public:

// Declare functions that implementing Blueprints should implement

UFUNCTION(BlueprintNativeEvent, BlueprintCallable, Category = "My Interface")

void MyFunction();

};
```

Now, any Blueprint class that implements IMyInterface will be required to provide an implementation for the MyFunction function.

Delegates and Multicast Delegates

DELEGATES AND MULTICAST Delegates in Blueprints allow you to bind functions to events dynamically. Delegates can be used for creating callbacks or responding to events in a more flexible manner.

Here's a simple example of how you can use Delegates:

```
DECLARE_DYNAMIC_MULTICAST_DELEGATE(FMyDelegate)

UCLASS()

class MYGAME_API AMyActor : public AActor

{

GENERATED_BODY()

public:

// Declare a multicast delegate
```

```
UPROPERTY(BlueprintAssignable, Category = "My Delegates")
FMyDelegate OnMyEvent;
};
```

In this example, we declare a multicast delegate OnMyEvent. We can then bind functions to this delegate, and when the event is triggered, all bound functions will be called.

Custom Structures and Enums

BLUEPRINTS SUPPORT custom structures and enums, allowing you to define your own data types and constants. This can help you organize and manage data within your Blueprints more effectively.

```
// Defining a custom structure
USTRUCT(BlueprintType)
struct FMyStructure
{
GENERATED_BODY()
UPROPERTY(BlueprintReadWrite, Category = "My Structure")
float MyFloatProperty;
UPROPERTY(BlueprintReadWrite, Category = "My Structure")
int32 MyIntProperty;
};
```

Custom structures can be used as variables, function inputs, or function outputs in Blueprints, providing a convenient way to package data.

Blueprint Native Events

BLUEPRINT NATIVE EVENTS are functions defined in a Blueprint class that can be overridden by child Blueprints. This is particularly useful for creating template classes with some default behavior that can be customized by derived Blueprints.

```
UCLASS(Blueprintable)

class MYGAME_API AMyBaseActor : public AActor

{

GENERATED_BODY()

public:

// Blueprint Native Event

UFUNCTION(BlueprintNativeEvent, BlueprintCallable, Category = "My Base Actor")

void MyEvent();

};
```

Derived Blueprints can choose to implement or override the MyEvent function as needed, allowing for flexible customization of behavior.

Conclusion

ADVANCED BLUEPRINT scripting concepts and techniques provide the means to create complex and modular game systems entirely within Unreal Engine's visual scripting environment. By mastering these concepts, you can take full advantage of the flexibility and power that Blueprints offer in game development. In the upcoming sections of this chapter, we will explore more advanced topics and practical examples to further enhance your Blueprint scripting skills.

2.2. Scripting Complex Game Mechanics

IN THIS SECTION, WE will explore the process of scripting complex game mechanics using Unreal Engine's Blueprint visual scripting system. Complex game mechanics often involve intricate interactions between various game elements, and Blueprint provides a versatile and efficient way to implement these mechanics.

Planning and Design

BEFORE DIVING INTO scripting complex game mechanics, it's crucial to plan and design your mechanics thoroughly. Define the desired behavior, interactions, and outcomes. Create flowcharts or diagrams to visualize the logic and connections between different elements.

For example, if you're working on a complex AI behavior, plan out the states, transitions, and conditions that dictate the AI's actions. Having a clear design in mind will make the scripting process more straightforward and organized.

State Machines

STATE MACHINES ARE a powerful tool for scripting complex behaviors, especially for characters, NPCs, and AI. Unreal Engine's Blueprint system includes a built-in State Machine framework that allows you to define states, transitions, and actions.

Here's a simplified example of implementing a character's state machine:

```
// Define custom states as enumerations

UENUM(BlueprintType)

enum class ECharacterState : uint8

{

Idle,

Walking,

Running,

Jumping,

// Add more states as needed

};

UCLASS()

class MYGAME_API AMyCharacter : public ACharacter

{

GENERATED_BODY()

public:
```

```
UPROPERTY(EditAnywhere, BlueprintReadWrite)

ECharacterState CurrentState;

// Functions to handle state transitions and actions

UFUNCTION(BlueprintCallable, Category = "Character State")

void SetCharacterState(ECharacterState NewState);

UFUNCTION(BlueprintCallable, Category = "Character Actions")

void PerformActionBasedOnState();

};
```

In this example, we define an enumeration ECharacterState to represent different character states. The AMyCharacter class has a CurrentState variable and functions to transition between states and perform actions based on the current state.

Input Handling

COMPLEX GAME MECHANICS often require responsive input handling. Unreal Engine's input system can be used in Blueprints to detect and respond to player input effectively.

For example, if you're creating a character with different movement modes (walk, run, crouch), you can use Blueprint functions like Input Key to detect input and change the character's behavior accordingly.

Custom Events and Functions

COMPLEX GAME MECHANICS often involve intricate sequences of actions and events. Use custom Blueprint events and functions to encapsulate and organize these sequences.

Here's an example of using custom events to script a puzzle mechanic:

```
UCLASS()

class MYGAME_API APuzzle : public AActor

{

GENERATED_BODY()

public:

UFUNCTION(BlueprintCallable, Category = "Puzzle")

void StartPuzzle();

UFUNCTION(BlueprintCallable, Category = "Puzzle")

void CompletePuzzle();

UFUNCTION(BlueprintCallable, Category = "Puzzle")

void ResetPuzzle();

UFUNCTION(BlueprintImplementableEvent, Category = "Puzzle")

void OnPuzzleStarted();

UFUNCTION(BlueprintImplementableEvent, Category = "Puzzle")
```

```
void OnPuzzleCompleted();

};
```

In this example, the APuzzle class has functions for starting, completing, and resetting the puzzle. It also defines Blueprint implementable events that can be customized in derived Blueprints to provide specific puzzle behaviors.

Debugging and Testing

COMPLEX GAME MECHANICS can be challenging to get right on the first try. Unreal Engine provides robust debugging tools for Blueprints, including breakpoints, watch windows, and execution flow visualization. Take advantage of these tools to diagnose and resolve issues in your scripts.

Additionally, thorough playtesting is crucial to ensure that your complex mechanics work as intended and provide an enjoyable player experience.

Conclusion

SCRIPTING COMPLEX GAME mechanics in Unreal Engine using Blueprints requires careful planning, design, and organization. State machines, input handling, custom events, and functions are essential tools for implementing intricate gameplay systems. Debugging and testing play a critical role in fine-tuning and ensuring the reliability of your mechanics. As you gain experience and familiarity with Blueprint scripting, you'll become more proficient in creating complex and engaging gameplay experiences.

2.3. Performance Optimization in Blueprints

IN THIS SECTION, WE will focus on performance optimization techniques when working with Blueprints in Unreal Engine. While Blueprints offer a powerful and accessible way to create gameplay logic, they can become resource-intensive if not optimized properly. Optimizing your Blueprints is crucial to ensure your game runs smoothly and efficiently.

Profile and Measure

BEFORE DIVING INTO optimization, it's essential to identify performance bottlenecks in your Blueprints. Unreal Engine provides a variety of profiling tools to help you pinpoint areas that need improvement. The key tools include:

- **Stat Commands**: Unreal Engine provides various console commands (e.g., stat fps, stat unit) that display real-time statistics, such as frame rate, rendering times, and more. Use these commands to monitor performance during gameplay.

- **Unreal Insights**: Unreal Insights is a comprehensive profiling tool that provides detailed insights into the performance of your game. It allows you to visualize CPU, GPU, and memory usage, making it easier to identify bottlenecks.

- **Print and Log Messages**: Use Print String or UE_LOG to output messages in the editor or log files. This can help you track the flow of your Blueprint scripts and identify areas where performance issues might occur.

Reduce Complexity

ONE OF THE PRIMARY ways to optimize Blueprints is by reducing their complexity. Here are some strategies:

- **Modularization**: Break down large Blueprints into smaller, more manageable components. This not only improves organization but also makes it easier to optimize individual parts.

- **Loop Optimization**: Be cautious when using loops in Blueprints, especially nested loops. Loops can quickly become performance bottlenecks. Consider whether the same functionality can be achieved with fewer iterations.

- **Conditional Checks**: Minimize the number of expensive conditional checks in your Blueprints. Use early exits (e.g., "Return" nodes) to skip unnecessary checks when conditions are not met.

Use Native Code When Necessary

WHILE BLUEPRINTS ARE a powerful tool, there are cases where implementing critical gameplay logic in native C++ code can significantly improve performance. Unreal Engine allows you to create custom C++ classes and seamlessly integrate them with your Blueprints. Here are some scenarios where native code can be beneficial:

- **Complex AI Behavior**: If your game features highly complex AI with intricate decision-making processes, consider implementing the AI logic in C++ to take advantage of low-level optimizations.

- **Physics and Collision**: For physics-heavy games or complex collision handling, native code can offer better performance.

- **Batch Processing**: When dealing with large datasets or batch processing tasks, C++ can be more efficient than Blueprints.

Reduce Tick and Event Overhead

EXCESSIVE USE OF TICK functions and events in Blueprints can impact performance. Here are some tips to reduce tick and event overhead:

- **Lower Tick Rates**: Consider reducing the tick rate of certain components or Blueprints that don't require frequent updates. This can save CPU cycles.

- **Event Batching**: Minimize the number of events and their frequency. Group multiple related actions into a single event where possible.

- **Event Disabling**: Temporarily disable events or tick functions when they are not needed. Re-enable them when the relevant conditions are met.

Use Blueprint Profiling Tools

UNREAL ENGINE PROVIDES Blueprint-specific profiling tools to help you optimize your scripts:

- **Performance Profiler**: The Blueprint Performance Profiler allows you to visualize the execution time of individual nodes within a Blueprint. Use it to identify nodes that contribute most to execution time.

- **Class Defaults Overrides**: Unreal Engine allows you to override default properties for Blueprint classes. Be cautious when making property changes, as excessive overrides can lead to performance issues. Use them judiciously.

Conclusion

PERFORMANCE OPTIMIZATION in Blueprints is a critical aspect of Unreal Engine game development. By profiling, reducing complexity, using native code when necessary, and managing ticks and events efficiently, you can ensure that your game runs smoothly and delivers a responsive player experience. Optimization is an iterative process, so regularly test and profile your game to identify and address performance bottlenecks as your project evolves.

2.4. Debugging and Refining Blueprint Scripts

IN THIS SECTION, WE will delve into the crucial aspects of debugging and refining Blueprint scripts in Unreal Engine. Debugging is an essential part of the development process, ensuring that your scripts work as intended and identifying and resolving issues.

Debugging Tools

UNREAL ENGINE PROVIDES several debugging tools specifically tailored for Blueprint debugging:

- **Print String Node**: This node allows you to print messages to the screen or log during gameplay. It's a simple but effective way to check the flow of your Blueprint scripts and inspect variable values.

- **Breakpoints**: You can set breakpoints in your Blueprint graphs. When execution reaches a breakpoint, the game will pause, allowing you to inspect variable values and step through the graph to understand the logic.

- **Watch Window**: The Watch Window allows you to monitor the values of specific variables or expressions during gameplay. You can add variables to the Watch Window and observe how they change in real-time.

- **Message Log**: The Message Log panel displays various messages, including warnings and errors. It can provide valuable information about issues in your Blueprint scripts.

Common Debugging Techniques

WHEN DEBUGGING BLUEPRINT scripts, consider the following techniques:

- **Use Print String Nodes**: Insert Print String nodes at different points in your Blueprint to log messages. This helps you trace the flow of execution and check the values of variables at specific moments.

- **Examine Variable Values**: You can inspect variable values by hovering over nodes connected to those variables while the game is running or by using the Watch

Window. This helps identify unexpected values or logic errors.

- **Breakpoints**: Set breakpoints at critical points in your Blueprint graphs, especially where you suspect issues might occur. When execution reaches a breakpoint, you can investigate the state of the graph.

- **Message Log**: Check the Message Log panel for any error or warning messages. Clicking on these messages can often take you directly to the Blueprint node causing the issue.

- **Step Through Execution**: When paused at a breakpoint, you can step through the execution one node at a time to see how the logic unfolds. This can be immensely helpful in understanding complex flows.

Tips for Refining Blueprints

REFINING BLUEPRINT scripts involves improving their readability, efficiency, and maintainability. Here are some tips:

- **Commenting**: Add comments to your Blueprint graphs to explain the purpose of specific nodes or sections. Clear comments make it easier for others (and your future self) to understand the logic.

- **Grouping and Organizing**: Use Blueprint nodes like Comment Boxes to group related nodes together. Organize your graphs logically to reduce clutter and improve readability.

- **Avoid Redundancy**: Look for duplicated or redundant logic in your Blueprints and refactor them into reusable functions or macros. This not only improves efficiency but also simplifies maintenance.

- **Modularization**: Break complex Blueprints into smaller, more manageable parts. This makes it easier to debug and maintain individual components.

- **Use Functions**: Create custom functions to encapsulate common logic or complex operations. Functions promote code reuse and make your Blueprints more structured.

- **Documentation**: Document your Blueprints, especially if they are part of a collaborative project. Describe the purpose of the Blueprint, its inputs and outputs, and any special considerations.

Best Practices

WHEN DEBUGGING AND refining Blueprints, follow these best practices:

- **Test Iteratively**: Test your Blueprints incrementally as you build them, rather than waiting until the entire system is complete. This allows you to catch and fix issues early.

- **Version Control**: Use version control systems like Git to track changes to your Blueprints. This helps you revert to previous versions if you encounter major issues.

- **Collaboration**: If you're working on a team, communicate with other team members about changes you make to Blueprints to avoid conflicts and ensure everyone is on the same page.

- **Continuous Testing**: After making changes or refinements to your Blueprints, thoroughly test them to ensure they still work as expected. Regression testing is crucial.

Conclusion

DEBUGGING AND REFINING Blueprint scripts are essential steps in Unreal Engine development. By using the debugging tools available, following common debugging techniques, and adhering to best practices for refining Blueprints, you can create more robust and reliable gameplay logic. Debugging is an iterative process, so be patient and persistent in identifying and addressing issues in your Blueprints.

2.5. Blueprint and C++ Interoperability

IN THIS SECTION, WE will explore the seamless interoperability between Blueprint and C++ in Unreal Engine. Unreal Engine offers the flexibility to use both visual scripting (Blueprints) and traditional programming (C++) within the same project. This combination allows you to leverage the strengths of each approach to create powerful and efficient game systems.

Advantages of Blueprint and C++ Integration

THE INTEGRATION OF Blueprint and C++ provides several advantages:

- **Accessibility**: Blueprint is a user-friendly visual scripting language that allows designers and artists to create gameplay logic without coding. This accessibility is invaluable for rapid prototyping and iterating on game mechanics.

• **Performance**: C++ is a compiled language that can offer better runtime performance compared to Blueprint. Critical and performance-sensitive components can be implemented in C++ for optimization.

• **Customization**: Blueprint exposes C++ functionality to designers, enabling them to customize and fine-tune gameplay logic without direct programming. This empowers designers to iterate on game mechanics independently.

• **Debugging**: Blueprint provides a visual debugging environment that simplifies the identification and resolution of issues. Designers can debug their logic without needing in-depth programming knowledge.

Blueprint-to-C++ Communication

UNREAL ENGINE FACILITATES seamless communication between Blueprint and C++. Here are common ways to pass data and invoke functions between the two:

• **BlueprintCallable Functions**: In C++, you can define functions with the UFUNCTION(BlueprintCallable) specifier. These functions can be called directly from Blueprints. This is a powerful way to expose C++ functionality to designers.

UFUNCTION(BlueprintCallable, Category = "My C++ Functions")

```
void MyCPPFunction();
```

- **BlueprintReadWrite Variables**: You can declare variables in C++ with the UPROPERTY(BlueprintReadWrite) specifier. These variables can be read and modified in Blueprints. This is useful for exposing data that designers need to tweak.

```
UPROPERTY(BlueprintReadWrite, Category = "My C++ Variables")

int32 MyCPPVariable;
```

- **Custom Events**: C++ can define custom Blueprint events using the DECLARE_DYNAMIC_MULTICAST_DELEGATE macro. These events can be fired in C++ code and bound to in Blueprints.

```
DECLARE_DYNAMIC_MULTICAST_DELEGATE(FMyDelegate);

UCLASS()

class MYGAME_API AMyActor : public AActor

{

GENERATED_BODY()

public:

UPROPERTY(BlueprintAssignable, Category = "My Delegates")

FMyDelegate OnMyEvent;

};
```

C++-to-Blueprint Communication

C++ CODE CAN ALSO INTERACT with Blueprints through a variety of mechanisms:

- **Blueprint Implementable Functions**: In Blueprints, you can declare functions as "Blueprint Implementable." These functions can be defined in C++ and overridden in Blueprint classes.

- **Blueprint Native Events**: C++ can declare events as "Blueprint Native." Blueprint classes can implement and customize the behavior of these events.

- **Event Dispatchers**: C++ code can define event dispatchers that Blueprint classes can bind to. When the event is triggered in C++, it invokes the bound functions in Blueprints.

Best Practices

WHEN INTEGRATING BLUEPRINT and C++ in your project, follow these best practices:

- **Clear Naming Conventions**: Use consistent naming conventions to make it clear which functions and variables are intended for use in Blueprints and which are for internal C++ logic.

- **Documentation**: Provide documentation for Blueprint-exposed C++ functions and variables to guide designers and artists on their usage.

- **Error Handling**: Implement proper error handling and validation in Blueprint-exposed C++ functions to prevent unexpected behavior in Blueprints.

- **Version Control**: Use version control to manage changes and avoid conflicts when multiple team members work on the same Blueprint and C++ codebase.

- **Collaboration**: Foster collaboration between programmers and designers to ensure that both sides understand the capabilities and limitations of each tool.

Conclusion

THE SYNERGY BETWEEN Blueprint and C++ in Unreal Engine empowers game developers to combine the accessibility of visual scripting with the performance and customization of traditional programming. By leveraging both approaches, you can create highly dynamic and efficient game systems while maintaining a flexible and collaborative development environment. Understanding how to communicate between Blueprint and C++ is essential for unlocking the full potential of Unreal Engine.

Chapter 3: Sophisticated 3D Modeling and Texturing

3.1. Advanced Modeling Techniques for Unreal

IN THIS SECTION, WE will explore advanced 3D modeling techniques tailored for Unreal Engine. Creating 3D assets that are optimized for real-time rendering and game development is crucial for achieving both visual quality and performance in your projects.

High-Quality Asset Creation

TO CREATE HIGH-QUALITY 3D assets for Unreal Engine, it's essential to follow these best practices:

- **Optimized Polygons**: Keep your polygon count as low as possible while maintaining the desired level of detail. Use techniques like LODs (Level of Detail) to reduce the polygon count for distant objects.

- **UV Mapping**: Efficient UV mapping is crucial for proper texturing. Avoid overlapping UVs, and aim for minimal distortion. Use tools like UV unwrapping to achieve clean UV layouts.

- **Normals and Smoothing**: Ensure that normals are correctly calculated and that smoothing groups are used where needed. This prevents shading artifacts and ensures smooth surfaces.

- **Texture Resolution**: Use texture resolutions appropriate for the target platform and object size. Unreal

Engine supports various texture compression formats to optimize memory usage.

PBR (Physically Based Rendering) Workflow

UNREAL ENGINE UTILIZES a PBR workflow for realistic material representation. When creating 3D models, adhere to PBR principles:

- **Albedo (Base Color)**: Use albedo maps to define the base color of your materials accurately. Ensure that albedo textures are color-corrected and physically accurate.

- **Metallic and Roughness Maps**: Create metallic and roughness maps that define how light interacts with your materials. Metallic maps specify metallicity, while roughness maps control surface roughness.

- **Normal Maps**: Generate normal maps to add fine surface details without increasing the polygon count. Normal maps simulate surface bumpiness and imperfections.

- **Ambient Occlusion**: Bake ambient occlusion maps to simulate the shadowing effect caused by nearby surfaces. This enhances the realism of your materials.

LODs (Level of Detail)

LODS ARE ESSENTIAL for optimizing the performance of your 3D assets in Unreal Engine. They involve creating multiple versions of an object with varying levels of detail. When an object is viewed from a distance, the engine switches to a lower LOD to reduce the polygon count and improve performance.

To create LODs for your 3D models:

- **Use Automatic LOD Generation**: Unreal Engine provides tools for automatically generating LODs based on a percentage reduction in polygon count. You can further refine these LODs manually.

- **Retopology**: For complex assets, consider manual retopology to create optimized, lower-poly versions of your models. This gives you more control over the LODs' quality and performance impact.

Collision Meshes

CREATING ACCURATE COLLISION meshes is crucial for physics interactions in your game. Unreal Engine offers several types of collision shapes, including simple primitives like boxes and spheres, as well as complex convex shapes.

To create collision meshes:

- **Use Simple Shapes**: For most objects, simple collision shapes like boxes or spheres are sufficient and offer good performance.

- **Complex Collisions**: For objects with irregular shapes, you can create complex collision shapes manually. This involves creating a simplified mesh that closely matches the object's form.

- **Simplify When Possible**: Keep in mind that complex collision meshes can impact performance, so try to simplify them as much as possible while retaining accuracy.

FBX Import Settings

WHEN IMPORTING 3D MODELS into Unreal Engine, pay attention to FBX import settings to ensure proper compatibility:

- **Scale Factor**: Set the scale factor appropriately to match the unit scale used in your modeling software.
- **Normals**: Ensure that "Import Normals" is enabled to preserve the model's normal information.
- **Tangents and Binormals**: Enable the import of tangents and binormals for normal mapping.
- **Static Mesh Generation**: Set the "Static Mesh Generation" option to "Auto Convex Collision" to generate collision meshes automatically.

Conclusion

ADVANCED 3D MODELING techniques tailored for Unreal Engine are essential for creating visually stunning and performance-optimized assets. By following best practices for asset creation, adhering to PBR workflows, implementing LODs, creating accurate collision meshes, and configuring FBX import settings, you can ensure that your 3D models seamlessly integrate with Unreal Engine and enhance the overall quality of your games. In the following sections, we will explore advanced texturing and material creation to further elevate the visual quality of your projects.

3.2. Creating Detailed and Realistic Textures

IN THIS SECTION, WE will delve into the process of creating detailed and realistic textures for your 3D models in Unreal Engine.

High-quality textures play a vital role in enhancing the visual appeal of your game environments and assets.

Texture Maps

UNREAL ENGINE RELIES on several types of texture maps to achieve realistic materials and surfaces. These maps are often referred to as PBR (Physically Based Rendering) textures and include:

- **Albedo (Base Color) Map**: The albedo map defines the base color of a material. It represents the actual color of the surface and contains details such as diffuse color, surface imperfections, and ambient occlusion.

- **Normal Map**: Normal maps simulate surface bumpiness and add fine details to materials. They affect how light interacts with the surface, giving the illusion of depth and relief.

- **Metallic Map**: The metallic map specifies which parts of a material are metallic and which are non-metallic. Values range from 0 (non-metallic) to 1 (fully metallic). It influences how light reflects off the surface.

- **Roughness Map**: The roughness map controls the surface roughness of a material. Lower values represent smoother surfaces, while higher values represent rougher surfaces. It impacts the micro-surface of the material.

- **Ambient Occlusion Map**: Ambient occlusion maps simulate the shadowing effect caused by nearby surfaces. They add depth and realism to materials by darkening crevices and corners.

Texture Resolution

WHEN CREATING TEXTURES for Unreal Engine, consider the appropriate texture resolution based on the object's size and importance in the scene. High-resolution textures can consume significant memory, so optimizing texture usage is crucial. Common texture resolutions include:

- **512x512 or 1024x1024**: Suitable for small props or objects that won't be viewed up close.
- **2048x2048 or 4096x4096**: Ideal for medium-sized objects and characters.
- **4096x4096 or 8192x8192**: Reserved for highly detailed objects or characters that require close-up shots.

Ensure that your textures are power-of-two in dimensions (e.g., 1024x1024, 2048x2048) to ensure optimal performance.

Texture Tiling and UV Mapping

PROPER UV MAPPING IS crucial for achieving seamless and realistic texture application to 3D models. Here are some UV mapping tips:

- **Non-Overlapping UVs**: Avoid overlapping UVs, as they can lead to texture artifacts. Overlapping UVs can also hinder the use of unique textures for different parts of the model.
- **Texture Tiling**: Plan your UV layout to take advantage of texture tiling. This allows you to tile textures across a surface without the need for extremely high-resolution textures.

- **Padding**: Add padding between UV islands to prevent bleeding of neighboring textures and to ensure that mipmaps generate correctly.

- **Avoid Stretching**: Minimize UV stretching, where the texture appears distorted. Stretching can affect the material's appearance.

Texture Painting Tools

FOR CREATING DETAILED and realistic textures, you can use dedicated texture painting software such as Substance Painter, Mari, or Photoshop with 3D painting capabilities. These tools offer features like layering, procedural texture generation, and real-time painting on 3D models.

Additionally, Unreal Engine provides its texture painting tool called the "Texture Editor," allowing you to make texture adjustments directly within the engine.

Material Layering

UNREAL ENGINE SUPPORTS material layering, allowing you to combine multiple textures and materials to create complex and realistic surfaces. Material layering enables you to blend materials based on height, slope, and other criteria.

Here's a simplified example of material layering in Unreal Engine using Blueprint:

```
// Define layers with their respective textures

UPROPERTY(EditAnywhere, BlueprintReadWrite, Category = "Material Layers")
```

```
TArray<UTexture2D*> BaseColorTextures;

UPROPERTY(EditAnywhere, BlueprintReadWrite, Category = "Material Layers")

TArray<UTexture2D*> NormalMaps;

// Function to blend materials based on specified parameters

UFUNCTION(BlueprintCallable, Category = "Material Layers")

UTexture2D* BlendMaterials(TArray<UTexture2D*> InBaseColorTextures, TArray<UTexture2D*> InNormalMaps);
```

In this example, you can blend multiple base color textures and normal maps based on specific criteria to create diverse and detailed surfaces.

Conclusion

CREATING DETAILED AND realistic textures is a fundamental aspect of achieving high-quality visuals in Unreal Engine. By understanding the various types of texture maps, considering texture resolution, mastering UV mapping, using texture painting tools effectively, and exploring material layering techniques, you can enhance the realism and visual appeal of your 3D models and environments in your Unreal Engine projects. Detailed textures contribute significantly to the overall immersion and aesthetics of your games.

3.3. Importing and Optimizing External 3D Models

IN THIS SECTION, WE will explore the process of importing external 3D models into Unreal Engine and optimizing them for use in your projects. Importing models from external sources is a common practice, as it allows you to leverage assets created in other 3D modeling software or acquired from online marketplaces.

Supported File Formats

UNREAL ENGINE SUPPORTS various 3D model file formats for import, including:

- **FBX**: Autodesk's FBX format is one of the most widely used formats for 3D asset exchange. It supports geometry, materials, animations, and more.

- **OBJ**: OBJ files are a versatile format for 3D geometry. While they don't support animations, they are excellent for static meshes.

- **Collada (DAE)**: The Collada format is suitable for geometry, materials, and animations. It's commonly used in some 3D modeling applications.

- **Alembic (ABC)**: Alembic is a format primarily used for animated assets with complex deformations, such as character animations or fluid simulations.

- **3DS**: The 3DS format is suitable for basic geometry and textures but lacks advanced features. It may require additional adjustments when imported.

Before importing, ensure that your 3D models are in one of these supported formats and that they are properly exported from the source software.

Import Settings

WHEN IMPORTING 3D MODELS into Unreal Engine, you can configure various import settings to optimize the process and ensure the assets are correctly interpreted. Here are some essential settings:

- **Scale Factor**: Set the scale factor to match the unit scale used in your modeling software. This ensures that the model's size is consistent with your Unreal Engine scene.

- **Import Materials**: Decide whether to import materials along with the model. Enabling this option can save time by preserving material assignments.

- **Import Textures**: If the model references textures, you can choose to import those textures. Ensure that the texture paths are correctly set for Unreal Engine to locate them.

- **Normals and Tangents**: Enable the import of normals and tangents if your model uses normal maps for detailing. This ensures that lighting calculations are accurate.

- **Generate Lightmap UVs**: If you intend to use baked lighting, enabling this option generates additional UVs optimized for lightmap baking.

- **Collision Generation**: Specify how collision geometry should be generated. Options include "Auto Convex Collision" for automatic convex hull generation or custom collision primitives.

Material Setup

AFTER IMPORTING YOUR 3D model, you may need to set up or adjust materials to achieve the desired look. Unreal Engine uses a physically based rendering (PBR) workflow, so it's essential to create or adapt materials accordingly. Here's a basic overview of material setup:

- **Material Instances**: Create material instances to customize materials without duplicating the base material. Material instances allow you to tweak properties like color, roughness, and metallic values.

- **Texture Assignments**: Assign textures to material properties, such as base color, normal maps, roughness, and metallic maps. Ensure that texture maps are correctly connected to the material.

- **Material Parameters**: Expose relevant material parameters to Blueprints, allowing you to change material properties at runtime. This is useful for creating dynamic materials.

- **Material Layering**: Utilize material layering techniques to blend multiple materials on a single mesh based on criteria like height, slope, or masks.

LODs (Level of Detail)

TO OPTIMIZE PERFORMANCE, consider creating LODs (Level of Detail) for your imported 3D models. Unreal Engine provides tools for automatically generating LODs based on a percentage reduction in polygon count. These simplified versions of your model are used when the object is viewed from a distance.

Optimizing LODs is essential for maintaining a consistent frame rate in your game and ensuring that less important details are not unnecessarily taxing on system resources.

Collision Setup

PROPER COLLISION SETUP is critical for physics interactions and gameplay in Unreal Engine. After importing your 3D model, you can define collision primitives that closely match the object's shape. Unreal Engine offers several types of collision shapes, including simple primitives like boxes and spheres, as well as complex convex shapes.

- **Simple Shapes**: For most objects, simple collision shapes like boxes or spheres are sufficient and offer good performance.

- **Complex Collisions**: For objects with irregular shapes, you can create complex collision shapes manually. This involves creating a simplified mesh that closely matches the object's form.

- **Simplify When Possible**: Keep in mind that complex collision meshes can impact performance, so try to simplify them as much as possible while retaining accuracy.

Conclusion

IMPORTING AND OPTIMIZING external 3D models in Unreal Engine is a fundamental part of game development. By following best practices for supported file formats, configuring import settings, setting up materials, creating LODs, and defining collision primitives, you can ensure that your imported assets integrate seamlessly into your Unreal Engine project. Efficient asset import and optimization contribute to better performance, reduced memory usage, and enhanced visual quality in your games.

3.4. Material Instances and Dynamic Materials

IN THIS SECTION, WE will explore the concept of material instances and dynamic materials in Unreal Engine. Material instances allow you to create variations of materials with different parameter values without duplicating the entire material, while dynamic materials enable real-time material manipulation for various in-game effects.

Material Instances

MATERIAL INSTANCES are derived from base materials and inherit their properties. However, you can customize the parameter values of material instances independently, making them extremely versatile for creating variations of materials without creating entirely new materials from scratch. Here's how to work with material instances:

1. **Create a Base Material**: Begin by creating a base material that defines the core properties of your material, such as textures, colors, and parameters.
2. **Create Material Instances**: Once you have your base material, you can create material instances based on it. Right-click the base material in the Content Browser and choose "Create Material Instance." This will generate a new asset linked to the base material.
3. **Customize Parameters**: Open the material instance in the Material Editor. Here, you can adjust parameter values,

such as colors, roughness, metallic, or any other exposed parameter. Changes made to the instance do not affect the base material or other instances.

4. **Apply Material Instances**: Apply material instances to your 3D models in Unreal Engine just like you would with base materials. Material instances are flexible and can be reused across different assets.

```
// Example of changing a material instance parameter in C++

UMaterialInstanceDynamic* DynamicMaterial = MeshComponent->CreateDynamicMaterialInstance(0, MaterialInstance);

if (DynamicMaterial)

{

// Adjust material parameter values

DynamicMaterial->SetScalarParameterValue("Roughness", 0.2f);

DynamicMaterial->SetVectorParameterValue("Color", FLinearColor(1.0f, 0.0f, 0.0f, 1.0f));

}
```

Dynamic Materials

DYNAMIC MATERIALS TAKE material customization to the next level by allowing real-time changes to materials during gameplay. This is especially useful for creating dynamic visual effects, such as changing a character's appearance or altering the state of an object. Here's how to work with dynamic materials:

1. **Create a Material with Parameters**: Start by creating a

material that includes parameters you intend to modify dynamically, such as colors, emissive values, or textures.
2. **Create a Material Instance Dynamic**: In your code or Blueprint, you can create an instance of the material using CreateDynamicMaterialInstance.
3. **Set Parameter Values**: Use functions like SetScalarParameterValue, SetVectorParameterValue, or SetTextureParameterValue to change the material's parameter values during runtime based on your game logic.
4. **Apply the Dynamic Material**: Assign the dynamic material instance to the appropriate mesh component or actor.

```
// Example of dynamic material creation and parameter modification in C++

UMaterialInstanceDynamic* DynamicMaterial = UMaterialInstanceDynamic::Create(BaseMaterial, this);

if (DynamicMaterial)

{

// Adjust material parameter values

DynamicMaterial->SetScalarParameterValue("EmissiveIntensity", 2.0f);

DynamicMaterial->SetVectorParameterValue("Color", FLinearColor(0.0f, 1.0f, 0.0f, 1.0f));

// Apply the dynamic material to a mesh component

MeshComponent->SetMaterial(0, DynamicMaterial);

}
```

Dynamic materials are particularly useful for implementing features like character customization, material reactions to in-game events (e.g., damage effects), or dynamic weather systems that alter the appearance of the environment.

Performance Considerations

WHILE DYNAMIC MATERIALS provide flexibility, they can also have performance implications, especially if you frequently change material parameters during gameplay. Keep the following performance considerations in mind:

- **Shader Complexity**: Dynamic material changes may result in shader recompilation, which can be costly. Minimize the number of dynamic material updates per frame.

- **Material Instances**: When possible, use material instances for parameter customization rather than dynamic materials. Material instances are more efficient for static or semi-static changes.

- **Texture Streaming**: Be mindful of texture streaming, especially if dynamic materials involve changing textures. Properly manage texture streaming to avoid excessive memory usage.

Conclusion

MATERIAL INSTANCES and dynamic materials are powerful tools in Unreal Engine that allow you to create diverse and customizable materials for your game objects. Material instances are excellent for creating variations of materials efficiently, while dynamic materials enable real-time material manipulation for dynamic effects and interactions in your game. Understanding when to use material instances or dynamic materials and managing their performance impact is essential for achieving the desired visual quality and gameplay experience in your Unreal Engine projects.

3.5. Procedural Content Generation in 3D

PROCEDURAL CONTENT generation is a powerful technique in game development, allowing you to create vast and diverse game worlds without manually designing every detail. In this section, we will explore the concept of procedural content generation in the context of 3D environments within Unreal Engine.

What Is Procedural Content Generation?

PROCEDURAL CONTENT generation (PCG) refers to the automatic creation of game content using algorithms and rules rather than manual authoring. It can be applied to various aspects of game development, including terrain, levels, textures, and even gameplay elements. PCG offers several advantages:

- **Scale**: PCG allows you to generate large, expansive worlds efficiently, saving time and resources compared to manual design.
- **Variety**: By using procedural techniques, you can introduce randomness and variety into your game, keeping players engaged with new experiences each playthrough.
- **Efficiency**: Procedural generation can create content on-the-fly, reducing the need for extensive pre-authored assets and decreasing load times.

Procedural Terrain Generation

TERRAIN GENERATION is a common application of procedural content generation. Unreal Engine provides several tools and techniques for procedurally generating terrain:

- **Landscape**: Unreal's Landscape system enables the creation of vast, detailed terrains. You can sculpt and paint terrain using brushes, import heightmaps, or use procedural algorithms to generate terrain at runtime.

- **Noise Functions**: Perlin noise, simplex noise, and other noise functions are commonly used to add natural variation to terrain. These functions can be used to generate heightmaps or texture maps.

- **Procedural Foliage**: You can procedurally place foliage, such as trees, rocks, and grass, on your terrain. Unreal Engine provides tools to distribute foliage based on rules and parameters.

Procedural Level Layout

PROCEDURAL CONTENT generation can also be applied to level layouts. You can use algorithms to create rooms, dungeons, or entire levels dynamically. Some key techniques include:

- **Dungeon Generation**: Algorithms like binary space partitioning (BSP) or cellular automata can be used to create procedural dungeons with interconnected rooms and corridors.

- **Road Networks**: Procedural road generation is essential for open-world games. You can use algorithms to generate road networks, highways, and intersections.

- **Cityscapes**: For urban environments, procedural generation can create city layouts, including streets, buildings, and parks.

Procedural Texturing

PROCEDURAL TEXTURES are generated algorithmically and can be applied to surfaces to add detail and realism. Unreal Engine's Material Editor supports the creation of procedural textures using nodes and functions:

- **Perlin Noise**: Perlin noise can be used to create various natural textures, such as clouds, marble, or terrain.

- **Voronoi Patterns**: Voronoi diagrams can be employed to generate patterns found in nature, such as cracked surfaces or cell-like structures.

- **Fractal Patterns**: Fractal algorithms, like the Mandelbrot set, can produce intricate and self-replicating textures.

Performance Considerations

WHILE PROCEDURAL CONTENT generation offers flexibility, it can also introduce performance challenges. Here are some considerations:

- **Optimization**: Optimize your procedural algorithms to run efficiently. Use data structures like spatial partitioning to speed up searches or limit the depth of recursive algorithms.

- **Streaming**: Procedural content can put a strain on memory and streaming. Implement streaming solutions to load and unload content dynamically as the player explores the world.

- **Visual Consistency**: Ensure that procedurally generated content matches the visual style of manually crafted assets to maintain a cohesive game world.

Conclusion

PROCEDURAL CONTENT generation is a valuable tool for creating vast and diverse 3D environments in Unreal Engine. By leveraging algorithms and rules, you can generate terrains, level layouts, textures, and more, providing players with unique and engaging experiences. However, careful consideration of performance, visual consistency, and optimization is crucial to make the most of procedural content generation in your Unreal Engine projects.

4. Lighting and Rendering Mastery

4.1. Advanced Lighting Techniques for Realism

IN THIS SECTION, WE will delve into advanced lighting techniques in Unreal Engine that can significantly enhance the realism and visual quality of your game environments. Lighting plays a crucial role in creating immersive and believable worlds, and Unreal Engine offers a wide range of tools and features to achieve stunning lighting effects.

Physically Based Rendering (PBR)

UNREAL ENGINE EMPLOYS Physically Based Rendering (PBR), a rendering technique that simulates the physical behavior of light in the real world. PBR materials and lighting provide a foundation for achieving realistic visuals. Here are key components of PBR in Unreal Engine:

- **Albedo (Base Color)**: The albedo texture defines the base color of a material. It represents the color and reflectivity of the surface.

- **Metallic**: The metallic parameter determines which parts of a material are metallic and which are dielectric (non-metallic). Metallic surfaces reflect light differently from dielectric surfaces.

- **Roughness**: The roughness parameter controls the surface roughness of a material. Lower values result in smoother surfaces, while higher values create rougher surfaces.

- **Normal Maps**: Normal maps add fine surface details to materials, affecting how light interacts with the surface.

Global Illumination (GI)

GLOBAL ILLUMINATION simulates the indirect bounce of light in the environment, enhancing the realism of scenes. Unreal Engine offers various GI techniques:

- **Static Lighting**: Lightmass is Unreal Engine's static GI solver. It precomputes lighting information and bakes it into lightmaps for static objects. It's suitable for architectural visualization and games with mostly static environments.

- **Dynamic Global Illumination**: Unreal Engine supports dynamic GI using methods like Distance Field Global Illumination (DFGI) and Screen Space Global Illumination (SSGI). These techniques provide real-time GI effects for dynamic objects and scenes.

- **Ray Tracing**: Ray tracing enables accurate real-time reflections, soft shadows, and global illumination. It simulates the path of light rays, resulting in highly realistic lighting effects.

Advanced Lighting Features

UNREAL ENGINE OFFERS several advanced lighting features that can enhance the realism of your scenes:

- **Real-Time Ray Tracing**: Real-time ray tracing introduces ray-traced reflections, shadows, and ambient occlusion for photorealistic visuals. It's especially beneficial for architectural visualization and high-end gaming.

- **Volumetric Fog**: Volumetric fog adds depth and atmosphere to scenes by simulating the interaction of light with fog and particles. It can create realistic god rays and atmospheric effects.

- **Cascade Shadow Maps (CSM)**: CSM improves the quality and performance of dynamic shadows by splitting the shadow map into multiple cascades. This is crucial for large outdoor environments with dynamic lighting.

Lighting Optimization

WHILE ADVANCED LIGHTING techniques can elevate the visual quality of your game, it's essential to consider performance and optimization:

- **Level of Detail (LOD)**: Implement LODs for lights to reduce the rendering cost of distant or less important lights.

- **Culling**: Use occlusion culling to avoid rendering objects and lights that are not visible to the camera, optimizing performance.

- **Lightmap Resolution**: Adjust lightmap resolution for static objects to balance quality and memory usage.

- **Lighting Complexity**: Unreal Engine provides tools to analyze lighting complexity and identify performance bottlenecks.

Conclusion

ADVANCED LIGHTING TECHNIQUES are a cornerstone of realistic and visually impressive environments in Unreal Engine. By leveraging PBR materials, global illumination, real-time ray tracing, and advanced lighting features, you can create stunning visuals that draw players into your game world. However, it's essential to strike a balance between realism and performance optimization to ensure a smooth and enjoyable gaming experience.

4.2. Mastering Unreal's Rendering Pipeline

IN THIS SECTION, WE will explore Unreal Engine's rendering pipeline and delve into the inner workings of how graphics are processed and displayed in your projects. Understanding the rendering pipeline is crucial for optimizing and achieving the desired visual quality in your Unreal Engine games.

The Rendering Pipeline Overview

UNREAL ENGINE'S RENDERING pipeline is a complex sequence of stages that transform 3D scene data into 2D images displayed on your screen. It involves several key processes:

1. **Scene Construction**: The first step is constructing the 3D scene, including geometry, materials, lights, and cameras. Unreal Engine provides a visual editor to create and manage these elements.
2. **Culling**: To optimize rendering, the engine performs occlusion culling to eliminate objects that are not visible to the camera. This reduces the workload of the subsequent stages.
3. **Transformations**: Geometry is transformed from world

space to camera space using matrices. This process prepares objects for rendering from the perspective of the camera.

4. **Rasterization**: During rasterization, the engine converts 3D objects into 2D pixels on the screen. This involves determining which pixels are covered by each triangle and interpolating vertex data across those pixels.
5. **Shading**: Shading involves calculating the color and illumination of each pixel. This step considers lighting, materials, and textures, resulting in the final pixel color.
6. **Post-Processing**: After the main rendering pass, post-processing effects are applied. This can include color grading, depth of field, bloom, and other enhancements.
7. **Output to Screen**: The final image is displayed on the screen, completing the rendering pipeline.

Rendering Optimizations

OPTIMIZING RENDERING performance is essential for achieving smooth gameplay and maintaining a high frame rate. Here are some key considerations:

- **Level of Detail (LOD)**: Implement LODs for 3D models, materials, and textures to reduce rendering complexity at a distance.

- **Culling Techniques**: Use frustum culling and occlusion culling to avoid rendering objects that are not visible to the camera.

- **Material Optimization**: Optimize materials by reducing shader complexity and minimizing texture usage.

- **Batching**: Minimize draw calls by batching objects with similar materials and shaders.

- **Lighting**: Carefully design and optimize your lighting setup to avoid performance bottlenecks.

Advanced Rendering Features

UNREAL ENGINE OFFERS a range of advanced rendering features that can enhance the visual quality of your projects:

- **Ray Tracing**: Real-time ray tracing introduces accurate reflections, soft shadows, and global illumination. It can significantly improve the realism of your scenes.

- **Volumetric Effects**: Volumetric fog, lighting, and particles add depth and atmosphere to environments.

- **High Dynamic Range (HDR)**: HDR rendering allows for a broader range of colors and luminance values, resulting in more vibrant visuals.

- **Screen Space Effects**: Effects like screen space reflections, ambient occlusion, and screen space global illumination can improve the realism of scenes.

Custom Shaders

FOR ADVANCED GRAPHICS programming, Unreal Engine allows you to create custom shaders using HLSL (High-Level Shading Language). This can be particularly useful for achieving unique visual effects or optimizing specific rendering tasks.

// Example of a custom shader function in Unreal Engine HLSL

```
float4 CustomShaderFunction(float2 UV : TEXCOORD0) : SV_Target

{

// Your shader code here

return float4(1.0, 0.0, 0.0, 1.0); // Red color as an example

}
```

Custom shaders can be integrated into your materials and used to achieve a wide range of visual effects, from stylized rendering to complex simulations.

Debugging and Profiling

UNREAL ENGINE PROVIDES tools for debugging and profiling rendering performance. Use the GPU Visualizer to identify rendering bottlenecks and analyze the performance of your materials and shaders. These tools are invaluable for optimizing your rendering pipeline.

Conclusion

MASTERING UNREAL ENGINE'S rendering pipeline is essential for achieving both visual excellence and optimal performance in your projects. Understanding the stages of the rendering pipeline, implementing optimization techniques, leveraging advanced rendering features, and experimenting with custom shaders can help you create visually stunning and efficient games. Additionally, the debugging and profiling tools provided by Unreal Engine are crucial for identifying and addressing performance issues within the rendering pipeline.

4.3. Real-Time Global Illumination Strategies

IN THIS SECTION, WE will explore real-time global illumination (GI) strategies in Unreal Engine. Global illumination is a crucial component of realistic lighting in 3D environments, and achieving it in real-time is a significant advancement in modern game development.

What Is Global Illumination?

GLOBAL ILLUMINATION refers to the indirect lighting that occurs when light rays bounce off surfaces and interact with other objects in a scene. It includes effects such as diffuse interreflection, color bleeding, and soft shadows. Global illumination is essential for creating realistic and visually appealing environments because it accurately simulates how light behaves in the real world.

Importance of Real-Time Global Illumination

REAL-TIME GLOBAL ILLUMINATION allows for dynamic lighting scenarios where objects move, change, or emit light sources, and their impact on the environment is instantly visible. This is crucial for games where players interact with the world and where time of day and weather conditions can change dynamically.

Unreal Engine's Real-Time Global Illumination Solutions

UNREAL ENGINE OFFERS several solutions for achieving real-time global illumination:

1. **Distance Field Global Illumination (DFGI)**: DFGI is a real-time global illumination technique that leverages

distance fields to approximate indirect lighting. It allows for dynamic changes in lighting conditions and is well-suited for games with complex, dynamic environments.

2. **Screen Space Global Illumination (SSGI)**: SSGI is another real-time global illumination method that works by analyzing screen space data. It can efficiently capture and simulate indirect lighting effects in real-time, improving the overall visual quality of scenes.
3. **Ray Tracing**: Unreal Engine's ray tracing features, such as ray-traced reflections and ray-traced global illumination, offer highly accurate and realistic global illumination effects. These features are computationally intensive but provide exceptional visual fidelity.

Optimizing Real-Time Global Illumination

WHILE REAL-TIME GLOBAL illumination is a powerful tool, it can be computationally expensive. Here are some optimization strategies:

- **Adjust Resolution**: Lowering the resolution of global illumination can significantly improve performance without a substantial loss of visual quality.
- **Limit Bounces**: Reducing the number of indirect light bounces can help manage computational costs.
- **Dynamic vs. Static**: Consider which parts of your environment require dynamic global illumination and which can use static baked lighting to save resources.

Dynamic Objects and Real-Time GI

ONE OF THE CHALLENGES with real-time global illumination is handling dynamic objects that move and change the lighting conditions. Unreal Engine's solutions, such as DFGI and SSGI, can handle dynamic objects to some extent. However, it's essential to strike a balance between visual quality and performance, especially in scenes with many dynamic objects.

```
// Example of enabling DFGI for a dynamic object in Unreal Engine

MeshComponent->SetEnableDFGIDynamic(true);
```

Conclusion

REAL-TIME GLOBAL ILLUMINATION is a crucial component of creating realistic and visually captivating 3D environments in Unreal Engine. By leveraging solutions like DFGI, SSGI, or ray tracing, you can achieve dynamic and accurate global illumination effects. However, it's essential to consider the computational cost and optimize your scenes to maintain a smooth and immersive gaming experience, especially in scenes with a high level of interactivity and dynamic objects.

4.4. Post-Processing Effects for Cinematic Quality

IN THIS SECTION, WE will explore post-processing effects in Unreal Engine that can elevate the visual quality of your scenes to achieve a cinematic look and feel. Post-processing effects are a crucial part of the rendering pipeline that allows you to enhance the final image and create specific visual styles and moods.

What Are Post-Processing Effects?

POST-PROCESSING EFFECTS, often referred to as "post-process" or "PP," are a set of techniques applied to the rendered image after the main rendering pass. They can modify various aspects of the image, such as color, contrast, depth, and more. Post-processing effects are widely used in film, photography, and video games to achieve specific artistic and visual goals.

Common Post-Processing Effects

UNREAL ENGINE PROVIDES a wide range of post-processing effects that can be combined and customized to achieve different visual styles. Some common post-processing effects include:

- **Color Grading**: Color grading allows you to adjust the color balance and tone of the image to create specific moods. You can achieve warm, cold, desaturated, or vibrant looks.

- **Bloom**: Bloom adds a glow or halo effect to bright areas of the image. It can make lights and other high-intensity objects appear more realistic and visually appealing.

- **Depth of Field (DOF)**: DOF simulates the selective focus of a camera, blurring objects in the foreground or background to draw attention to the subject.

- **Motion Blur**: Motion blur adds blur to moving objects, enhancing the sense of speed and realism in fast-paced scenes.

- **Lens Flares:** Lens flares are optical artifacts created by light interacting with the camera lens. They can add a cinematic and realistic touch to scenes with intense light sources.

- **Chromatic Aberration**: Chromatic aberration simulates the separation of colors at the edges of objects, mimicking a lens defect. It can create a subtle, immersive effect.

Cinematic Post-Processing

TO ACHIEVE A CINEMATIC look in Unreal Engine, you can combine specific post-processing effects and settings. Here are some techniques commonly used for cinematic quality:

- **Contrast and Saturation**: Adjust the contrast and saturation to create a distinct visual style. Lower contrast and desaturation can give a moody or dramatic look.

- **Film Grain**: Add a film grain effect to simulate the texture of film stock. It can evoke a nostalgic or cinematic atmosphere.

- **Vignette**: Apply a vignette effect to darken the corners of the screen, drawing the viewer's focus toward the center.

```
// Example of setting post-processing effects in Unreal Engine C++

APlayerController* PlayerController = GetWorld()->GetFirstPlayerController();

if (PlayerController)

{
```

```
APlayerCameraManager* CameraManager = PlayerController->PlayerCameraManager;

if (CameraManager)

{

// Adjust post-processing settings

CameraManager->SetManualCameraFStop(2.8f); // Adjust aperture for depth of field

CameraManager->SetManualLensSettings(true); // Enable manual lens settings

}

}
```

Performance Considerations

WHILE POST-PROCESSING effects can enhance visual quality, they can also impact performance, especially on lower-end hardware. Here are some considerations:

- **Performance Impact**: Each post-processing effect consumes GPU resources. Avoid overloading your scene with too many effects.

- **Quality vs. Performance**: Some effects, like ray tracing-based effects, are computationally expensive. Balance visual quality with performance based on your target platform.

- **Optimization**: Unreal Engine provides tools for profiling and optimizing post-processing effects. Use these tools to identify and address performance bottlenecks.

Conclusion

POST-PROCESSING EFFECTS are a vital tool for achieving cinematic quality visuals in Unreal Engine. By carefully selecting and customizing these effects, you can create specific visual styles and moods that enhance the storytelling and immersion in your game. However, it's essential to balance visual quality with performance optimization, especially when targeting a wide range of hardware configurations.

4.5. Optimizing Rendering for Different Platforms

IN THIS SECTION, WE will explore the importance of optimizing your game's rendering for different platforms in Unreal Engine. Ensuring that your game runs smoothly and looks great on various hardware configurations is crucial for reaching a broader audience and providing an enjoyable gaming experience.

Platform Considerations

UNREAL ENGINE ALLOWS you to develop games for a wide range of platforms, including PC, consoles, mobile devices, and VR/AR headsets. Each platform has its unique hardware capabilities and performance characteristics, which should be considered during development.

- **PC**: PCs offer a wide range of hardware configurations, from high-end gaming rigs to budget laptops. Optimizing for PC involves providing scalability options to accommodate different setups.

- **Consoles**: Consoles have fixed hardware specifications, making optimization more predictable. However, you still need to maximize performance to achieve the target frame rate and resolution.

- **Mobile Devices**: Mobile devices have limited processing power and memory compared to PCs and consoles. Optimizing for mobile platforms often requires reducing graphical complexity and implementing efficient rendering techniques.

- **VR/AR Headsets**: VR and AR devices demand high frame rates and low latency to prevent motion sickness. Optimization is critical to maintain a smooth and immersive experience.

Scalability Settings

UNREAL ENGINE PROVIDES scalability settings that allow you to adjust graphical fidelity based on the platform and performance requirements. These settings include:

- **Resolution Scaling**: Dynamically adjust the rendering resolution to maintain performance while preserving visual quality.

- **Texture Quality**: Lower texture resolutions or use compressed textures on less powerful hardware.

- **Shadow Quality**: Reduce the quality and resolution of shadows for better performance.

- **Post-Processing Effects**: Enable or disable specific post-processing effects based on performance targets.

Level of Detail (LOD)

IMPLEMENTING LOD (LEVEL of Detail) is essential for optimizing rendering on all platforms. LOD involves using lower-polygon models, lower-resolution textures, and simplified materials for objects at a distance. Unreal Engine provides tools to generate LODs automatically and optimize asset rendering.

// Example of setting LOD settings for a static mesh in Unreal Engine C++

StaticMesh->SetForcedLod(0); *// Set the LOD level to use (0 is the highest quality)*

Occlusion Culling

OCCLUSION CULLING IS the process of preventing the rendering of objects that are not visible to the camera. Unreal Engine uses occlusion culling techniques to improve performance by skipping the rendering of hidden objects. It's particularly important for open-world games and large environments.

Testing and Profiling

TO ENSURE OPTIMAL PERFORMANCE on different platforms, rigorous testing and profiling are essential. Unreal Engine provides profiling tools to identify performance bottlenecks, including GPU Visualizer, CPU Profiler, and Frame Profiler. Use these tools to diagnose and address performance issues specific to each platform.

Platform-Specific Optimization

OPTIMIZING FOR DIFFERENT platforms may require platform-specific considerations and adjustments. For example:

- **Console Optimization**: On consoles, optimize memory usage, and utilize platform-specific features and APIs for improved performance.

- **Mobile Optimization**: Reduce draw calls, minimize texture sizes, and consider mobile-specific rendering techniques like mobile HDR and Vulkan rendering.

- **VR/AR Optimization**: Achieve low-latency rendering and high frame rates for VR/AR experiences by optimizing CPU and GPU performance.

Conclusion

OPTIMIZING RENDERING for different platforms is a critical aspect of game development in Unreal Engine. To reach a broad audience and deliver an enjoyable gaming experience, you must consider the hardware capabilities and performance characteristics of each platform. Implement scalability settings, LOD, occlusion culling, and conduct thorough testing and profiling to ensure that your game runs smoothly and looks great on all target platforms. Platform-specific optimization may be necessary to leverage the unique features and capabilities of each platform.

Chapter 5: Physics and Simulations

5.1. Implementing Realistic Physics Behaviors

IN THIS SECTION, WE will explore how to implement realistic physics behaviors in your Unreal Engine projects. Physics simulations are essential for creating interactive and dynamic game worlds, allowing objects to move, collide, and respond to forces in a lifelike manner.

The Importance of Realistic Physics

REALISTIC PHYSICS ADD depth and immersion to your games. They enable objects to obey the laws of physics, making the virtual world feel more tangible and believable. Whether you're creating a racing game with realistic vehicle physics, a platformer with precise character movements, or a puzzle game with dynamic object interactions, implementing physics accurately is crucial.

Unreal Engine's Physics System

UNREAL ENGINE COMES with a robust physics system powered by NVIDIA's PhysX technology. This system allows you to simulate a wide range of physical behaviors, including:

- **Rigid Body Dynamics**: Objects can have mass, collide with each other, and respond to forces like gravity and user interactions.

- **Collision Detection**: Unreal Engine provides collision detection and response systems to handle object interactions and prevent objects from intersecting.

- **Joints and Constraints**: You can create complex structures by connecting objects with constraints like hinges, sliders, and ball joints.

- **Ragdoll Physics**: Simulate realistic character and object animations with ragdoll physics for lifelike reactions to impacts.

- **Particle Systems**: Implement realistic particle systems for effects like fire, smoke, and fluid simulations.

Setting up Physics in Unreal Engine

TO ENABLE PHYSICS FOR an object in Unreal Engine, you need to do the following:

1. **Enable Physics Simulation**: Select the object you want to simulate physics for, go to the Details panel, and check the "Simulate Physics" option.
2. **Adjust Mass and Collision**: Configure the object's mass, collision settings, and physical materials to control its behavior and interactions.
3. **Constraints and Joints**: Create constraints or joints to connect objects and define their relationship, such as a swinging door hinge.

```
// Example of creating a physics constraint in Unreal Engine C++

UPhysicsConstraintComponent* PhysicsConstraint = CreateDefaultSubobject<UPhysicsConstraintComponent>(TEXT("Ph

PhysicsConstraint->SetupAttachment(RootComponent);

PhysicsConstraint->SetConstrainedComponents(Comp1, NAME_None, Comp2, NAME_None);
```

Realistic Character Physics

IMPLEMENTING REALISTIC character physics is crucial for games involving player-controlled characters. Unreal Engine provides character movement components that handle complex behaviors like walking, running, jumping, and interacting with the environment.

```
// Example of setting up character movement in Unreal Engine C++

ACharacter* MyCharacter = GetMyCharacter();

if (MyCharacter)

{

UCharacterMovementComponent* MovementComp = MyCharacter->GetCharacterMovement();

MovementComp->MaxWalkSpeed = 600.0f; // Set maximum walking speed

MovementComp->JumpZVelocity = 600.0f; // Set jump height

}
```

Optimizing Physics Simulations

WHILE REALISTIC PHYSICS are essential, it's crucial to optimize them to maintain performance, especially in complex scenes. Consider the following optimization techniques:

- **Collision Complexity**: Simplify collision geometry to reduce computational overhead.
- **LOD**: Implement level of detail for physics representations to reduce complexity at a distance.

- **Physics Profiling**: Use Unreal Engine's physics profiling tools to identify performance bottlenecks and optimize accordingly.

Conclusion

IMPLEMENTING REALISTIC physics behaviors in your Unreal Engine projects enhances immersion and gameplay quality. Whether you're simulating rigid bodies, character movements, or complex object interactions, Unreal Engine's physics system provides the tools and features needed to create lifelike simulations. To ensure optimal performance, balance realism with optimization techniques and leverage Unreal Engine's built-in physics profiling tools to fine-tune your physics simulations.

5.2. Creating Interactive Environments with Physics

IN THIS SECTION, WE will explore how to create interactive environments with physics in Unreal Engine. Interactive environments add depth and realism to your games by allowing objects to respond dynamically to player actions and environmental changes.

Physics-Based Interactions

PHYSICS-BASED INTERACTIONS enable objects to move, collide, and react to forces in real-time. Unreal Engine's physics system allows you to create various interactive elements, such as:

- **Dynamic Objects**: Objects that can be picked up, thrown, pushed, or affected by in-game forces.

• **Destructible Environments**: Create destructible objects and structures that break apart realistically when subjected to damage.

• **Environmental Interactions**: Implement interactive elements in your environments, like levers, switches, doors, and elevators.

• **Simulated Water**: Create realistic water simulations with buoyancy and fluid dynamics.

Setting up Interactive Objects

TO CREATE INTERACTIVE objects in Unreal Engine, follow these steps:

1. **Enable Physics**: Enable physics simulation for the object by checking the "Simulate Physics" option in the Details panel.
2. **Collision Setup**: Configure the collision settings to ensure that the object interacts correctly with other objects in the scene.
3. **Physics Materials**: Apply physics materials to objects to control friction, bounciness, and other physical properties.
4. **Blueprints**: Use Blueprints to define the behavior of interactive objects, such as how a lever activates a door or how an object responds to player interactions.

```
// Example of Blueprint scripting for an interactive lever in Unreal Engine

void ALever::OnInteract()

{
```

```
if (bActivated)
{
// Deactivate the lever
RotateLever(FRotator(0.0f, 0.0f, -45.0f));
bActivated = false;
// Perform associated actions, such as closing a door
if (LinkedDoor)
{
LinkedDoor->CloseDoor();
}
}
else
{
// Activate the lever
RotateLever(FRotator(0.0f, 0.0f, 45.0f));
bActivated = true;
// Perform associated actions, such as opening a door
if (LinkedDoor)
{
LinkedDoor->OpenDoor();
```

```
}
}
}
```

Destructible Environments

CREATING DESTRUCTIBLE environments can add excitement and realism to your game. Unreal Engine provides a Destructible Mesh system that allows you to break objects into pieces based on physical interactions or predefined damage thresholds.

```
// Example of setting up a destructible mesh in Unreal Engine
UDestructibleComponent* DestructibleComponent = CreateDefaultSubobject<UDestructibleComponent>(TEXT("Destructib
DestructibleComponent->SetDestructibleMesh(DestructibleMesh);
```

Water and Fluid Simulations

IMPLEMENTING WATER and fluid simulations can enhance your game's realism. Unreal Engine provides tools for simulating water, including buoyancy and fluid dynamics. You can create realistic water bodies, such as rivers, lakes, and oceans, with interactive properties.

Optimization for Interactive Environments

TO MAINTAIN OPTIMAL performance in interactive environments, consider the following optimization techniques:

- **Level of Detail (LOD)**: Implement LODs for physics representations of objects to reduce complexity at a distance.

- **Culling**: Use occlusion culling to avoid rendering objects that are not visible to the camera.

- **Physics Profiling**: Use Unreal Engine's physics profiling tools to identify and optimize performance bottlenecks.

- **Simplified Collision**: Simplify collision geometry for objects that don't require precise collisions.

Conclusion

CREATING INTERACTIVE environments with physics in Unreal Engine adds depth and immersion to your games. Whether you're implementing dynamic objects, destructible environments, or complex environmental interactions, Unreal Engine's physics system provides the tools and features needed to create realistic and engaging experiences. To ensure optimal performance, optimize your interactive environments using techniques like LOD, culling, and physics profiling while balancing realism with efficiency.

5.3. Advanced Particle Systems and Effects

IN THIS SECTION, WE will delve into advanced particle systems and effects in Unreal Engine. Particle systems are a powerful tool for creating a wide range of visual effects, from natural phenomena like fire and smoke to magical spells and futuristic sci-fi visuals. Understanding and mastering particle systems can greatly enhance the visual appeal and immersion of your game.

Particle Systems in Unreal Engine

UNREAL ENGINE PROVIDES a sophisticated particle system that allows you to create complex and dynamic effects. Here are some key components and concepts related to particle systems:

- **Emitter**: An emitter is a source of particles. It defines where and how particles are spawned and their initial properties, such as size, color, and velocity.

- **Modules**: Particle systems consist of multiple modules that control different aspects of particle behavior, including lifetime, collision, forces, and rendering.

- **Cascade**: Cascade is Unreal Engine's dedicated particle editing and authoring tool. It provides a visual interface for designing and fine-tuning particle systems.

Types of Particle Effects

PARTICLE EFFECTS CAN be categorized into various types, including:

- **Environmental Effects**: These include weather-related effects like rain, snow, and wind-blown leaves. They add realism and atmosphere to outdoor scenes.

- **Combat and Weapon Effects**: Particle effects are commonly used to represent gunfire, explosions, magic spells, and other combat-related visuals.

- **Ambient Effects**: Ambient effects can simulate dust, fog, mist, and other subtle atmospheric elements that contribute to the mood of a scene.

- **UI and Feedback Effects**: Particles can be used for user interface elements, such as health bars, damage indicators, and feedback animations.

Creating Particle Systems

TO CREATE A PARTICLE system in Unreal Engine, follow these steps:

1. **Access Cascade**: Open the Cascade particle editor by right-clicking in the Content Browser, selecting "Create," and choosing "Particle System."
2. **Edit Emitters**: Inside Cascade, you can create and edit emitters, adjust emitter properties, and add modules to control particle behavior.
3. **Materials and Textures**: You can use materials and textures to define particle appearance. Materials can be animated to create dynamic effects.
4. **Particle Templates**: Unreal Engine provides particle templates that you can use as starting points for various effects.

Realistic Effects with GPU Particles

UNREAL ENGINE SUPPORTS GPU particles, which allow for a massive number of particles to be simulated and rendered efficiently on modern graphics hardware. GPU particles can achieve highly detailed and realistic effects, such as fluid simulations, volumetric fire, and dynamic smoke.

Optimization and Performance

WHILE PARTICLE EFFECTS can enhance visuals, they can also impact performance, especially when dealing with a large number of particles. To optimize particle systems:

- **LOD**: Implement level of detail (LOD) for particle systems to reduce complexity at a distance.

- **Culling**: Use occlusion culling and frustum culling to avoid rendering particles that are not visible to the camera.

- **Pooling**: Implement particle pooling to reuse particles and reduce the overhead of spawning and destroying them.

- **Particle Size and Lifetimes**: Adjust particle sizes and lifetimes based on their importance and visual impact.

Conclusion

ADVANCED PARTICLE SYSTEMS and effects are valuable tools for creating immersive and visually stunning experiences in Unreal Engine. Whether you're aiming for realistic environmental effects, cinematic combat visuals, or intricate ambient atmospheres, mastering particle systems and leveraging GPU particles can take your game's visuals to the next level. However, it's crucial to optimize particle systems to ensure smooth performance, especially in scenes with many particles.

5.4. Fluid, Fire, and Smoke Simulations

IN THIS SECTION, WE will explore the creation of fluid, fire, and smoke simulations in Unreal Engine. These simulations are essential for various types of games, from realistic fire and smoke in survival horror games to fluid dynamics in adventure and simulation games. Unreal Engine provides tools and features to achieve convincing and dynamic fluid and smoke effects.

Fluid Simulations

FLUID SIMULATIONS IN Unreal Engine enable you to create realistic water bodies, lava flows, and other liquid-based environments. Unreal Engine's fluid simulation system allows for the dynamic interaction of fluids with objects and the environment.

Key aspects of fluid simulations in Unreal Engine include:

- **Realistic Flow**: Create fluid flow patterns that respond to environmental forces like wind and gravity.
- **Buoyancy**: Objects within the fluid can have buoyant forces applied to them, making them float or sink.
- **Surface Tension**: Control the surface tension of the fluid to influence the behavior of droplets and waves.
- **Viscosity**: Adjust the viscosity of the fluid to make it more or less sticky or resistant to flow.

Fire and Smoke Simulations

IMPLEMENTING CONVINCING fire and smoke effects is crucial for creating immersive game experiences. Unreal Engine's Niagara Particle System allows you to simulate fire and smoke with dynamic behavior and realistic visuals.

Key features of fire and smoke simulations include:

- **Particle Systems**: Use particle systems to create the appearance of smoke and fire. These particles can be manipulated to create various fire and smoke behaviors.

- **Volumetric Effects**: Unreal Engine supports volumetric rendering, allowing you to create dense and realistic smoke volumes.

- **Dynamic Lighting**: Simulated fire and smoke can emit light and cast shadows, enhancing the realism of the effect.

- **Environmental Interaction**: Fire and smoke can interact with the environment, affecting objects, characters, and lighting.

Creating Fluid Simulations

TO CREATE FLUID SIMULATIONS in Unreal Engine, you can use the Chaos Physics and Chaos Destruction systems, which are integrated into the engine. These systems provide tools for simulating liquids and rigid bodies interacting with fluids.

// Example of creating a fluid simulation in Unreal Engine C++

```
UFluidSimulationComponent* FluidSim = CreateDefaultSubobject<UFluidSimulationComponent>(TEXT("FluidSi

FluidSim->SetupAttachment(RootComponent);

FluidSim->InitializeFluidSimulation();
```

Optimizing Fluid and Smoke Simulations

REALISTIC FLUID AND smoke simulations can be computationally intensive. To maintain performance:

- **Level of Detail (LOD)**: Implement LOD for fluid and smoke representations to reduce complexity at a distance.

- **Culling**: Use occlusion culling to avoid rendering fluid and smoke that are not visible to the camera.

- **GPU Acceleration**: Utilize GPU acceleration when available to speed up fluid simulations.

- **Particle Pooling**: Implement particle pooling to reuse particles and reduce the overhead of spawning and destroying them.

Conclusion

FLUID, FIRE, AND SMOKE simulations in Unreal Engine are powerful tools for creating immersive and visually stunning game environments. Whether you're aiming to simulate flowing rivers, blazing fires, or billowing smoke, Unreal Engine provides the features and tools needed to achieve realistic and dynamic effects. However, optimizing these simulations is crucial to ensure smooth performance, especially in scenes with complex fluid and smoke interactions.

5.5. Custom Physics Engines Integration

IN THIS SECTION, WE will explore the integration of custom physics engines into Unreal Engine. While Unreal Engine comes with its robust physics simulation system, there are cases where you may want to implement a custom physics engine to achieve specific gameplay mechanics, simulations, or optimizations. Integrating a custom physics engine can provide you with more control and flexibility over your game's physics.

Why Use Custom Physics Engines?

THERE ARE SEVERAL REASONS to consider integrating a custom physics engine into Unreal Engine:

- **Specialized Requirements**: If your game has unique physics requirements that Unreal Engine's built-in system cannot fulfill, a custom physics engine may be necessary.

- **Performance Optimization**: Custom physics engines can be tailored to your game's specific performance needs, allowing for optimization beyond what the general-purpose physics system offers.

- **Unique Mechanics**: If your game relies on unconventional physics or interactions, a custom engine can be designed to accommodate these mechanics.

- **Research and Development**: For research projects or experimental gameplay, a custom physics engine can be a valuable tool for exploring new ideas and concepts.

Steps to Integrate a Custom Physics Engine

INTEGRATING A CUSTOM physics engine into Unreal Engine involves several steps:

1. **Engine Integration**: Integrate the custom physics engine's codebase into your Unreal Engine project. This may involve modifying Unreal Engine's source code to accommodate the custom physics engine's requirements.
2. **Binding and Interface**: Create a bridge or interface that allows communication between Unreal Engine and the custom physics engine. Define how Unreal Engine

components interact with the custom physics engine.

3. **Initialization**: Implement initialization routines to set up the custom physics engine when the game starts.
4. **Object Interactions**: Define how Unreal Engine actors and objects interact with the custom physics engine. This includes handling collision detection, rigid body dynamics, and other physics interactions.
5. **Simulation Update**: Implement the custom physics simulation update loop, which calculates the behavior of physical objects in the game world.
6. **Synchronization**: Ensure that the custom physics engine synchronizes with Unreal Engine's main game loop and other subsystems, such as rendering.

```
// Example of initializing a custom physics engine in Unreal Engine

void UCustomPhysicsComponent::InitializeCustomPhysics()

{

CustomPhysicsEngine::Initialize(); // Replace with your custom engine's initialization function

}
```

Debugging and Testing

INTEGRATING A CUSTOM physics engine can be complex, and debugging is crucial to ensure that physics interactions behave as expected. Unreal Engine provides debugging tools and visualization options to help identify issues in the physics simulation.

- **Logging**: Implement logging and debugging output in your custom physics engine to track and diagnose issues.

- **Visual Debugging**: Use Unreal Engine's visual debugging tools to visualize physics interactions and collision geometry.

- **Simulated Time**: Test your custom physics engine with varying time scales to ensure that physics interactions are stable and consistent.

Performance Considerations

OPTIMIZING A CUSTOM physics engine's integration is essential to maintain smooth gameplay performance. Consider the following performance-related aspects:

- **Parallelization**: Leverage multi-threading and parallel processing to distribute physics calculations across CPU cores.

- **Data Streaming**: Optimize memory usage and data streaming to minimize CPU and memory overhead.

- **Collision Detection**: Implement efficient collision detection algorithms to reduce computational cost.

- **Profiler Integration**: Integrate profiling and performance monitoring tools to identify and address bottlenecks.

Conclusion

INTEGRATING A CUSTOM physics engine into Unreal Engine offers unique advantages when your game requires specialized physics behaviors, optimizations, or experimental gameplay mechanics. While the process can be complex and requires careful planning, the flexibility and control it provides can lead to innovative and engaging gameplay experiences. However, thorough testing, debugging, and performance optimization are crucial to ensure that the custom physics engine functions seamlessly within Unreal Engine.

Chapter 6: Complex AI and Pathfinding

6.1 Crafting Advanced AI Behaviors

IN THIS SECTION, WE will delve into the intricacies of crafting advanced AI behaviors for your Unreal Engine projects. Creating lifelike and responsive AI is essential for immersive gameplay experiences. Whether you're developing non-player characters (NPCs) or wildlife, mastering advanced AI techniques will set your game apart.

Understanding AI Behavior Trees

ONE OF THE CORE COMPONENTS of advanced AI is the Behavior Tree. Behavior Trees are a visual representation of AI decision-making processes. They consist of nodes that define actions, conditions, and sequences of actions. Here's an example of a simple Behavior Tree snippet:

```
Selector
├─ Sequence (Move to Player)
│ ├─ Is Player In Range?
│ └─ Move Toward Player
└─ Sequence (Attack)
```

├─ Is Player In Attack Range?

└─ Attack Player

In this example, the AI checks if the player is in range, and if so, it moves toward the player. If the player is within attack range, it initiates an attack. Behavior Trees allow you to create complex decision-making logic for AI entities.

Implementing Finite State Machines (FSMs)

FINITE STATE MACHINES are another crucial tool in crafting advanced AI. They model AI behavior as a set of states, transitions between these states, and actions associated with each state. Consider a simple example of an NPC's FSM:

State: *Idle*

- Actions: Stand still, look around

State: Patrol

- Actions: Move along a predefined path, occasionally stop to observe

State: Alert

- Actions: Investigate suspicious noises, prepare for combat

State: Combat

- Actions: Attack the player, dodge, and take cover

FSMs help AI entities react differently to changing situations and create more dynamic gameplay.

Implementing Advanced Sensory Perception

ADVANCED AI OFTEN RELIES on sensory perception to interact with the game world realistically. Implementing sensory systems like sight, hearing, and smell can significantly enhance AI behavior. Here's an example of a simple sight perception system:

On See Player:

- Set Player Location as Target

- Transition to Alert State

This code represents how an AI character reacts when it sees the player. Advanced AI may use raycasting or more complex algorithms to simulate realistic sensory perception.

Using Utility-Based AI Decision Making

UTILITY-BASED AI DECISION making involves assigning values to different actions or behaviors based on their importance or desirability. The AI then chooses the action with the highest utility value. For instance:

Utility for Attacking Player = 0.8

Utility for Fleeing = 0.2

Decision: Attack Player (0.8 > 0.2)

This approach allows AI to make nuanced decisions, considering multiple factors simultaneously.

Creating Adaptive AI

ADAPTIVE AI IS CAPABLE of learning and evolving during gameplay. Machine learning techniques like neural networks can be employed to achieve adaptive behavior. These networks can be trained to improve AI performance over time, making AI opponents more challenging as players progress.

In summary, crafting advanced AI behaviors involves understanding Behavior Trees, implementing Finite State Machines, using sensory perception, incorporating utility-based decision making, and exploring adaptive AI techniques. By mastering these concepts, you can create AI that adds depth and challenge to your Unreal Engine games.

6.2 Implementing Dynamic Pathfinding Systems

IN THIS SECTION, WE will explore the implementation of dynamic pathfinding systems for AI in Unreal Engine. Dynamic pathfinding is crucial for AI to navigate complex and changing environments effectively. We will discuss techniques and algorithms that enable AI characters to adapt to obstacles and dynamic changes in the game world.

A Algorithm for Static Pathfinding*

BEFORE DIVING INTO dynamic pathfinding, it's essential to understand the A* (A-star) algorithm, a popular choice for static pathfinding. A* is a graph traversal algorithm that finds the shortest path from a start node to a goal node while considering the cost of moving through nodes. It uses a heuristic to guide the search efficiently.

Here's a simplified representation of the A* algorithm in pseudocode:

OpenSet = {start}

ClosedSet = {}

while OpenSet is not empty:

current = node in OpenSet with the lowest f_score

if current is the goal:

return reconstruct_path(current)

remove current from OpenSet

add current to ClosedSet

for neighbor in neighbors of current:

if neighbor is in ClosedSet:

continue

tentative_g_score = g_score[current] + distance_between(current, neighbor)

if neighbor is not in OpenSet or tentative_g_score < g_score[neighbor]:

came_from[neighbor] = current

g_score[neighbor] = tentative_g_score

f_score[neighbor] = g_score[neighbor] + heuristic(neighbor, goal)

if neighbor is not in OpenSet:

add neighbor to OpenSet

This basic A* implementation is suitable for static environments, but it doesn't handle dynamic changes well.

Dynamic Pathfinding with Recast Navigation

FOR DYNAMIC PATHFINDING in Unreal Engine, the Recast Navigation system is a powerful tool. It's a C++ library integrated into Unreal Engine that provides real-time navigation mesh generation and dynamic pathfinding capabilities.

Recast Navigation can dynamically update navigation meshes to adapt to changes in the environment, such as doors opening or obstacles moving. It uses a voxel grid to represent the environment and efficiently computes paths for AI characters.

Here's a high-level overview of using Recast Navigation in Unreal Engine:

1. **Navigation Mesh Generation:** Use the NavMeshBoundsVolume to define the area where the navigation mesh should be generated. The system automatically creates and updates the navigation mesh based on this volume.
2. **Navigation Queries:** Unreal Engine's AI system provides functions to perform navigation queries, such as finding a path from point A to point B or checking if a location is reachable. These queries use the navigation mesh generated by Recast Navigation.
3. **Dynamic Updates:** When the environment changes, you can use functions like BuildNavigation to update the navigation mesh dynamically. For example, if a door opens,

you can update the navigation mesh to account for the new path.
4. **Path Following:** Unreal Engine's AIController and AICharacter classes include built-in path following behavior. You can set a destination for an AI character, and it will automatically navigate to that location using the generated path.

Recast Navigation simplifies the process of implementing dynamic pathfinding, making it a valuable tool for creating responsive AI in Unreal Engine.

Handling Dynamic Obstacles

DYNAMIC PATHFINDING is particularly useful when dealing with moving obstacles. Consider a scenario where AI characters need to navigate around dynamically moving objects, such as other characters, vehicles, or objects in the game world.

One approach is to continuously update the navigation mesh to reflect the current state of the environment. For example, if an AI character is following another character, the pathfinding system can periodically update the navigation mesh to account for the movement of both characters.

```
// Pseudocode for dynamic obstacle handling

while game is running:

if dynamic_obstacle_has_moved:

update_navigation_mesh()

AI_character_follow_path()
```

This ensures that the AI characters can adapt to changing conditions and continue to navigate effectively.

Conclusion

IMPLEMENTING DYNAMIC pathfinding systems is essential for creating realistic and responsive AI in Unreal Engine. Understanding the A* algorithm for static pathfinding is a foundation, but for dynamic environments, tools like Recast Navigation provide efficient solutions. With dynamic pathfinding, AI characters can navigate around obstacles and adapt to changes in the game world, enhancing the overall gameplay experience.

6.3 AI for Non-Player Characters and Wildlife

IN THIS SECTION, WE will explore the implementation of AI for non-player characters (NPCs) and wildlife in Unreal Engine. NPCs and wildlife play crucial roles in game worlds, adding depth, immersion, and challenges for players. We will discuss various techniques and considerations for creating lifelike and engaging AI behaviors for these entities.

NPC Behavior Design

DESIGNING AI BEHAVIOR for NPCs involves defining their roles, personalities, and interactions within the game world. Consider the following aspects when creating NPC behaviors:

- **Roles:** Determine the primary roles of NPCs, such as quest givers, vendors, or hostile enemies. Each role requires specific AI behaviors and interactions with the player.

- **Personality:** Assign personalities or traits to NPCs to make them feel more realistic. For example, a friendly NPC may approach the player with helpful information, while a hostile NPC may attack on sight.

- **Dialogues:** Create dialogue systems that allow NPCs to communicate with the player. Implement branching dialogues and responses to player choices, enhancing the narrative experience.

- **Schedules:** NPCs can follow schedules, moving between locations or performing tasks at specific times. This adds realism and immersion to the game world.

Behavior Trees for NPCs

BEHAVIOR TREES, AS discussed earlier, are valuable for defining the decision-making processes of NPCs. NPCs can have complex Behavior Trees that govern their actions, reactions to events, and interactions with the player.

Here's an example of a simplified Behavior Tree snippet for an NPC guard:

```
Selector
├─ Sequence (Patrol)
│ ├─ Is Player in Sight?
│ ├─ Chase Player
```

```
│ └─ If Player Escapes, Resume Patrol
├─ Sequence (Alert)
│ ├─ Investigate Suspicious Activity
│ ├─ Call for Backup
│ └─ Chase Intruders
└─ Sequence (Idle)
├─ Wander Randomly
└─ Occasionally Socialize with Other NPCs
```

This Behavior Tree outlines how an NPC guard behaves when the player is encountered, when alerted to suspicious activity, and during idle moments.

Wildlife AI

WILDLIFE AI IS OFTEN used to populate open-world games with animals, creating a more immersive environment. Wildlife AI focuses on natural behaviors, such as hunting, grazing, or fleeing from danger.

- **Navigation:** Wildlife AI often uses navigation systems similar to those of NPCs. However, animals may follow more natural movement patterns, such as herding or flocking.

- **Behavioral States:** Define different behavioral states for wildlife, such as feeding, resting, and fleeing. Each state corresponds to specific actions and interactions with the environment.

- **Predator-Prey Dynamics:** Implement predator-prey interactions among wildlife to create ecological realism. Predators hunt prey, and prey animals may exhibit evasion behaviors.

- **Environmental Awareness:** Wildlife AI should be aware of their surroundings, including terrain, water sources, and other animals. This helps them make informed decisions based on their environment.

Advanced Wildlife Simulations

FOR ADVANCED WILDLIFE simulations, consider using advanced techniques like finite state machines (FSMs) and neural networks. FSMs can model complex wildlife behaviors, while neural networks can provide adaptive learning for animals, allowing them to respond to changing conditions and learn from their interactions.

// Pseudocode for wildlife FSM

State: Grazing

- Actions: Graze on nearby vegetation, move slowly

State: Fleeing

- Actions: Run away from perceived threats, such as predators or loud noises

State: Hunting

- Actions: Pursue prey, coordinate with other predators for group hunting

State: Resting

- Actions: Find a suitable resting spot, conserve energy

These advanced techniques add depth to wildlife AI and make them more convincing within the game world.

Conclusion

CREATING AI FOR NPCS and wildlife in Unreal Engine involves a combination of design considerations, Behavior Trees, and specialized behaviors. NPCs bring life and storytelling elements to your game, while wildlife adds realism to open-world environments. By carefully designing their behaviors and interactions, you can enhance the player's immersion and create memorable gaming experiences.

6.4 Environmental and Adaptive AI

IN THIS SECTION, WE will explore the concept of environmental and adaptive AI in Unreal Engine. Environmental AI refers to AI entities that interact with and respond to their surroundings, while adaptive AI focuses on AI systems that can learn and adapt to changing conditions. These AI techniques can greatly enhance the realism and complexity of your game world.

Environmental Interaction

ENVIRONMENTAL AI INVOLVES AI entities that interact with the game environment in meaningful ways. This can include NPCs that pick up objects, creatures that create nests or burrows, or characters that dynamically respond to weather and terrain changes.

Environmental Awareness

TO CREATE ENVIRONMENTAL interactions, AI needs to be aware of its surroundings. Implementing a sensory system that allows AI to perceive and react to the environment is essential. For example, an NPC might seek shelter when it starts raining, or animals might dig holes in the ground to create nests.

```
// Pseudocode for environmental awareness

if (weather == rain) {

if (entity.type == NPC) {

entity.seekShelter();

} else if (entity.type == Animal) {

entity.digNest();

}

}
```

Dynamic Obstacles

ENVIRONMENTAL AI SHOULD also be able to navigate around dynamic obstacles or changes in the environment. For example, an NPC vendor might move their stall to avoid a crowd, or animals might change their grazing patterns when a new object is placed in their path.

```
// Pseudocode for dynamic obstacle avoidance

if (obstacle.type == crowd) {
```

```
if (entity.type == NPC) {

entity.moveStall();

} else if (entity.type == Animal) {

entity.changeGrazingPattern();

}

}
```

Adaptive AI Learning

ADAPTIVE AI GOES A step further by allowing AI entities to learn from their experiences and adapt to changing conditions. This can be achieved using machine learning techniques, such as neural networks or reinforcement learning.

Reinforcement Learning

REINFORCEMENT LEARNING is a popular technique for adaptive AI. In this approach, AI entities receive rewards or penalties based on their actions, and they learn to maximize their cumulative rewards over time. For example, an AI character in a strategy game might learn to make better decisions in battles through reinforcement learning.

```
// Pseudocode for reinforcement learning

while (game is running) {

state = getCurrentGameState();

action = agent.selectAction(state);
```

```
performAction(action);

reward = calculateReward();

agent.updateQTable(state, action, reward);

}
```

Neural Networks

NEURAL NETWORKS CAN be used for more complex adaptive AI behaviors. For instance, an AI character in a racing game can use a neural network to learn how to navigate tracks efficiently, adapt to different cars, and improve its racing skills over time.

```
// Pseudocode for neural network-based learning

while (game is running) {

state = getCurrentGameState();

action = agent.selectAction(state);

performAction(action);

new_state = getCurrentGameState();

agent.trainNeuralNetwork(state, action, new_state);

}
```

Challenges and Considerations

IMPLEMENTING ENVIRONMENTAL and adaptive AI can be challenging. It requires robust sensory systems, complex decision-making algorithms, and significant computational resources, especially for machine learning-based approaches. Debugging and fine-tuning these systems can also be time-consuming.

However, the rewards are substantial. Environmental AI adds depth and realism to your game world, making it more immersive. Adaptive AI can make your AI opponents or allies more challenging and engaging, enhancing the overall gameplay experience.

Conclusion

ENVIRONMENTAL AND ADAPTIVE AI are advanced techniques that can elevate your game to new heights. By enabling AI entities to interact meaningfully with the environment and adapt to changing conditions, you create a dynamic and engaging gaming experience. Whether you're developing NPCs that respond to weather or characters that learn from their actions, these AI techniques can make your game world come alive.

6.5 Balancing and Fine-Tuning AI Difficulty

BALANCING THE DIFFICULTY of AI opponents and characters is a critical aspect of game design. It ensures that your game remains challenging and enjoyable for players of all skill levels. In this section, we will explore various techniques for balancing and fine-tuning AI difficulty in Unreal Engine.

Difficulty Levels

ONE COMMON APPROACH to balancing AI difficulty is to implement multiple difficulty levels, such as easy, medium, and hard. Each difficulty level adjusts various AI parameters to provide a different level of challenge. For example, in a first-person shooter game, the easy difficulty level might reduce the accuracy of enemy shots, while the hard difficulty level increases enemy accuracy and reaction time.

```
// Pseudocode for difficulty levels

if (difficulty == easy) {

enemy.accuracy = low;

} else if (difficulty == medium) {

enemy.accuracy = medium;

} else if (difficulty == hard) {

enemy.accuracy = high;

}
```

Dynamic Difficulty Adjustment

DYNAMIC DIFFICULTY adjustment (DDA) is a technique that continuously adapts the game's difficulty based on the player's performance. DDA algorithms monitor player actions, such as the number of wins or losses, and adjust AI parameters accordingly to maintain an optimal level of challenge.

```
// Pseudocode for DDA

while (game is running) {

if (playerWins > playerLosses) {

increaseEnemyDifficulty();

} else if (playerLosses > playerWins) {
```

```
decreaseEnemyDifficulty();
}
}
```

DDA ensures that players are neither overwhelmed by AI opponents nor bored due to lack of challenge.

Player Skill-Based AI

ANOTHER APPROACH IS to create AI that adapts to the player's skill level. This can be achieved by modeling the player's skill through various metrics, such as accuracy, reaction time, or completion time, and adjusting AI behavior accordingly.

```
// Pseudocode for skill-based AI
while (game is running) {
playerSkill = calculatePlayerSkill();
adjustAIParametersBasedOnSkill(playerSkill);
}
```

For example, if the player's accuracy is high, AI opponents may become more agile and employ evasive maneuvers to maintain a challenge.

Playtesting and Feedback

BALANCING AI DIFFICULTY often requires extensive playtesting and player feedback. Game designers and developers should actively playtest the game to identify areas where AI difficulty needs adjustment. Collecting feedback from players, both internally and through beta testing, is invaluable for fine-tuning AI behaviors.

Fairness and Transparency

WHEN ADJUSTING AI DIFFICULTY, it's essential to maintain fairness and transparency. Players should understand how difficulty levels affect the game and have the option to choose their preferred level. Avoid creating situations where AI opponents have unfair advantages or behave unpredictably, as this can lead to frustration.

AI Behavior Variety

TO KEEP THE GAMEPLAY engaging, consider implementing AI behavior variety within the same difficulty level. AI opponents with diverse tactics and strategies can make the game more interesting. For example, in a strategy game, different AI factions might have distinct playstyles, even within the same difficulty tier.

```
// Pseudocode for AI behavior variety

if (faction == aggressive) {

employ aggressive tactics;

} else if (faction == defensive) {

use defensive strategies;

} else if (faction == balanced) {

combine offense and defense;

}
```

Conclusion

BALANCING AND FINE-tuning AI difficulty is a crucial aspect of game design that directly impacts the player's experience. Whether you implement difficulty levels, dynamic difficulty adjustment, or player skill-based AI, the goal is to create an enjoyable and appropriately challenging gaming experience. Playtesting and player feedback are essential tools for achieving the right balance in your game.

Chapter 7: Multiplayer and Networking Mastery

7.1 Advanced Networking Concepts in Unreal

IN THIS SECTION, WE will delve into advanced networking concepts in Unreal Engine, focusing on creating robust and seamless multiplayer experiences for your games. Multiplayer functionality is essential for many modern games, and Unreal Engine provides a powerful networking framework to support it. We'll explore key networking concepts and techniques to help you master multiplayer development.

Replication in Unreal Engine

REPLICATION IS A FUNDAMENTAL concept in Unreal Engine's networking framework. It involves synchronizing game state information between the server and connected clients. Unreal Engine uses a client-server model, where one machine acts as the server, responsible for authoritative gameplay decisions, while others are clients, rendering the game and sending input to the server.

Replication can be applied to various game elements, including actors, variables, and functions. For example, replicating the position and rotation of a character allows clients to see the character's movements as determined by the server.

```
// Pseudocode for replicating actor's position and rotation

if (IsServer) {

ReplicatePositionAndRotation();
```

```
}
if (IsClient) {
UpdatePositionAndRotation();
}
```

Remote Function Calls (RCPs)

REMOTE FUNCTION CALLS (RPCs) are used to execute functions on remote machines. This is crucial for triggering actions that affect gameplay across the network. Unreal Engine provides various types of RPCs, including Unreliable, Reliable, and Multicast, each suited for different scenarios.

Unreliable RPCs are used for non-critical information that can be lost without a significant impact on gameplay, while Reliable RPCs ensure that the function call reaches its destination. Multicast RPCs are used to broadcast actions to all connected clients.

```
// Example of a Reliable RPC call
UFUNCTION(Reliable, Server)
void ServerSpawnProjectile(FVector SpawnLocation, FRotator SpawnRotation);
// Example of a Multicast RPC call
UFUNCTION(NetMulticast, Reliable)
void MulticastNotifyGameStart();
```

Networking Optimization

EFFICIENT NETWORKING is crucial for a smooth multiplayer experience. Unreal Engine provides several optimization techniques, including network relevancy, to minimize the amount of data sent over the network. Network relevancy ensures that only relevant information is replicated to clients based on their proximity to game elements.

```
// Pseudocode for network relevancy

if (IsServer && IsNetRelevantFor(Client)) {

ReplicateDataTo(Client);

}
```

Client Prediction and Server Correction

TO IMPROVE THE RESPONSIVENESS of multiplayer games, Unreal Engine supports client-side prediction and server correction. Client prediction allows clients to simulate their actions locally without waiting for server validation. The server then corrects any discrepancies between the client's predictions and the actual game state.

```
// Pseudocode for client prediction and server correction

if (IsClient) {

SimulateLocalMovement();

SendInputToServer();

}
```

```
if (IsServer) {
ValidateClientInput();
UpdateGameState();
SendGameStateToClients();
}
```

Security and Anti-Cheat Measures

MULTIPLAYER GAMES OFTEN face security challenges, such as cheating and hacking. Unreal Engine provides tools and techniques for implementing security measures, including server-side validation of actions and detection of cheating behaviors. It's essential to implement anti-cheat measures to maintain fair and enjoyable multiplayer experiences.

Conclusion

ADVANCED NETWORKING concepts in Unreal Engine are essential for creating engaging and seamless multiplayer games. Replication, RPCs, networking optimization, client prediction, and anti-cheat measures are key elements to master. Understanding and implementing these concepts will help you create multiplayer experiences that captivate players and stand out in the world of online gaming.

7.2 Building Scalable Multiplayer Systems

IN THIS SECTION, WE will explore the development of scalable multiplayer systems in Unreal Engine. Scalability is crucial for multiplayer games to handle various player loads and maintain a stable gaming experience. We will discuss architecture, techniques, and best practices for building multiplayer systems that can grow with the demands of your player base.

Client-Server Architecture

UNREAL ENGINE FOLLOWS a client-server model, where one machine acts as the authoritative server, and others are clients. This architecture allows for centralized control of game logic, making it easier to maintain consistency across clients.

When designing a scalable multiplayer system, consider the server's hardware capabilities, as it will handle the bulk of the processing. Ensure that the server can scale horizontally by adding more instances as player demand increases.

Load Balancing

LOAD BALANCING IS ESSENTIAL for distributing player connections across multiple game servers efficiently. It ensures that no single server becomes overloaded, leading to degraded performance.

Popular load balancing techniques include round-robin DNS, where players are directed to different servers in a cyclical manner, and more advanced solutions like dedicated load balancers that distribute connections based on server load.

```
// Pseudocode for round-robin DNS

if (newPlayerConnection) {

server = getNextAvailableServer();
```

```
redirectPlayerTo(server);

}
```

Replication and Network Traffic

EFFICIENT REPLICATION of game data is critical for scalable multiplayer systems. To reduce network traffic and maintain smooth gameplay, consider the following techniques:

- **Network relevancy:** Only replicate data that is relevant to nearby players to minimize unnecessary traffic.
- **Caching:** Cache frequently accessed data on the client to reduce the need for constant server queries.
- **Compression:** Use network compression to reduce the size of data packets sent over the network.

```
// Pseudocode for caching and compression

if (IsClient) {

CacheFrequentlyUsedData();

CompressNetworkPackets();

}
```

Dynamic Server Allocation

TO HANDLE FLUCTUATIONS in player load, implement dynamic server allocation and deallocation. This involves automatically spawning or shutting down game servers based on player demand.

Cloud service providers like AWS, Azure, and Google Cloud offer solutions for auto-scaling game servers based on predefined rules, ensuring that your multiplayer system can adapt to varying player populations.

```
// Pseudocode for dynamic server allocation

if (playerCount > threshold) {

spawnNewGameServer();

} else if (playerCount < threshold) {

shutDownIdleGameServers();

}
```

Database Scalability

DATABASE SCALABILITY is often overlooked but crucial for multiplayer games that require persistent player data, such as profiles, achievements, and leaderboards. Consider using distributed databases or NoSQL databases that can scale horizontally to handle increased player data.

Monitoring and Analytics

IMPLEMENTING COMPREHENSIVE monitoring and analytics tools is essential for identifying performance bottlenecks, tracking player behavior, and making data-driven decisions to improve scalability.

Tools like Unreal Insights and third-party analytics platforms can provide valuable insights into your multiplayer system's performance and player engagement.

Conclusion

BUILDING SCALABLE MULTIPLAYER systems in Unreal Engine requires careful planning, architecture design, and the implementation of various techniques. A well-designed scalable system can accommodate player growth, ensure a stable gaming experience, and position your multiplayer game for success in a competitive market. By following best practices and staying informed about emerging technologies, you can create multiplayer games that scale with confidence.

7.3 Synchronizing States in Networked Games

IN THIS SECTION, WE will delve into the crucial topic of synchronizing states in networked games using Unreal Engine. When developing multiplayer games, ensuring that all players have a consistent view of the game world is essential for a fair and enjoyable experience. We will explore various synchronization techniques and considerations to achieve this goal.

Deterministic Simulation

TO ACHIEVE SYNCHRONIZED game states, multiplayer games often rely on deterministic simulation. Determinism ensures that given the same initial conditions and inputs, all game instances will produce the same outcomes. This property is crucial for maintaining consistency across clients and the server.

Unreal Engine provides replication and networking features that enable deterministic simulation. By replicating game-relevant actions and events to all clients, you can ensure that everyone observes the same game state. Additionally, using fixed time steps for simulation helps achieve determinism.

```
// Pseudocode for deterministic simulation

if (IsServer) {

ReplicateGameActionsToClients();

SimulateGameAtFixedTimeStep();

}
```

Time Synchronization

SYNCHRONIZING TIME across networked game instances is another critical aspect of maintaining consistent game states. When players experience different frame rates or network delays, time synchronization ensures that game events occur in the correct order.

Unreal Engine offers built-in support for time synchronization through network time manager classes. These classes help adjust the timing of game events based on network conditions to maintain synchronization.

```
// Pseudocode for time synchronization

if (IsServer) {

ReplicateGameActionsToClients();

SynchronizeGameTimeAcrossClients();

SimulateGameAtFixedTimeStep();

}
```

Input Authority and Validation

IN MULTIPLAYER GAMES, it's essential to determine which actions and inputs should be authoritative. Generally, the server should have authority over critical gameplay decisions to prevent cheating. Client-side prediction and server correction mechanisms can help maintain fairness and synchronization.

```
// Pseudocode for input authority and validation

if (IsServer) {

ValidateClientInputs();

SimulateGameAtFixedTimeStep();

ReplicateGameActionsToClients();

}
```

Lag Compensation

LAG COMPENSATION TECHNIQUES are used to ensure that players' actions are still relevant, even when there is network latency. For example, when shooting at a moving target in a first-person shooter game, the game may compensate for lag by predicting the target's position based on the player's input.

```
// Pseudocode for lag compensation

if (IsClient) {

LagCompensateShots();

ReplicateClientActionsToServer();
```

```
}
if (IsServer) {
ValidateClientActionsWithLagCompensation();
SimulateGameAtFixedTimeStep();
ReplicateGameActionsToClients();
}
```

Interpolation and Extrapolation

TO IMPROVE THE VISUAL experience in networked games, interpolation and extrapolation techniques are often used. Interpolation smooths out the movement of remote players, while extrapolation predicts their future positions.

Unreal Engine provides built-in support for these techniques, allowing you to create visually appealing multiplayer games.

```
// Pseudocode for interpolation and extrapolation
if (IsClient) {
InterpolateRemotePlayerMovement();
ExtrapolateRemotePlayerMovement();
}
```

Conclusion

SYNCHRONIZING STATES in networked games is a complex but essential task for delivering enjoyable multiplayer experiences.

Deterministic simulation, time synchronization, input authority, lag compensation, and interpolation/extrapolation techniques are key components in achieving consistent game states across all players. By carefully implementing and fine-tuning these aspects, you can create multiplayer games that offer fair and synchronized gameplay, ensuring player satisfaction and engagement.

7.4 Implementing Security and Anti-Cheat Systems

IN THIS SECTION, WE will explore the critical aspects of implementing security and anti-cheat systems in multiplayer games using Unreal Engine. Security measures are essential to maintain fair gameplay and protect the integrity of your game. We will discuss various techniques and strategies to deter cheating and ensure a level playing field for all players.

Server Authority

ONE FUNDAMENTAL PRINCIPLE of multiplayer game security is server authority. The server should have the final say in all critical game decisions, such as hit detection, player positions, and score calculations. By making the server authoritative, you prevent clients from manipulating game data to gain an unfair advantage.

```
// Pseudocode for server authority

if (IsServer) {

ValidateClientActions();

CalculateGameState();

ReplicateGameStateToClients();
```

}

Client-Side Prediction and Server Correction

TO MAINTAIN SMOOTH gameplay and responsiveness, many multiplayer games use client-side prediction and server correction. Clients simulate actions locally before receiving confirmation from the server. The server then validates and corrects any discrepancies, ensuring fair gameplay.

```
// Pseudocode for client-side prediction and server correction

if (IsClient) {

SimulateLocalActions();

SendActionsToServer();

}

if (IsServer) {

ValidateClientActions();

CorrectClientActions();

UpdateGameState();

ReplicateGameStateToClients();

}
```

Encryption and Secure Communication

PROTECTING NETWORK traffic through encryption is vital to prevent data tampering and eavesdropping. Unreal Engine supports secure communication protocols like HTTPS and SSL/TLS, ensuring that data exchanged between clients and the server remains confidential and secure.

```
// Pseudocode for encrypted communication

if (IsClient) {

EstablishSecureConnection();

SendEncryptedData();

}

if (IsServer) {

ReceiveEncryptedData();

DecryptAndValidateData();

}
```

Cheat Detection and Reporting

IMPLEMENTING CHEAT detection algorithms is essential to identify and penalize cheaters. Unreal Engine provides tools to detect common cheating behaviors, such as aimbots or wallhacks. When a cheat is detected, you can take appropriate actions, such as banning the cheater or applying penalties to their account.

```
// Pseudocode for cheat detection and reporting

if (IsServer) {

DetectCheatingBehavior();

if (CheatingDetected) {
```

```
ApplyPenalties();

ReportToAdmins();

}

}
```

Secure Data Storage

PROTECTING PLAYER DATA and accounts is crucial for maintaining player trust. Implement secure data storage practices to safeguard sensitive information, including usernames, passwords, and payment details. Utilize encryption and access control mechanisms to secure databases and player profiles.

Regular Updates and Patching

FREQUENTLY UPDATE YOUR game to address known vulnerabilities and exploits. Cheaters often exploit outdated versions of games. Regular patches and updates not only improve gameplay but also ensure that security measures remain effective.

Player Reporting and Moderation

ENCOURAGE PLAYERS TO report suspicious behavior or cheaters within the game. Implement moderation tools and teams to review reports and take necessary actions, such as banning or warning offending players. Transparency in handling reports can help maintain a fair gaming environment.

Conclusion

IMPLEMENTING SECURITY and anti-cheat systems in multiplayer games is essential to provide a fair and enjoyable experience for all players. Server authority, client-side prediction, encryption, cheat detection, and secure data storage are critical components of a robust security strategy. By combining these measures and staying vigilant against emerging threats, you can create a secure and cheat-free multiplayer gaming environment, fostering player trust and long-term success.

7.5 Optimizing Network Performance and Latency

IN THIS SECTION, WE will explore techniques and strategies for optimizing network performance and reducing latency in multiplayer games developed using Unreal Engine. Network performance is crucial for providing a smooth and responsive gameplay experience, and minimizing latency is essential for ensuring that players' actions are reflected in the game world with minimal delay.

Network Bandwidth Management

EFFECTIVE NETWORK BANDWIDTH management is vital to optimize network performance. Unreal Engine provides tools for controlling the amount of data transmitted over the network, helping to reduce congestion and prevent packet loss. Key techniques include:

- **Replication relevancy:** Use Unreal's replication system to replicate only relevant data to each player based on their proximity to in-game objects. This reduces unnecessary data transmission to distant players.

```
// Pseudocode for replication relevancy

if (IsServer && IsNetRelevantFor(Client)) {

ReplicateDataTo(Client);

}
```

- **Bandwidth throttling:** Implement bandwidth throttling to limit the amount of data sent by individual players. This helps prevent one player from monopolizing the network resources and causing lag for others.

```
// Pseudocode for bandwidth throttling

if (IsClient) {

ThrottleOutgoingData();

}
```

Server-Side Optimization

OPTIMIZING THE SERVER'S performance is critical for reducing latency and ensuring a responsive gaming experience. Consider the following server-side optimization techniques:

- **Server hardware:** Use powerful server hardware to handle game logic and network communication efficiently. High CPU and RAM resources are essential for maintaining a smooth server performance.

- **Load balancing:** Distribute player connections across multiple server instances to prevent overloading a single server. Load balancing ensures that server performance remains consistent.

- **Server tick rate:** Adjust the server tick rate to balance simulation accuracy and network performance. A lower tick rate reduces server load but may affect gameplay responsiveness.

```
// Pseudocode for server tick rate adjustment

if (IsServer) {

SetServerTickRate(30); // Adjust the tick rate as needed

}
```

Client-Side Prediction and Lag Compensation

CLIENT-SIDE PREDICTION and lag compensation techniques, as discussed in previous sections, help minimize the perceived effects of network latency. By allowing clients to simulate actions locally and compensating for lag, you can create a more responsive gaming experience.

```
// Pseudocode for client-side prediction and lag compensation

if (IsClient) {

SimulateLocalActions();

SendActionsToServer();

}
```

```
if (IsServer) {
ValidateClientActions();
CorrectClientActionsWithLagCompensation();
UpdateGameState();
ReplicateGameStateToClients();
}
```

Network Protocols and Transport

CHOOSING THE RIGHT network protocols and transport layers can significantly impact network performance. Unreal Engine supports various network protocols and transport layers, including TCP, UDP, and custom solutions. Consider the specific requirements of your game and select the most appropriate protocol for your networking needs.

Network Debugging and Profiling

REGULARLY MONITOR AND profile network performance using Unreal's debugging and profiling tools. Identifying network bottlenecks and latency issues early allows for timely optimization and maintenance of a responsive multiplayer experience.

Conclusion

OPTIMIZING NETWORK performance and reducing latency in multiplayer games is essential for providing an enjoyable and competitive gaming experience. Effective bandwidth management, server-side optimization, client-side prediction, and careful protocol selection are key factors in achieving this goal. By implementing these strategies and continuously monitoring and refining your networking solution, you can create multiplayer games that are responsive, engaging, and free from frustrating latency issues.

Chapter 8: Virtual Reality and Augmented Reality Development

8.1 Crafting Immersive VR and AR Experiences

IN THIS SECTION, WE will explore the exciting world of virtual reality (VR) and augmented reality (AR) development using Unreal Engine. VR and AR technologies offer immersive and interactive experiences that can transport players to new worlds or enhance their real-world surroundings. We'll delve into the fundamentals of creating compelling VR and AR experiences and discuss key considerations for successful development.

Understanding VR and AR

VIRTUAL REALITY (VR) immerses users in a fully simulated digital environment, typically using headsets that track head movements and often hand controllers for interaction. VR experiences can range from immersive games to architectural visualizations and training simulations.

Augmented Reality (AR), on the other hand, overlays digital content onto the real world. AR applications can be seen through smartphones, tablets, AR glasses, or other devices, enhancing the user's perception of reality with digital elements.

Unreal Engine's VR and AR Support

UNREAL ENGINE PROVIDES robust support for both VR and AR development. It includes a wide range of tools, APIs, and plugins that make it easier to create immersive experiences. Unreal Engine supports popular VR and AR platforms such as Oculus Rift, HTC Vive, PlayStation VR, and ARKit/ARCore for mobile AR.

Building VR Environments

CREATING IMMERSIVE VR environments in Unreal Engine involves several key steps:

- **Designing 3D Assets:** Design and model 3D assets that fit your VR world's theme and purpose. Ensure that assets are optimized for VR performance.
- **VR Camera Setup:** Configure the VR camera system to respond to head movements and user interactions. Unreal Engine provides built-in support for VR cameras.
- **Interaction Mechanics:** Implement interaction mechanics that allow users to interact with objects and navigate the VR environment. This may include hand controllers or gaze-based interactions.
- **Performance Optimization:** VR experiences demand high performance to maintain immersion. Optimize your VR project for a stable frame rate and low latency.

Developing AR Applications

FOR AR DEVELOPMENT in Unreal Engine, you'll need to consider:

- **Markerless Tracking:** Implement markerless tracking using ARKit or ARCore to track the user's device in the real world accurately.

- **Scene Augmentation:** Develop digital assets and animations to overlay on the real world. Consider how these elements will interact with the user's surroundings.

- **User Interaction:** Create intuitive interaction methods, such as touch or gesture-based controls, to allow users to interact with AR content.

- **Environmental Understanding:** Leverage AR features like environmental understanding to anchor digital objects in the real world, creating a seamless blend of virtual and real elements.

Performance and Optimization

BOTH VR AND AR EXPERIENCES require careful performance optimization. To maintain a consistent frame rate and minimize motion sickness in VR, you may need to reduce the complexity of 3D models, use level-of-detail (LOD) techniques, and optimize lighting and rendering.

For AR, optimizing real-time rendering while maintaining high-quality visual effects is crucial. Balancing performance and visual fidelity is a key challenge in AR development.

User Comfort and Accessibility

CONSIDER USER COMFORT and accessibility in your VR and AR experiences. Minimize motion sickness in VR by providing comfortable locomotion options and ensuring that the frame rate remains stable. Make AR experiences accessible by considering user mobility and device compatibility.

Conclusion

CREATING IMMERSIVE VR and AR experiences with Unreal Engine opens up exciting possibilities for game development, training simulations, architectural visualization, and more. Understanding the differences between VR and AR, leveraging Unreal Engine's VR and AR support, optimizing performance, and prioritizing user comfort are essential elements for crafting compelling and enjoyable VR and AR experiences. With the right approach and creative vision, you can transport users to new dimensions and enhance their reality through immersive technology.

8.2 Performance and Optimization for VR/AR

IN THIS SECTION, WE will focus on the crucial aspect of performance and optimization when developing virtual reality (VR) and augmented reality (AR) experiences using Unreal Engine. Achieving high performance is essential to deliver smooth and immersive VR/AR interactions while maintaining visual quality. We will explore optimization strategies, best practices, and tools to help you create responsive and visually stunning VR/AR applications.

Frame Rate and Latency

MAINTAINING A HIGH and consistent frame rate is paramount in VR and AR development. Low frame rates can lead to motion sickness and discomfort for users. In VR, a frame rate of at least 90 frames per second (FPS) is recommended for a comfortable experience, while AR applications should aim for 60 FPS or higher.

Reducing latency is equally important. Latency refers to the delay between a user's action and the corresponding visual or auditory feedback. Lower latency improves the sense of presence in VR/AR. Unreal Engine provides tools and optimizations to minimize latency, including asynchronous timewarp and predictive tracking.

Level of Detail (LOD) and Optimization

OPTIMIZING 3D ASSETS through level-of-detail (LOD) techniques is crucial for VR/AR performance. LOD involves creating simplified versions of 3D models for different distances from the user's viewpoint. Unreal Engine allows you to set up LODs for assets, automatically switching to lower-detail models when they are distant from the camera. This significantly reduces rendering workload and improves performance.

```
// Pseudocode for LOD setup in Unreal Engine

if (IsClient) {

SetupLODFor3DModel();

}
```

Texture and Material Optimization

OPTIMIZING TEXTURES and materials is another vital aspect of VR/AR performance. High-resolution textures and complex materials can consume GPU resources, leading to reduced frame rates. To optimize textures, you can:

- Use texture streaming to load textures only when needed.
- Compress textures to reduce memory usage.

• Implement mipmapping for smooth texture transitions at varying distances.

For materials, consider simplifying shaders and avoiding unnecessary complexity. Use the Material Editor in Unreal Engine to optimize material settings.

Dynamic Lighting and Shadows

REAL-TIME DYNAMIC LIGHTING and shadows can be resource-intensive. In VR/AR, it's essential to strike a balance between visual quality and performance. Consider using baked lighting for static objects and minimizing the use of dynamic lights. Implementing level streaming techniques can help load and unload parts of the scene as needed, reducing the rendering workload.

```
// Pseudocode for level streaming setup in Unreal Engine

if (IsClient) {

SetupLevelStreaming();

}
```

Particle Systems and Effects

PARTICLE SYSTEMS AND visual effects can enhance VR/AR experiences but also impact performance. Optimize particle systems by adjusting particle counts, using GPU particles, and culling particles that are outside the user's field of view. Unreal Engine's Niagara system offers advanced tools for creating and optimizing particle effects.

```
// Pseudocode for Niagara particle system optimization
```

```
if (IsClient) {
OptimizeNiagaraParticleSystem();
}
```

Profiling and Testing

REGULARLY PROFILE YOUR VR/AR application to identify performance bottlenecks. Unreal Engine provides profiling tools that help you analyze CPU and GPU performance, memory usage, and frame timings. Testing on target hardware is crucial to ensure that your application performs well on the intended VR/AR devices.

Conclusion

PERFORMANCE AND OPTIMIZATION are fundamental considerations when developing VR and AR experiences in Unreal Engine. Maintaining a high frame rate, minimizing latency, optimizing 3D assets, textures, materials, lighting, and particle systems are key strategies to deliver immersive and responsive applications. Regular profiling and testing help ensure that your VR/AR application provides a smooth and enjoyable experience for users, enhancing immersion and engagement.

8.3 Implementing Advanced Interaction Systems

IN THIS SECTION, WE will delve into the implementation of advanced interaction systems for virtual reality (VR) and augmented reality (AR) experiences using Unreal Engine. Interactivity is a key factor in creating engaging VR/AR applications, allowing users to interact with the virtual world in a natural and immersive way. We will explore various interaction techniques, input methods, and best practices to enhance user engagement.

Motion Controllers and Input Devices

MOTION CONTROLLERS are essential tools for enabling interaction in VR. These controllers can track users' hand movements and gestures, allowing them to manipulate objects and interact with the environment. Unreal Engine provides built-in support for popular VR controllers such as Oculus Touch, HTC Vive controllers, and PlayStation Move controllers.

```
// Pseudocode for motion controller setup in Unreal Engine

if (IsClient) {

SetupMotionControllers();

}
```

Hand Tracking

HAND TRACKING TECHNOLOGY has become increasingly popular in VR/AR development. It allows users to interact with the virtual world using their bare hands, eliminating the need for physical controllers. Unreal Engine supports hand tracking devices like the Oculus Quest hand tracking feature, making it easier to create natural and intuitive interactions.

Physics-Based Interactions

IMPLEMENTING PHYSICS-based interactions adds realism to VR/AR experiences. Unreal Engine's physics engine can simulate object interactions, allowing users to pick up, throw, and manipulate objects as they would in the real world. Consider using physics constraints and interactions to make objects behave naturally.

```
// Pseudocode for physics-based interactions

if (IsClient) {

ImplementPhysicsInteractions();

}
```

Gesture Recognition

GESTURE RECOGNITION enhances user interaction by recognizing predefined hand gestures or movements. You can use gesture recognition to trigger actions, activate UI elements, or perform in-game gestures. Unreal Engine provides tools for recognizing gestures and mapping them to specific actions in your VR/AR application.

```
// Pseudocode for gesture recognition in Unreal Engine

if (IsClient) {

RecognizeGestures();

MapGesturesToActions();

}
```

Haptic Feedback

HAPTIC FEEDBACK PROVIDES tactile sensations to users, enhancing the sense of immersion in VR/AR environments. Unreal Engine supports haptic feedback for motion controllers, allowing you to provide users with realistic touch sensations when they interact with objects or surfaces.

```
// Pseudocode for haptic feedback in Unreal Engine

if (IsClient) {

ImplementHapticFeedback();

}
```

UI and Menu Interaction

INCORPORATING USER interfaces (UI) and menus into VR/AR applications is essential for navigation and interaction. Unreal Engine offers tools for creating 3D UI elements that users can interact with using motion controllers or gestures. Ensure that UI elements are designed for readability and ease of interaction in a 3D space.

User Testing and Iteration

USER TESTING IS A CRUCIAL step in refining your VR/AR interaction systems. Gather user feedback to identify areas for improvement and iterate on your interaction design. Pay attention to user comfort and ergonomics, as uncomfortable or awkward interactions can lead to a less enjoyable experience.

Conclusion

IMPLEMENTING ADVANCED interaction systems in VR and AR applications using Unreal Engine allows you to create immersive and engaging experiences. Whether you are using motion controllers, hand tracking, physics-based interactions, gesture recognition, or haptic feedback, the goal is to provide users with natural and intuitive ways to interact with the virtual world. Through careful design, testing, and iteration, you can deliver compelling VR/AR applications that captivate users and enhance their sense of presence in the virtual environment.

8.4 Overcoming VR/AR Development Challenges

IN THIS SECTION, WE will address some of the common challenges and considerations that developers face when creating virtual reality (VR) and augmented reality (AR) experiences using Unreal Engine. While VR and AR offer exciting possibilities, they also come with unique technical and design challenges that need to be overcome for a successful project.

Motion Sickness and Comfort

MOTION SICKNESS REMAINS one of the significant challenges in VR development. Developers must design experiences that minimize motion sickness by optimizing frame rates, reducing latency, and providing comfortable locomotion options. Techniques like teleportation and snap turning can help mitigate discomfort for some users.

```
// Pseudocode for teleportation implementation

if (IsClient) {

ImplementTeleportation();

}
```

Performance Optimization

VR/AR APPLICATIONS demand high performance to maintain immersion. Developers need to optimize assets, textures, materials, and lighting while still delivering high-quality visuals. Regular profiling and testing on target hardware are essential to identify and address performance bottlenecks.

User Interface Design

DESIGNING USER INTERFACES (UI) for VR/AR can be challenging due to the 3D spatial aspect. UI elements must be placed in the virtual world effectively, ensuring readability and usability. Developers should consider gaze-based interactions, gesture controls, and 3D UI design principles.

```
// Pseudocode for 3D UI design in Unreal Engine
if (IsClient) {
Design3DUIElements();
}
```

Content Creation

CREATING 3D CONTENT for VR/AR requires specialized skills and tools. Developers must model, texture, and animate assets for the virtual world. Asset optimization, LODs, and effective use of physics are critical considerations. Unreal Engine's content creation tools can streamline this process.

Platform Fragmentation

VR/AR DEVELOPMENT OFTEN involves targeting multiple platforms, each with its own hardware specifications and capabilities. Developers must optimize and test their applications for each target platform, which can be time-consuming and resource-intensive.

User Testing and Feedback

USER TESTING IS ESSENTIAL to identify usability issues and gather feedback on VR/AR experiences. It may involve conducting playtesting sessions, observing user behavior, and making iterative improvements based on user input.

Accessibility

ENSURING THAT VR/AR experiences are accessible to a wide range of users is vital. Consider factors like user mobility, visual impairments, and physical limitations. Implement accessibility features, such as voice commands or alternative interaction methods, to accommodate diverse user needs.

```
// Pseudocode for accessibility features in Unreal Engine

if (IsClient) {

ImplementAccessibilityFeatures();

}
```

Legal and Ethical Considerations

VR/AR DEVELOPERS MUST navigate legal and ethical considerations, including privacy concerns, intellectual property rights, and ethical design practices. Familiarize yourself with relevant regulations and ethical guidelines to ensure compliance.

Future-Proofing

THE VR/AR LANDSCAPE is continually evolving. Developers should stay informed about emerging technologies, hardware advancements, and industry trends to future-proof their projects. Regularly updating and optimizing applications to leverage new capabilities is crucial for long-term success.

Conclusion

VR AND AR DEVELOPMENT offer exciting opportunities but also come with challenges that developers must address. From mitigating motion sickness to optimizing performance and ensuring accessibility, overcoming these challenges requires careful planning, testing, and iteration. By staying up-to-date with industry developments and prioritizing user experience, developers can create compelling and successful VR/AR applications using Unreal Engine.

8.5 Future Trends in VR/AR with Unreal

IN THIS SECTION, WE will explore the future trends and emerging technologies in the field of virtual reality (VR) and augmented reality (AR) development using Unreal Engine. The VR/AR landscape is continually evolving, presenting exciting opportunities for developers to create cutting-edge experiences. We'll discuss some of the key trends and technologies to watch out for in the coming years.

1. Mixed Reality (MR): Mixed Reality combines elements of both

VR and AR, allowing users to interact with both digital and physical worlds seamlessly. Unreal Engine is well-positioned to support MR experiences, making it easier to create applications that blur the line between the virtual and real.

2. 5G Connectivity: The rollout of 5G networks will significantly enhance the capabilities of mobile AR applications. Unreal Engine's support for mobile platforms makes it a powerful tool for creating 5G-powered AR experiences with low latency and high bandwidth.

3. AI and Machine Learning: Integrating AI and machine learning into VR/AR applications can enable more realistic interactions and adaptive content. Unreal Engine's extensible architecture allows developers to incorporate AI-driven features into their projects.

4. Hand and Gesture Tracking: Advances in hand and gesture tracking technologies will make VR/AR interactions even more natural. Unreal Engine's support for hand tracking devices and gesture recognition enables developers to leverage these technologies easily.

5. Spatial Computing: Spatial computing refers to the ability of AR devices to understand and interact with the physical world's spatial context. Unreal Engine's capabilities in environmental understanding and scene anchoring make it suitable for spatial computing applications.

6. WebXR: The WebXR standard aims to bring VR/AR experiences to web browsers, making them more accessible to users. Unreal Engine's support for WebXR allows developers to

create web-based VR/AR content that reaches a broader audience.

7. Realistic Physics and Interactions: Unreal Engine's ongoing development focuses on enhancing physics simulation and interactions, making it easier to create lifelike VR/AR experiences with realistic physics and object behavior.

```
// PSEUDOCODE FOR PHYSICS interaction in Unreal Engine
if (IsClient) {
CreateRealisticPhysicsInteractions();
}
```

8. Cross-Platform Development: Cross-platform VR/AR development will become increasingly important as the market diversifies. Unreal Engine's ability to target multiple platforms from a single project simplifies cross-platform development.

9. Content Creation Tools: Unreal Engine continues to evolve its content creation tools, making it more accessible for artists and designers to create 3D assets and environments. These improvements streamline the content creation pipeline for VR/AR projects.

10. Community and Collaboration: The Unreal Engine developer community is vibrant and collaborative. Leveraging community resources, forums, and marketplace assets can accelerate VR/AR development and provide valuable insights into emerging trends.

Conclusion

THE FUTURE OF VR AND AR development using Unreal Engine is full of exciting possibilities. As technology continues to advance, developers have access to a growing toolkit of features and capabilities to create immersive and engaging experiences. Staying informed about emerging trends, experimenting with new technologies, and collaborating with the Unreal Engine community will be essential for harnessing the full potential of VR and AR in the years to come.

Chapter 9: Advanced Animation and Character Design

9.1 Rigging and Skinning for Complex Characters

IN THIS SECTION, WE will dive deep into the world of character rigging and skinning for complex characters in Unreal Engine. Rigging is the process of creating a skeleton or armature for a character, while skinning involves attaching the character's mesh to the skeleton. Proper rigging and skinning are essential for realistic character animations and interactions. We'll explore the techniques, tools, and best practices for rigging and skinning complex characters.

Importance of Rigging and Skinning

RIGGING AND SKINNING are fundamental steps in character animation. A well-rigged character can perform a wide range of realistic movements and expressions. Skinning ensures that the character's mesh deforms smoothly as the skeleton moves, creating lifelike animations.

Skeletal Meshes and Skeletons

IN UNREAL ENGINE, CHARACTER rigging involves creating a skeleton composed of bones, each representing a part of the character's body. Skeletal meshes are 3D models associated with a skeleton. The process of rigging connects the skeletal mesh to the skeleton.

Bone Hierarchy and Naming Conventions

MAINTAINING A CLEAR bone hierarchy and adhering to naming conventions is crucial for rigging. Bones should be organized logically, with child bones attached to parent bones. Consistent naming conventions make it easier to work with rigs and animations.

```
// Pseudocode for defining bone hierarchy

if (IsClient) {

DefineBoneHierarchy();

ApplyNamingConventions();

}
```

Weight Painting

WEIGHT PAINTING IS the process of assigning influence to each bone on the character's mesh. Different parts of the mesh are affected by different bones. Weight painting ensures that deformations appear natural during animation.

```
// Pseudocode for weight painting in Unreal Engine

if (IsClient) {

ApplyWeightPainting();

}
```

Inverse Kinematics (IK) and Forward Kinematics (FK)

UNREAL ENGINE SUPPORTS both inverse kinematics (IK) and forward kinematics (FK) for character animation. IK allows you to manipulate the end of a limb (e.g., a hand or foot), and the rest of the limb follows naturally. FK involves rotating each bone individually.

Animation Blueprints

ANIMATION BLUEPRINTS in Unreal Engine are essential for defining how characters move and interact. They allow you to create complex animations, blend between different states, and control character behaviors.

```
// Pseudocode for Animation Blueprint setup
if (IsClient) {
CreateAnimationBlueprint();
DefineCharacter Behaviors();
ImplementAnimation Logic();
}
```

Retargeting and Animation Sharing

UNREAL ENGINE PROVIDES tools for retargeting animations between characters with different skeletons. This allows you to reuse animations across multiple characters, saving development time and resources.

Blend Spaces and Animation Blending

BLEND SPACES ENABLE smooth transitions between different animations based on input parameters. For example, you can create blend spaces for character movement speed, smoothly transitioning between walking, running, and sprinting animations.

```
// Pseudocode for blend space setup in Unreal Engine

if (IsClient) {

CreateBlendSpace();

DefineTransition Parameters();

ImplementAnimation Blending();

}
```

Facial Animation

FACIAL ANIMATION IS a critical aspect of character design. Unreal Engine provides tools for creating expressive facial animations, including morph targets and blend shapes.

Conclusion

RIGGING AND SKINNING for complex characters in Unreal Engine are essential skills for character animators and game developers. These processes lay the foundation for realistic and expressive character animations. By following best practices, organizing bone hierarchies, weight painting accurately, and utilizing Unreal Engine's animation features, you can create characters that come to life with lifelike movements and emotions in your game or interactive project.

9.2 Facial Animation and Expressive Characters

IN THIS SECTION, WE will explore the fascinating world of facial animation and creating expressive characters in Unreal Engine. Facial animation is crucial for bringing characters to life, conveying emotions, and enhancing the storytelling in games and interactive experiences. We'll delve into the techniques, tools, and best practices for achieving realistic and emotionally engaging facial animations.

Importance of Facial Animation

FACIAL ANIMATION PLAYS a significant role in character design and storytelling. It allows characters to express emotions, communicate non-verbally, and connect with the audience on a deeper level. Whether it's a smile, a frown, or a raised eyebrow, facial animations can convey a character's thoughts and feelings effectively.

Morph Targets and Blend Shapes

UNREAL ENGINE SUPPORTS morph targets, also known as blend shapes in some 3D modeling software. Morph targets involve creating a series of pre-modeled facial expressions or deformations that can be blended together in real-time to create various facial animations. These morph targets can represent different emotions, mouth shapes for speech, and more.

```
// Pseudocode for creating and blending morph targets

if (IsClient) {

CreateMorphTargets();

BlendMorphTargets();
```

```
}
```

Rigging for Facial Animation

RIGGING FOR FACIAL animation involves setting up a bone or joint system that controls the movement of different parts of the face, such as the jaw, eyebrows, and eyelids. These bones or joints can be manipulated to create a wide range of facial expressions. Rigging for facial animation often uses a combination of bone-based rigging and morph targets.

```
// Pseudocode for facial rigging setup in Unreal Engine

if (IsClient) {

SetupFacialRig();

}
```

Facial Animation Blueprints

UNREAL ENGINE ALLOWS you to create Facial Animation Blueprints to control and blend different facial animations. These blueprints enable you to map input data, such as microphone input or performance capture data, to the movement of facial bones or morph targets.

```
// Pseudocode for Facial Animation Blueprint setup

if (IsClient) {

CreateFacialAnimationBlueprint();

MapInputData();

ControlFacialExpressions();
```

```
}
```

Performance Capture and Scanning

FOR HIGHLY REALISTIC facial animations, performance capture and 3D scanning technologies can be employed. These methods capture an actor's facial movements and expressions in detail and apply them to a 3D character model. Unreal Engine supports performance capture workflows, making it possible to achieve lifelike facial animations.

Real-Time Rendering and Shading

REAL-TIME RENDERING and shading techniques play a significant role in the quality of facial animations. Unreal Engine's advanced rendering capabilities allow for realistic skin shading, subsurface scattering, and dynamic lighting that enhance the appearance of characters during facial animations.

Lip Sync and Speech Animation

CREATING ACCURATE LIP sync and speech animations is crucial for characters that speak. Unreal Engine provides tools for synchronizing character lip movements with spoken dialogue, making it possible to create realistic conversations and cinematic sequences.

```
// Pseudocode for lip sync and speech animation setup
if (IsClient) {
CreateDialogueSystem();
ImplementLipSync();
```

```
SyncSpeech with Facial Expressions();
}
```

Conclusion

FACIAL ANIMATION IS a powerful tool for character expression and storytelling in Unreal Engine. Whether you're creating characters for video games, simulations, or animated films, mastering facial animation techniques is essential to engage and immerse your audience. By leveraging morph targets, facial rigging, animation blueprints, and real-time rendering, you can breathe life into your characters and convey emotions effectively, enhancing the overall quality of your projects.

9.3 Motion Capture Integration and Processing

IN THIS SECTION, WE will delve into the world of motion capture (MoCap) integration and processing in Unreal Engine. Motion capture is a technique used to capture the movements of actors or objects and apply them to 3D characters or models. Integrating MoCap data into your Unreal Engine project can bring a new level of realism to character animations and interactions. We will explore the steps involved in MoCap integration, data processing, and best practices.

Understanding Motion Capture

MOTION CAPTURE INVOLVES recording the movements of real-world objects or actors using specialized equipment like motion capture suits, markers, or cameras. The captured data is then processed and applied to virtual characters or models, allowing them to mimic the recorded movements accurately.

MoCap Hardware and Software

TO BEGIN WITH MOCAP integration, you need access to suitable hardware and software. This includes motion capture cameras, sensors, or suits, as well as MoCap software for data recording and processing. Unreal Engine supports various MoCap hardware and software solutions, making it versatile for integration.

```
// Pseudocode for connecting MoCap hardware to Unreal Engine

if (IsClient) {

ConnectMotionCaptureHardware();

}
```

Data Capture and Recording

THE FIRST STEP IN MOCAP integration is capturing motion data. Actors or objects equipped with motion capture markers or sensors perform the desired actions while being recorded. MoCap cameras or sensors track the movements and create a dataset for further processing.

Data Processing and Cleanup

MOCAP DATA IS OFTEN noisy and may require cleaning and processing. Unreal Engine provides tools for filtering and refining motion data, removing outliers, and ensuring smooth and accurate animations.

```
// Pseudocode for MoCap data processing in Unreal Engine
if (IsClient) {
CleanAndRefineMotionData();
}
```

Skeleton Mapping

MAPPING THE MOCAP DATA to your character's skeleton is a crucial step. Unreal Engine allows you to define a mapping between the motion capture rig and your character's skeleton, ensuring that the movements align correctly.

```
// Pseudocode for skeleton mapping in Unreal Engine
if (IsClient) {
MapMoCapDataToCharacterSkeleton();
}
```

Animation Retargeting

IN CASES WHERE THE motion capture data comes from different sources or actors, retargeting may be necessary. Unreal Engine provides retargeting tools to adapt MoCap data to characters with different proportions or skeletons.

```
// Pseudocode for animation retargeting in Unreal Engine
if (IsClient) {
RetargetMoCapAnimations();
```

```
}
```

Animation Blueprints and Blending

ONCE THE MOCAP DATA is integrated, you can use Animation Blueprints in Unreal Engine to control character animations and blending. This allows you to combine MoCap animations with other animations or procedural animations for more complex and realistic movements.

```
// Pseudocode for Animation Blueprint setup with MoCap data

if (IsClient) {

CreateMoCapAnimationBlueprint();

BlendMoCapAnimations();

}
```

Fine-Tuning and Artistic Control

WHILE MOCAP PROVIDES realistic animations, artistic control is essential to achieve the desired look and feel. Unreal Engine's animation tools allow animators to fine-tune and adjust animations to match the project's artistic vision.

Conclusion

MOTION CAPTURE INTEGRATION and processing in Unreal Engine open up a world of possibilities for creating lifelike character animations and interactions. Whether you're working on video games, simulations, or cinematic experiences, MoCap data can add a level of realism and authenticity that is hard to achieve through manual animation alone. By understanding the MoCap pipeline, mastering data processing, and utilizing Unreal Engine's animation tools, you can elevate the quality of character animations in your projects.

9.4 Advanced Animation Blending Techniques

IN THIS SECTION, WE will explore advanced animation blending techniques in Unreal Engine. Animation blending is a critical aspect of character animation, allowing for smooth transitions between different animations and creating complex character behaviors. We'll delve into the tools, methods, and best practices for achieving advanced animation blending in Unreal Engine.

Importance of Animation Blending

ANIMATION BLENDING enables characters to respond dynamically to in-game events and player inputs. Whether it's transitioning from walking to running, seamlessly switching between combat stances, or smoothly blending between idle and interaction animations, advanced blending techniques enhance the overall gameplay experience.

Blend Spaces

BLEND SPACES ARE A powerful tool in Unreal Engine for creating smooth transitions between animations based on multiple input parameters. These parameters can include variables like movement speed, aiming direction, or any custom gameplay variables. Blend spaces allow for complex, multidimensional animation blending.

```
// Pseudocode for creating a blend space in Unreal Engine

if (IsClient) {

CreateBlendSpace();

DefineInput Parameters();

ImplementComplexBlendTransitions();

}
```

Animation Layers

UNREAL ENGINE SUPPORTS animation layers, which allow you to stack multiple animations on top of each other. This enables the blending of animations for different body parts independently. For example, you can have a character walking while separately animating their upper body to aim or perform other actions.

```
// Pseudocode for setting up animation layers in Unreal Engine

if (IsClient) {

CreateAnimationLayers();

BlendAnimationsInLayers();

}
```

State Machines

ANIMATION STATE MACHINES are used to define complex logic for transitioning between different animation states. They are particularly useful for handling character behaviors in response to various game events. Unreal Engine's Animation Blueprint Graph provides a visual way to design and control animation state machines.

```
// Pseudocode for creating an animation state machine in Unreal Engine

if (IsClient) {

CreateAnimationStateMachine();

DefineTransitionsandConditions();

ImplementComplexBehavior Logic();

}
```

Animation Montages

ANIMATION MONTAGES in Unreal Engine allow you to combine multiple animations into a single sequence. They are useful for creating dynamic and cinematic sequences, such as combat combos or interactive cutscenes. Montages can be triggered programmatically during gameplay.

```
// Pseudocode for setting up animation montages in Unreal Engine

if (IsClient) {

CreateAnimationMontage();
```

```
DefineMontageSections();

TriggerMontagesInGameplay();

}
```

Blending for Different States

EFFECTIVE ANIMATION blending often involves smoothly transitioning between various character states, such as walking, running, crouching, or performing specific actions. By carefully configuring the blending parameters and transitions, you can create responsive and visually appealing character animations.

Inverse Kinematics (IK)

INVERSE KINEMATICS can be integrated into animation blending to ensure that characters interact realistically with the environment. For example, IK can be used to align a character's hands with objects they are holding or surfaces they are touching.

```
// Pseudocode for implementing inverse kinematics in Unreal Engine

if (IsClient) {

IntegrateInverseKinematics();

AlignCharacter Limbs Accurately();

}
```

Testing and Iteration

EFFECTIVE ANIMATION blending often requires thorough testing and iteration to fine-tune transitions and ensure that animations feel responsive and seamless during gameplay. Playtesting and user feedback are crucial for identifying areas that need improvement.

Conclusion

ADVANCED ANIMATION blending techniques are essential for creating immersive and dynamic character animations in Unreal Engine. Whether you're developing a video game, interactive experience, or simulation, mastering these techniques will enable you to create characters that move and behave realistically in response to player actions and in-game events. By combining blend spaces, animation layers, state machines, and montages, you can achieve a high level of animation fidelity and create compelling character-driven gameplay.

9.5 Procedural Animation and Dynamic IK Systems

IN THIS SECTION, WE will explore the exciting world of procedural animation and dynamic Inverse Kinematics (IK) systems in Unreal Engine. Procedural animation allows characters and objects to move and interact with their environment dynamically, without relying solely on pre-made animations. Dynamic IK systems enable characters to adapt and react realistically to changes in the game world. We'll delve into the techniques, tools, and best practices for incorporating procedural animation and dynamic IK into your Unreal Engine projects.

The Power of Procedural Animation

PROCEDURAL ANIMATION is a game-changer in character and object animation. It allows for realistic and responsive movements that adapt to the game's context. Rather than relying solely on a library of pre-crafted animations, procedural animation generates animations on the fly based on game events and physics simulations.

Ragdoll Physics

UNREAL ENGINE PROVIDES robust support for ragdoll physics, which enables characters to react dynamically to forces and collisions. When a character is defeated or knocked back, the physics-based ragdoll simulation takes over, creating natural and unpredictable movements.

```
// Pseudocode for enabling ragdoll physics in Unreal Engine

if (IsClient) {

EnableRagdollPhysics();

SimulateRagdollReactions();

}
```

Animation Blueprints for Procedural Animation

ANIMATION BLUEPRINTS in Unreal Engine are versatile tools for implementing procedural animations. They allow you to define complex logic that influences character movements and animations based on various conditions. This is particularly useful for locomotion, aiming, and reacting to environmental changes.

```
// Pseudocode for Animation Blueprint setup with procedural animation

if (IsClient) {

CreateProceduralAnimationBlueprint();

DefineProceduralBehaviorLogic();

ImplementDynamicCharacter Movements();

}
```

Dynamic IK Systems

DYNAMIC IK SYSTEMS in Unreal Engine are essential for characters to interact convincingly with the environment. These systems allow characters to adapt their limb positions and orientations based on factors like terrain slopes, object interactions, and physical constraints.

```
// Pseudocode for implementing dynamic IK in Unreal Engine

if (IsClient) {

IntegrateDynamicIKSystem();

AdaptLimbPositionsToTerrain();

}
```

Physics Constraints and Interactions

CHARACTERS AND OBJECTS can be equipped with physics constraints that enable them to grasp, push, or manipulate objects realistically. These constraints are particularly useful for implementing physical interactions in games and simulations.

Blend Spaces and Blending Procedural Animations

BLEND SPACES ARE NOT limited to predefined animations; they can also blend procedural animations seamlessly. This allows for fluid transitions between different character behaviors and interactions.

Realistic Locomotion

PROCEDURAL ANIMATION can greatly enhance character locomotion. Whether it's adapting to slopes, uneven terrain, or reacting to external forces, dynamic locomotion ensures that characters move realistically in various situations.

Player Input and Interaction

PROCEDURAL ANIMATION can also respond to player input and interactions. For example, a character's hand can reach out to touch objects, walls, or other characters based on player actions, creating immersive and interactive experiences.

Conclusion

PROCEDURAL ANIMATION and dynamic IK systems bring a new level of realism and interactivity to Unreal Engine projects. By leveraging ragdoll physics, Animation Blueprints, dynamic IK, and physics constraints, you can create characters and objects that respond dynamically to the game world, enhancing immersion and gameplay. Mastering these techniques allows for more flexible and responsive animations, making your projects feel alive and dynamic. Whether you're developing games, simulations, or other interactive experiences, procedural animation and dynamic IK are valuable tools for achieving realism and immersion.

Chapter 10: Audio Design and Spatial Sound

10.1 Implementing Advanced Audio Systems

IN THIS SECTION, WE will explore the implementation of advanced audio systems in Unreal Engine. Audio design plays a crucial role in creating immersive and engaging experiences in games and interactive projects. We'll dive into the tools, techniques, and best practices for crafting rich audio environments, spatial soundscapes, and interactive audio elements using Unreal Engine's audio capabilities.

The Role of Audio in Immersion

AUDIO IS A POWERFUL tool for immersing players and users in virtual worlds. Well-designed audio can enhance the atmosphere, provide important feedback, and convey narrative elements. Advanced audio systems enable you to create dynamic, responsive, and convincing soundscapes.

Unreal Engine's Audio Engine

UNREAL ENGINE FEATURES a robust audio engine that supports both 2D and 3D audio, allowing sound to be positioned in the game world. It supports various audio formats, effects, and features for creating diverse and realistic audio experiences.

Sound Classes and Mixing

UNREAL ENGINE USES sound classes to categorize and control audio assets. These classes help manage audio properties like volume, pitch, and effects. Effective mixing and balancing of sound classes are essential for creating a coherent and immersive audio experience.

```
// Pseudocode for managing sound classes in Unreal Engine

if (IsClient) {

CreateSoundClasses();

ImplementSoundMixing();

BalanceAudioLevels();

}
```

Spatial Audio and 3D Soundscapes

UNREAL ENGINE'S SPATIAL audio features enable sound to be emitted from specific points in the game world. This creates a sense of depth and realism, as sounds appear to come from their sources. Spatial audio is crucial for games, VR, and AR experiences, where accurate sound positioning enhances immersion.

```
// Pseudocode for implementing spatial audio in Unreal Engine

if (IsClient) {

PositionAudioSources();

Create3DSoundscapes();

ImplementSpatialSound Effects();
```

```
}
```

Interactive Music and Sound Effects

INTERACTIVE AUDIO ELEMENTS allow the game to respond dynamically to player actions and events. Unreal Engine provides tools for implementing interactive music, adaptive soundscapes, and dynamic sound effects that enhance gameplay and storytelling.

Audio Optimization and Balancing

OPTIMIZING AUDIO IS crucial for performance and resource management. This involves reducing unnecessary audio asset sizes, adjusting streaming settings, and ensuring that audio quality is maintained while keeping performance in check.

```
// Pseudocode for audio optimization in Unreal Engine
if (IsClient) {
OptimizeAudioAssets();
AdjustStreamingSettings();
EnsureAudio Quality();
}
```

Middleware Integration for Enhanced Audio

UNREAL ENGINE CAN INTEGRATE with various audio middleware solutions, such as FMOD and Wwise, to provide even more advanced audio capabilities. Middleware allows for complex audio interactions, procedural audio, and additional audio authoring tools.

Realistic Sound Propagation

UNREAL ENGINE SUPPORTS sound propagation systems that simulate how sound travels and interacts with the environment. This can include audio occlusion, reverb, and reflection effects, adding realism to audio experiences.

Audio Debugging and Testing

TESTING AND DEBUGGING audio interactions are essential to ensure that audio behaves as intended. Unreal Engine provides debugging tools and audio profiling to identify and resolve issues in the audio system.

Conclusion

IMPLEMENTING ADVANCED audio systems in Unreal Engine is essential for creating immersive and memorable experiences in games and interactive projects. By understanding the role of audio in immersion, leveraging Unreal Engine's audio engine and features, and following best practices for sound class management, spatial audio, interactive audio elements, and optimization, you can craft audio experiences that enhance gameplay and storytelling. Whether you're developing games, simulations, or interactive narratives, advanced audio design is a key component of creating compelling and immersive worlds.

10.2 Spatial Audio and 3D Soundscapes

IN THIS SECTION, WE will delve into the world of spatial audio and 3D soundscapes in Unreal Engine. Spatial audio is a vital component of creating immersive experiences, as it allows sounds to be positioned in 3D space, providing a sense of direction and depth. We will explore the techniques, tools, and best practices for implementing spatial audio and crafting realistic soundscapes in your Unreal Engine projects.

The Importance of Spatial Audio

SPATIAL AUDIO ENHANCES immersion by making the virtual world feel more convincing. Sounds that are positioned correctly in 3D space can provide players or users with crucial spatial cues, such as the direction of approaching enemies, the location of hidden items, or the ambiance of the environment.

Positioning Audio Sources

UNREAL ENGINE ENABLES you to position audio sources within the game world. You can specify the location and orientation of these sources, allowing sounds to appear as if they are coming from specific points or objects. This feature is especially valuable for VR, AR, and immersive games.

```
// Pseudocode for positioning audio sources in Unreal Engine

if (IsClient) {

PositionAudioSource();

SetAudioOrientation();
```

```
Create3DSoundEmitter();
}
```

Attenuation and Distance Effects

SOUNDS IN THE REAL world diminish in volume as the listener moves away from the source. Unreal Engine replicates this phenomenon through attenuation settings, which control how audio volume decreases with distance. You can adjust attenuation curves and settings to achieve realistic distance-based audio effects.

```
// Pseudocode for configuring audio attenuation in Unreal Engine
if (IsClient) {
ConfigureAttenuation();
SetDistance-based Effects();
Fine-tuneAudio Settings();
}
```

3D Soundscapes

CREATING 3D SOUNDSCAPES involves placing multiple audio sources throughout the game world to mimic the ambiance of different environments. For instance, you can have birds chirping in the distance, footsteps echoing in a cave, or the hum of machinery in a factory. These soundscapes add depth and richness to the auditory experience.

```
// Pseudocode for crafting 3D soundscapes in Unreal Engine
if (IsClient) {
```

```
CreateEnvironmentalSoundscapes();

LayerAmbient Audio Sources();

BlendSounds Seamlessly();

}
```

Realistic Sound Propagation

SOUND IN THE REAL WORLD doesn't travel through obstacles in a straight line; it's affected by the environment. Unreal Engine supports sound propagation systems that simulate audio occlusion (when sounds are blocked by objects), reverb (sound reflections off surfaces), and other acoustic properties. These effects contribute to a more realistic auditory experience.

```
// Pseudocode for implementing sound propagation in Unreal Engine

if (IsClient) {

SimulateAudio Occlusion();

GenerateRealistic Reverb();

Enhance EnvironmentalAudio Effects();

}
```

Interactive Audio Environments

FOR GAMES AND INTERACTIVE experiences, audio environments must adapt to the player's actions and position. Implementing dynamic audio environments, where the audio changes based on the player's location and interactions, adds depth to the gameplay experience.

Testing and Fine-Tuning

IMPLEMENTING SPATIAL audio and 3D soundscapes is a creative and iterative process. Regular testing and fine-tuning are essential to ensure that audio elements work seamlessly together and provide the intended level of immersion.

Conclusion

SPATIAL AUDIO AND 3D soundscapes are indispensable for creating immersive and convincing environments in Unreal Engine. By positioning audio sources, configuring attenuation, crafting 3D soundscapes, simulating sound propagation, and implementing interactive audio environments, you can engage players or users on a deeper level by immersing them in a rich and believable auditory world. Whether you're developing games, architectural visualizations, or simulations, spatial audio is a crucial tool for enhancing the overall experience and making it more memorable.

10.3 Interactive Music and Sound Effects

IN THIS SECTION, WE will explore the implementation of interactive music and sound effects in Unreal Engine. Interactive audio elements are essential for creating dynamic and engaging audio experiences that respond to player actions and in-game events. We'll delve into the techniques, tools, and best practices for integrating interactive music and sound effects into your Unreal Engine projects.

The Role of Interactive Audio

INTERACTIVE AUDIO ENHANCES gameplay by providing real-time feedback, heightening tension during critical moments, and immersing players in the game world. Whether it's adaptive music that changes with the action or dynamic sound effects triggered by in-game events, interactive audio can significantly impact the player's experience.

Audio Cues and Triggers

UNREAL ENGINE ALLOWS you to define audio cues and triggers that respond to specific in-game events or conditions. These cues can be used to trigger sound effects, music changes, or voiceovers based on player interactions, scripted events, or gameplay states.

```
// Pseudocode for implementing audio cues and triggers in Unreal Engine

if (IsClient) {

DefineAudioCues();

SetAudioTriggers();

ReactToIn-Game Events();

}
```

Adaptive Music

ADAPTIVE MUSIC SYSTEMS adjust the music's tempo, intensity, or instrumentation based on the gameplay situation. For example, music can become more intense during combat, shift to a peaceful melody during exploration, or change dynamically to match the mood of a cinematic sequence.

```
// Pseudocode for implementing adaptive music in Unreal Engine

if (IsClient) {

CreateAdaptiveMusicSystem();

DefineMusic Layers();

ImplementDynamic Music Transitions();

}
```

Dynamic Sound Effects

DYNAMIC SOUND EFFECTS add depth and immersion to the game world. Unreal Engine enables you to trigger sound effects in response to various in-game events, such as footsteps, gunfire, object interactions, or environmental changes. These sound effects enhance the player's awareness and create a more immersive experience.

```
// Pseudocode for implementing dynamic sound effects in Unreal Engine

if (IsClient) {

SetSoundEffect Triggers();

ReactToIn-Game Events();

CreateRealistic Audio Feedback();

}
```

Sound Occlusion and Occlusion Traces

IN COMPLEX GAME ENVIRONMENTS, sound may be blocked by objects or structures, affecting what the player can hear. Unreal Engine offers sound occlusion and occlusion traces, allowing you to simulate how sound interacts with the environment. This adds realism and enhances gameplay by providing auditory cues about the player's surroundings.

```
// Pseudocode for simulating sound occlusion in Unreal Engine

if (IsClient) {

ImplementSound Occlusion System();

TraceSound Occlusion Paths();

EnhanceSpatial Audio Realism();

}
```

Audio State Machines

UNREAL ENGINE'S AUDIO state machines are essential for managing complex audio interactions. They enable you to define logic for transitioning between different audio states based on game events or conditions. This is particularly useful for orchestrating interactive audio experiences.

```
// Pseudocode for creating audio state machines in Unreal Engine

if (IsClient) {

DefineAudio States();

CreateAudio State Transitions();
```

```
ImplementComplex Audio Logic();

}
```

Testing and Player Feedback

TESTING AND ITERATING on interactive audio elements are crucial to ensure that audio cues, music transitions, and sound effects enhance the player's experience rather than detract from it. Player feedback and playtesting help identify areas for improvement and fine-tuning.

Conclusion

IMPLEMENTING INTERACTIVE music and sound effects in Unreal Engine adds depth and immersion to your projects. By leveraging audio cues, triggers, adaptive music, dynamic sound effects, sound occlusion, audio state machines, and player feedback, you can create audio experiences that respond dynamically to gameplay events and enrich the overall gaming experience. Whether you're developing games, simulations, or interactive narratives, interactive audio design is a powerful tool for enhancing player engagement and creating memorable audio-driven experiences.

10.4 Audio Optimization and Balancing

IN THIS SECTION, WE will explore the importance of audio optimization and balancing in Unreal Engine. While creating immersive audio experiences is crucial, it's equally important to ensure that your audio assets are well-optimized to maintain performance and resource efficiency. We will delve into techniques, tools, and best practices for optimizing and balancing audio in your Unreal Engine projects.

The Significance of Audio Optimization

AUDIO ASSETS, ESPECIALLY high-quality ones, can consume significant memory and processing power. To maintain a smooth and responsive experience, it's essential to optimize audio to strike a balance between audio quality and performance.

Asset Compression and Format Selection

UNREAL ENGINE SUPPORTS various audio formats, each with its own compression and quality trade-offs. When importing audio assets, choose appropriate formats and compression settings to reduce file size without compromising audio quality.

```
// Pseudocode for selecting audio formats and compression settings in Unreal Engine

if (IsClient) {

ChooseAudio Formats();

SetCompression Settings();

OptimizeAudio Files();

}
```

Audio Streaming

FOR LARGE AUDIO ASSETS or environments with many audio cues, streaming can be a valuable optimization technique. It allows audio assets to load dynamically as needed, reducing the initial load time and memory footprint.

```
// Pseudocode for implementing audio streaming in Unreal Engine
```

```
if (IsClient) {

EnableAudio Streaming();

ConfigureStreaming Settings();

OptimizeMemory Usage();

}
```

Priority and Sound Class Balancing

BALANCING AUDIO PRIORITIES and sound classes is essential to maintain a consistent audio experience. Assigning appropriate priorities ensures that crucial audio cues are always audible, while less important sounds are attenuated or prioritized accordingly.

```
// Pseudocode for balancing audio priorities and sound classes in Unreal Engine

if (IsClient) {

SetSound Priorities();

BalanceSound Classes();

Ensure Consistent Audio Levels();

}
```

Sound Mixing

UNREAL ENGINE'S AUDIO mixer allows you to create complex sound mixes and audio effects. Careful sound mixing helps ensure that different audio elements blend well together and that they are balanced correctly in the final mix.

```
// Pseudocode for sound mixing in Unreal Engine

if (IsClient) {

CreateSound Mixes();

ImplementSound Effects();

BalanceAudio Levels();

}
```

Multithreaded Audio

TO LEVERAGE THE FULL power of modern hardware, Unreal Engine supports multithreaded audio rendering. Enabling this option can improve audio performance, especially in complex and demanding scenes.

```
// Pseudocode for enabling multithreaded audio rendering in Unreal Engine

if (IsClient) {

EnableMultithreaded Audio();

OptimizeAudio Performance();

}
```

Real-time Parameter Control

IN INTERACTIVE AUDIO experiences, real-time parameter control allows you to adjust audio properties dynamically based on gameplay conditions. For example, you can modify the pitch, volume, or effects of a sound based on in-game events.

```
// Pseudocode for real-time parameter control in Unreal Engine

if (IsClient) {

Implement Real-time Audio Parameter Control();

React to In-game Events();

Enhance Dynamic Audio Feedback();

}
```

Profiling and Testing

REGULAR PROFILING AND testing are crucial to identify audio-related performance bottlenecks and issues. Profiling tools in Unreal Engine can help you pinpoint areas where audio optimization is needed.

Conclusion

AUDIO OPTIMIZATION and balancing are essential steps in ensuring that your Unreal Engine projects perform well without sacrificing audio quality. By compressing audio assets appropriately, enabling streaming, prioritizing sound cues, balancing sound classes, fine-tuning sound mixes, optimizing for multithreaded audio, and implementing real-time parameter control, you can strike the right balance between audio fidelity and performance. This ensures that players or users can enjoy a seamless and immersive audio experience in your games, simulations, or interactive projects, even on a variety of hardware configurations.

10.5 Middleware Integration for Enhanced Audio

IN THIS SECTION, WE will explore the integration of middleware solutions for enhanced audio capabilities in Unreal Engine. Middleware serves as an extension to Unreal Engine's built-in audio tools, providing additional features, authoring capabilities, and control over your audio assets. We will discuss the benefits of middleware integration, common middleware options, and the steps to integrate them into your Unreal Engine projects.

The Role of Middleware

MIDDLEWARE SOLUTIONS are third-party audio engines or tools that can be seamlessly integrated into Unreal Engine. They offer advanced audio authoring, interactive audio capabilities, complex sound interactions, and procedural audio generation, among other features. Middleware bridges the gap between traditional audio authoring and game engine integration.

Popular Middleware Options

SEVERAL MIDDLEWARE solutions are widely used in the game development industry, each with its unique strengths. Some of the most popular middleware options for enhanced audio in Unreal Engine include:

• **FMOD Studio**: FMOD is known for its flexibility and real-time audio capabilities. It offers a comprehensive toolset for creating complex audio interactions and adaptive music systems.

• **Wwise**: Wwise is renowned for its robust audio authoring tools and deep integration with game engines. It excels in interactive audio design and supports a wide range of platforms.

• **Fabric**: Fabric is known for its procedural audio capabilities, allowing you to generate audio procedurally based on in-game events and interactions. It's ideal for creating dynamic and adaptive soundscapes.

• **ADL (Audiokinetic Dynamic Libraries)**: ADL is a low-level audio middleware solution that offers fine-grained control over audio processing. It's suitable for projects that require low-level audio programming.

Integration Steps

INTEGRATING MIDDLEWARE into your Unreal Engine project involves several key steps:

1. **Middleware Installation**: Begin by downloading and installing the middleware of your choice. Follow the middleware's documentation for installation instructions.
2. **Project Setup**: Configure your Unreal Engine project to work with the middleware. This typically involves adding the middleware's plugin to your project.
3. **Asset Import**: Import your audio assets into the middleware's authoring environment. This is where you

will create complex sound interactions, adaptive music systems, and other advanced audio features.

4. **Sound Event Creation**: Define sound events in the middleware, specifying how audio assets will be triggered, manipulated, and interact with the game world.
5. **Integration with Unreal Engine**: Use middleware-specific integration scripts or blueprints to connect the sound events in the middleware with in-game events and triggers in Unreal Engine.
6. **Testing and Debugging**: Thoroughly test the audio interactions and integration to ensure they work as intended. Use debugging tools provided by the middleware for fine-tuning.
7. **Performance Optimization**: Optimize audio assets and middleware settings to balance audio quality with performance requirements. Consider platform-specific optimizations.

Benefits of Middleware Integration

INTEGRATING MIDDLEWARE offers several advantages:

- **Advanced Audio Authoring**: Middleware provides a more extensive set of tools for crafting complex audio interactions, interactive music, and dynamic soundscapes.

- **Real-time Control**: Middleware often allows real-time control of audio parameters, enabling dynamic adjustments based on gameplay events.

- **Platform Flexibility**: Middleware solutions support multiple platforms, making it easier to develop for various target devices and platforms.

- **Procedural Audio**: Some middleware solutions, like Fabric, excel in procedural audio generation, enabling dynamic audio responses to in-game events.

- **Community and Support**: Middleware options like FMOD and Wwise have large communities and extensive documentation, making it easier to find resources and get support.

Conclusion

MIDDLEWARE INTEGRATION enhances the audio capabilities of Unreal Engine, enabling you to create more sophisticated and interactive audio experiences. Whether you need advanced sound interactions, adaptive music, procedural audio, or platform flexibility, middleware solutions like FMOD, Wwise, Fabric, or ADL can empower you to take your audio design to the next level. By following the integration steps and leveraging the strengths of your chosen middleware, you can elevate the audio quality and immersion in your games, simulations, or interactive projects.

Chapter 11: Advanced Material Creation and Shaders

11.1 Writing Custom Shaders for Unique Effects

IN THIS SECTION, WE will delve into the exciting world of custom shader development in Unreal Engine. Shaders are essential components in creating unique visual effects, and understanding how to write your own shaders can take your game's visuals to the next level. Custom shaders allow you to achieve effects that are not possible with standard materials and can be used for a wide range of purposes, from creating distinctive visual styles to simulating complex physical phenomena.

The Basics of Shaders

SHADERS ARE PROGRAMS that run on the GPU (Graphics Processing Unit) and are responsible for determining how the surface of objects in your scene should be rendered. There are two primary types of shaders in Unreal Engine: Vertex Shaders and Pixel Shaders.

Vertex Shaders

VERTEX SHADERS OPERATE on each vertex (corner point) of a 3D model. They are responsible for transforming the model's vertices from local space to world space, and eventually to screen space. This transformation includes operations like translation, rotation, and scaling. Additionally, vertex shaders can compute values that are interpolated across the surface of the triangle formed by the vertices, which can be used in pixel shaders for effects like per-pixel lighting.

Pixel Shaders

PIXEL SHADERS, ALSO known as fragment shaders, work at the pixel level. They determine the color of each pixel on the screen. Pixel shaders can sample textures, perform lighting calculations, apply materials, and create various visual effects. This is where you have the most control over the final appearance of your objects.

HLSL (High-Level Shader Language)

UNREAL ENGINE USES HLSL (High-Level Shader Language) for writing shaders. HLSL is a C-like language that allows you to express complex calculations and operations in a shader-friendly way. It provides a rich set of functions and data types specifically designed for graphics programming.

Here's a simple example of a custom shader written in HLSL:

```
// Vertex shader

float4 mainVS(VertexInput input) : SV_POSITION

{

float4 position;

// Perform vertex transformations here

return position;

}

// Pixel shader

float4 mainPS(VertexOutput input) : SV_TARGET

{
```

```
float4 color;

// Calculate pixel color here

return color;

}
```

In this example, we have a basic vertex shader (mainVS) that takes a VertexInput structure and returns a position (SV_POSITION). The pixel shader (mainPS) takes a VertexOutput structure and returns a color (SV_TARGET). These shaders are responsible for processing vertices and pixels, respectively.

Shader Development Workflow

WHEN DEVELOPING CUSTOM shaders in Unreal Engine, it's essential to follow a structured workflow:

1. **Define Shader Inputs**: Determine what data your shader needs as input. This may include vertex positions, normals, textures, and custom parameters.
2. **Write Vertex and Pixel Shaders**: Create your vertex and pixel shaders using HLSL. Implement the logic for transforming vertices and determining pixel colors.
3. **Compile Shaders**: Compile your HLSL code into shader bytecode that Unreal Engine can understand. This is typically done using the Shader Compiler provided by Unreal.
4. **Create Material Instances**: In Unreal, you'll typically create Material Instances that use your custom shader. These instances can be applied to objects in your scene.
5. **Adjust Shader Parameters**: Define parameters that can be adjusted in the Material Instance. This allows artists and

designers to tweak the shader's behavior without modifying the code.

6. **Apply Materials**: Apply your materials to objects in the scene to see the custom shader in action.
7. **Iterate and Refine**: Fine-tune your shader by iterating on its parameters and code to achieve the desired visual effects.

Custom shaders open up a world of possibilities for creating unique and stunning visuals in your Unreal Engine projects. Whether you want to simulate realistic materials, create special effects, or achieve a distinctive art style, understanding shader development is a valuable skill for any game developer.

11.2 Material Layering and Blending Techniques

MATERIAL LAYERING AND blending are fundamental techniques in shader development that allow you to create complex and realistic materials by combining multiple layers of textures and effects. In this section, we will explore the concept of material layering, various blending modes, and how to implement these techniques in Unreal Engine.

Understanding Material Layering

MATERIAL LAYERING INVOLVES stacking multiple material layers on top of each other to create a composite material. Each layer can have its own texture maps, properties, and shaders. This approach is particularly useful for creating surfaces with intricate details, such as terrain, skin, or weathered objects.

In Unreal Engine, you can achieve material layering using the Material Layer Blend node. This node allows you to blend two or more material functions or shaders together based on a mask or weight map. Common use cases for material layering include adding dirt and grime to a surface, blending different types of rocks on a terrain, or simulating wear and tear on objects.

Here's a basic example of material layering using the Material Layer Blend node in Unreal Engine's Material Editor:

```
// Base Material Function

float3 BaseMaterial(float2 UV)

{

// Perform base material calculations here

return BaseColor;

}

// Dirt Material Function

float3 DirtMaterial(float2 UV)

{

// Perform dirt material calculations here

return DirtColor;

}

// Blend Factor (from a mask or weight map)

float BlendFactor(float2 UV)
```

```
{
// Calculate blend factor from a mask or weight map
return MaskValue;
}
// Final Material Function using Material Layer Blend
float3 FinalMaterial(float2 UV)
{
float3 Base = BaseMaterial(UV);
float3 Dirt = DirtMaterial(UV);
float Blend = BlendFactor(UV);
return lerp(Base, Dirt, Blend);
}
```

In this example, we have a base material function (BaseMaterial) and a dirt material function (DirtMaterial). The BlendFactor function calculates the blending factor based on a mask or weight map. Finally, the FinalMaterial function combines the base and dirt materials using the lerp function based on the blend factor.

Blending Modes

WHEN LAYERING MATERIALS, you can choose from various blending modes to determine how the layers interact. Some common blending modes include:

• **Additive**: This mode adds the colors of the layers, resulting in a brighter appearance. It's often used for effects like flames, glows, and light sources.

• **Multiplicative**: Multiplicative blending multiplies the colors of the layers together, creating a darker and more saturated result. It's useful for simulating shadows and occlusion.

• **Alpha Blending**: Alpha blending combines the layers based on their alpha (transparency) values. This allows for smooth transitions between materials and is commonly used for foliage and glass materials.

• **Overlay**: Overlay blending combines the layers in a way that preserves the highlights and shadows of the base material while adding details from the top layer. It's useful for adding surface imperfections and grunge.

• **Height-based Blending**: In some cases, you may want to blend materials based on height information, such as for terrain materials. This can create a more realistic transition between materials at different elevations.

Implementing these blending modes involves writing custom shader code that performs the appropriate calculations for each mode. Unreal Engine provides a range of blending nodes and functions to simplify this process.

Use Cases and Best Practices

MATERIAL LAYERING AND blending are versatile techniques that find application in various aspects of game development. Here are some common use cases and best practices:

- Terrain Materials: Create complex terrain materials by blending multiple layers of textures, such as rock, sand, and grass, based on height, slope, or other criteria.

- Character Materials: Achieve realistic skin textures by layering different skin tones, subsurface scattering effects, and blemishes.

- Weathering and Damage: Simulate wear and tear on objects by blending dirt, rust, or scratches onto their surfaces.

- Foliage: Blend different types of foliage, such as leaves and moss, on trees and vegetation.

- Realistic Ground Cover: Layer various ground cover materials like pebbles, twigs, and leaves for a natural look.

When using material layering, consider the performance impact, especially on older or less powerful hardware. To optimize, use LOD (Level of Detail) techniques and cull unnecessary layers based on distance or visibility.

In conclusion, material layering and blending are powerful tools for creating complex and visually appealing materials in Unreal Engine. Understanding the principles of layering, choosing the right blending modes, and optimizing for performance will enable you to create stunning and immersive game worlds.

11.3 Using Subsurface Scattering for Realism

SUBSURFACE SCATTERING (SSS) is a rendering technique that plays a crucial role in achieving realistic and natural-looking materials in computer graphics and game development. SSS simulates the behavior of light as it penetrates and scatters within translucent objects like skin, wax, and various organic materials. In this section, we'll explore the concept of subsurface scattering and how to implement it in Unreal Engine for enhanced realism in your materials.

Understanding Subsurface Scattering

TO UNDERSTAND SUBSURFACE scattering, consider how light interacts with different materials. When light hits a surface, it can either bounce off the surface (specular reflection) or penetrate into the material (subsurface scattering). Subsurface scattering occurs when light travels through a translucent material and interacts with the molecules and particles within it. This interaction causes the light to scatter in various directions before eventually emerging from the surface at a different point. The result is a soft, diffused appearance that is characteristic of materials like skin.

In the context of computer graphics, simulating subsurface scattering is essential for achieving lifelike skin, organic materials, and other translucent surfaces. Without SSS, materials may appear flat and artificial, lacking the natural translucency that we observe in the real world.

SSS in Unreal Engine

UNREAL ENGINE PROVIDES tools and shaders to simulate subsurface scattering effectively. To utilize SSS in your materials, follow these key steps:

1. **Use SSS Profiles**: Unreal Engine allows you to define subsurface scattering profiles that describe how light scatters within a specific material. These profiles are essential for accurately simulating the behavior of light in

materials like skin, wax, or jade. Profiles determine the distance and direction that light travels within the material.

2. **SSS Materials**: Create or adjust materials to include subsurface scattering properties. Unreal Engine offers a dedicated Subsurface Scattering Profile node that you can use in your material graph to define the SSS profile for the material. This node lets you specify the material's SSS parameters, such as color, scale, and radius.
3. **Shader Settings**: Configure the material shader settings to enable subsurface scattering. This includes specifying the SSS profile you created and adjusting parameters like subsurface color and intensity. Unreal Engine's Material Editor provides an intuitive interface for making these adjustments.
4. **Texture Maps**: SSS can be influenced by texture maps, such as diffuse and normal maps. Ensure that your material uses the appropriate texture maps to control the appearance of subsurface scattering, especially for skin and organic materials.

Here's a simplified example of how to enable subsurface scattering in a material in Unreal Engine's Material Editor:

```
// Subsurface Scattering Profile

SubsurfaceScatteringProfile SSSProfile;

// Material Properties

float3 BaseColor;

float3 SubsurfaceColor;

float SubsurfaceIntensity;
```

```
float SubsurfaceRadius;

// Shader Entry Point

float4 main(float2 UV) : SV_TARGET

{

// Calculate subsurface scattering

float3 SSS = SubsurfaceScattering(SSSProfile, SubsurfaceColor,
SubsurfaceIntensity, SubsurfaceRadius);

// Final color with subsurface scattering

float3 FinalColor = BaseColor + SSS;

return float4(FinalColor, 1.0f);

}
```

In this example, we define a subsurface scattering profile (SSSProfile) and specify material properties such as base color, subsurface color, intensity, and radius. The SubsurfaceScattering function is used to calculate the subsurface scattering effect based on the defined profile and material properties. Finally, the final color is computed by combining the base color and subsurface scattering.

Use Cases and Considerations

SUBSURFACE SCATTERING is particularly useful for achieving realistic skin in character models, as well as for materials like wax, marble, fruits, and leaves. When implementing SSS, consider the following:

- **Tuning Parameters**: Adjust the SSS parameters (color, intensity, radius, etc.) to match the specific material you are simulating. Different materials exhibit varying degrees of subsurface scattering.

- **Texture Maps**: Utilize texture maps to control SSS properties and variations across the surface. For skin, use maps that define areas with more or less scattering, such as veins or areas with thicker or thinner skin.

- **Performance**: Subsurface scattering can be computationally intensive, especially in real-time applications. Use LOD (Level of Detail) techniques and optimize your shaders to balance realism and performance.

In conclusion, subsurface scattering is a vital technique for achieving realism in materials, especially in rendering human characters and organic objects. Unreal Engine provides robust tools and shaders to implement SSS effectively, allowing you to create visually stunning and lifelike materials in your games and simulations.

11.4 Real-Time Reflections and Refractions

REAL-TIME REFLECTIONS and refractions are essential elements in achieving visually stunning and immersive environments in computer graphics and game development. In this section, we'll explore the concepts of reflections and refractions, and how to implement them in Unreal Engine to enhance the realism and visual appeal of your scenes.

Understanding Reflections

REFLECTIONS SIMULATE the behavior of light as it bounces off surfaces and reflects back to the viewer's perspective. In the real world, reflections can be observed in mirrors, water surfaces, and glossy materials. Accurately rendering reflections in real-time graphics is crucial for creating convincing and immersive environments.

In Unreal Engine, you can implement real-time reflections using techniques like Screen Space Reflections (SSR), Reflection Capture Actors, and Planar Reflections. Each method has its advantages and use cases:

- **Screen Space Reflections (SSR)**: SSR is a technique that calculates reflections based on the screen space information of the scene. It's relatively fast and suitable for rendering reflections on surfaces that are close to the camera. However, it has limitations and may not handle complex scenes or off-screen reflections well.

- **Reflection Capture Actors**: Reflection Capture Actors are components that capture the environment's reflection information from a specific point in the scene. These actors are especially useful for capturing static or semi-static reflections, such as those on metallic surfaces or glass.

- **Planar Reflections**: Planar reflections involve rendering a scene from the perspective of a reflective plane (e.g., a body of water or a glass surface) and then mapping that rendering onto the reflective surface. This method provides accurate reflections but can be more performance-intensive.

Implementing Real-Time Reflections

TO IMPLEMENT REAL-TIME reflections in Unreal Engine, follow these general steps:

1. **Enable Reflections**: Ensure that reflections are enabled in your project settings and the rendering pipeline.
2. **Choose the Reflection Technique**: Depending on your scene's requirements, choose the appropriate reflection technique (SSR, Reflection Capture Actors, or Planar Reflections).
3. **Assign Materials**: Apply materials to reflective surfaces that specify how reflections should behave. Unreal Engine's Material Editor provides features like the "Specular" and "Roughness" parameters to control reflectivity.
4. **Set Up Reflection Captures**: If you're using Reflection Capture Actors, place them strategically in your scene to capture reflection data. Adjust the capture settings to match the quality and performance requirements.
5. **Use Planar Reflection Actors**: For accurate planar reflections, add Planar Reflection Actors to reflective surfaces like water or glass. Configure the actors to match the reflective area.
6. **Adjust Reflection Settings**: Fine-tune reflection settings in the Engine's post-processing volume or within materials to achieve the desired look. Parameters like reflection intensity, resolution, and fade distance can be adjusted.
7. **Optimize for Performance**: Keep in mind that real-time reflections can be computationally intensive. Implement LOD and culling techniques to manage the rendering load. Additionally, consider using lower-resolution reflection captures for distant objects.

Understanding Refractions

REFRACTIONS OCCUR WHEN light passes through a transparent or semi-transparent material, causing it to change direction. This phenomenon is observed in materials like glass, water, and lenses. Accurate rendering of refractions is crucial for creating realistic transparent materials and lenses in your scenes.

In Unreal Engine, refractions can be achieved using techniques like Screen Space Refraction (SSR) and Refraction Capture Actors. Similar to reflections, each method has its strengths and use cases:

- **Screen Space Refraction (SSR)**: SSR can be used to simulate simple refractions based on screen space information. It's suitable for rendering basic refractions on nearby transparent surfaces.

- **Refraction Capture Actors**: Refraction Capture Actors capture the refraction information from specific points in the scene. They are useful for capturing and rendering accurate refractions on semi-static or static transparent surfaces.

Implementing Real-Time Refractions

TO IMPLEMENT REAL-TIME refractions in Unreal Engine, follow these general steps:

1. **Enable Refractions**: Ensure that refractions are enabled in your project settings and rendering pipeline.
2. **Choose the Refraction Technique**: Depending on your scene's requirements, choose the appropriate refraction technique (SSR or Refraction Capture Actors).
3. **Assign Materials**: Apply materials to transparent or semi-transparent surfaces that specify how refractions should behave. Unreal Engine's Material Editor provides parameters like "Refraction" and "IOR" (Index of Refraction) for controlling refraction effects.
4. **Set Up Refraction Captures**: If you're using Refraction

Capture Actors, position them strategically in your scene to capture refraction data. Adjust the capture settings to match the quality and performance requirements.

5. **Adjust Refraction Settings**: Fine-tune refraction settings in the Engine's post-processing volume or within materials to achieve the desired refraction appearance. Parameters like refraction intensity and IOR can be adjusted.
6. **Optimize for Performance**: Similar to reflections, real-time refractions can impact performance. Implement LOD and culling techniques to manage the rendering load. Use lower-resolution refraction captures for distant objects when necessary.

In conclusion, real-time reflections and refractions are essential tools for achieving visual realism and immersion in your Unreal Engine projects. By understanding the principles of these techniques and choosing the right method for your scene, you can enhance the quality of your graphics and create stunning and lifelike environments.

11.5 Performance Considerations for Materials

EFFICIENTLY MANAGING and optimizing materials is crucial in game development to ensure smooth performance and maintain a stable frame rate. In this section, we'll discuss various performance considerations and best practices for materials in Unreal Engine.

Material Complexity

MATERIALS CAN SIGNIFICANTLY impact a game's performance, especially if they are overly complex or resource-intensive. To optimize material complexity:

1. **Use Material Instances**: Utilize Material Instances to create variations of a base material with different parameter values. This reduces shader recompilation overhead and allows artists to tweak materials without modifying the base material.
2. **Keep Shader Instructions in Check**: Monitor the number of shader instructions in your materials. Excessive instructions can lead to slower rendering. Use Unreal Engine's Material Editor's built-in statistics to identify costly instructions.
3. **Limit Material Layers**: While material layering is powerful, excessive layers can be performance-intensive. Use layering judiciously, and consider combining layers when possible.
4. **Texture Size and Compression**: Choose appropriate texture sizes and compression settings. Higher resolution textures demand more memory and can affect performance, especially on lower-end hardware.

Texture Streaming

TEXTURE STREAMING IS a technique used to efficiently manage and load textures based on the player's view and proximity to objects. To optimize texture streaming:

1. **Mipmapping**: Enable automatic mipmapping for textures. Mipmaps are smaller versions of textures used for distant objects, reducing texture memory consumption and improving performance.
2. **Texture Streaming Budget**: Define a texture streaming budget to control the memory allocated to texture streaming. Prioritize critical textures while lowering quality for less important ones.

3. **Level of Detail (LOD)**: Implement LODs for materials. Lower LODs use simplified shaders and textures to improve performance when objects are at a distance.

Shader Complexity

SHADERS ARE A SIGNIFICANT part of material performance. To optimize shader complexity:

1. **Shader Culling**: Use efficient culling techniques to avoid rendering unnecessary objects or materials. Implement occlusion culling, frustum culling, and distance-based culling to reduce the number of shaders being processed.
2. **Dynamic Material Instances**: For objects with materials that change at runtime (e.g., character customization), use dynamic material instances sparingly. These instances can incur a performance cost due to shader recompilation.
3. **Material Quality Levels**: Implement different material quality levels based on the player's hardware capabilities. Allow players to adjust material quality settings in the game's options.

Material Transitions

SMOOTH TRANSITIONS between materials can enhance visual quality but may introduce performance overhead. To optimize material transitions:

1. **Use Material Blending**: When transitioning between materials, use techniques like alpha blending or lerping to create smooth transitions without abrupt changes.
2. **Fade Effects**: Implement fade effects during material transitions to mask any potential visual artifacts.
3. **Distance-Based Transitions**: Opt for distance-based

material transitions. Fade in higher-quality materials as the player approaches objects, and fade out lower-quality materials as they move away.

Material Instances and Instancing

UNREAL ENGINE SUPPORTS Material Instances and Material Instancing to optimize materials:

1. **Material Instances**: Use Material Instances to create variations of materials with unique parameter values. This reduces shader recompilation and improves performance.
2. **Material Instancing**: When dealing with many instances of the same material (e.g., foliage or particles), use Material Instancing to share a single shader across multiple instances, reducing CPU overhead.

Mobile and Console Optimization

FOR MOBILE PLATFORMS and consoles, specific optimizations may be necessary:

1. **Platform-Specific Settings**: Adjust material settings and quality levels based on the target platform's capabilities and limitations.
2. **Texture Compression**: Utilize platform-specific texture compression formats to optimize texture memory usage.
3. **Shader Complexity**: Optimize shaders to meet the performance requirements of the target platform, as different platforms may have varying shader capabilities.
4. **Performance Profiling**: Use performance profiling tools to identify and address bottlenecks related to materials, such as high shader compilation times or excessive GPU load.

In conclusion, optimizing materials is a critical aspect of game development for achieving excellent performance without sacrificing visual quality. By following best practices and considering the specific requirements of your target platform, you can create efficient and visually impressive materials in Unreal Engine.

Chapter 12: Cinematics and Storytelling Techniques

12.1 Advanced Sequencer and Cinematic Tools

IN THIS SECTION, WE will delve into the world of cinematic storytelling in Unreal Engine, focusing on the advanced features of Sequencer and cinematic tools. Cinematics play a vital role in modern game development, enhancing storytelling, immersion, and player engagement. Unreal Engine provides a robust suite of tools to create cinematic sequences, cutscenes, and interactive storytelling experiences.

Understanding Sequencer

SEQUENCER IS UNREAL Engine's powerful and flexible cinematic editing and animation tool. It allows you to create complex cinematic sequences by combining cameras, actors, animations, audio, and visual effects. Sequencer is ideal for crafting storytelling experiences, in-game cinematics, and trailers.

Key Features of Sequencer:

- **Track-Based Timeline**: Sequencer uses a track-based timeline interface, making it easy to organize and edit cinematic elements over time. Each track can represent various properties, such as camera movement, character animations, and audio cues.

- **Keyframing and Animation**: You can keyframe properties and create animations directly in Sequencer.

This includes camera movement, actor animations, and even post-processing effects.

• **Blendable Cameras**: Sequencer supports blendable cameras, allowing smooth transitions between different camera setups. This is crucial for creating dynamic and engaging camera movements during cinematic sequences.

• **Visual Effects Integration**: You can integrate visual effects and particle systems seamlessly within Sequencer, enhancing the cinematic experience with explosions, fire, smoke, and more.

• **Audio Sync**: Sequencer provides tools for syncing audio tracks with visuals. You can add dialogue, music, and sound effects to your cinematics and ensure they match the on-screen action.

• **Interactive Cinematics**: Unreal Engine allows you to create interactive cinematics where player choices influence the outcome of a scene or story. This is useful for branching narratives and dynamic storytelling.

Creating Cinematic Sequences

TO CREATE CINEMATIC sequences in Unreal Engine using Sequencer:

1. **Open Sequencer**: Access Sequencer by going to the "Cinematics" tab in the main editor toolbar and selecting "Sequencer."
2. **Create a Sequence**: Start by creating a new cinematic sequence. You can name it and set its properties, such as frame rate and resolution.

3. **Add Tracks**: In Sequencer, add tracks for various elements like cameras, characters, animations, and audio. You can import assets from your project to populate these tracks.
4. **Keyframing**: Keyframe properties over time to create animations and camera movements. Use the "Record" button to record keyframes interactively.
5. **Blend Cameras**: Use blendable cameras to transition smoothly between different viewpoints or shots. Adjust camera properties to achieve the desired look.
6. **Audio Sync**: Add audio tracks and synchronize dialogue, music, and sound effects with your cinematic. You can import audio files and precisely time their playback.
7. **Visual Effects**: Integrate visual effects and particle systems to enhance your cinematic. Configure particle systems to emit smoke, sparks, or other effects as needed.
8. **Timeline Editing**: Refine the timing and pacing of your cinematic by editing the timeline and adjusting keyframes. Use easing curves to control animation interpolation.
9. **Rendering**: Once your cinematic is complete, you can render it to create a video file for playback or integration into your game.

Interactive Storytelling

UNREAL ENGINE'S SEQUENCER also supports interactive storytelling, where player choices influence the narrative. This is accomplished through Blueprint scripting and Sequencer's ability to trigger events and sequences based on gameplay events.

To create interactive storytelling:

1. **Define Player Choices**: Identify points in the story where player choices can impact the narrative.

2. **Blueprint Integration**: Use Blueprints to implement gameplay mechanics and events triggered by player choices.
3. **Sequencer Integration**: In Sequencer, create multiple sequences corresponding to different narrative branches or outcomes.
4. **Trigger Sequences**: Use Blueprint scripting to trigger the appropriate sequence based on player choices or events. Sequencer allows you to play, pause, or stop sequences via Blueprint nodes.
5. **Branching Narratives**: Construct branching narratives by organizing sequences to reflect the story's diverging paths.
6. **Dynamic Cinematics**: Craft dynamic cinematics that respond to player actions, creating a more engaging and personalized storytelling experience.

In conclusion, Sequencer is a versatile tool for creating cinematic sequences and storytelling experiences in Unreal Engine. Whether you're crafting cutscenes, trailers, or interactive narratives, understanding the advanced features of Sequencer empowers you to deliver compelling and immersive storytelling in your games.

12.2 Directing Cinematic Scenes in Unreal

DIRECTING CINEMATIC scenes in Unreal Engine is a creative and technical process that involves crafting visually captivating and emotionally engaging storytelling sequences. In this section, we will explore the art of cinematic direction, including camera composition, shot planning, and directing performances to convey your narrative effectively.

Cinematic Storytelling Principles

SUCCESSFUL CINEMATIC direction in Unreal Engine is founded on several key principles:

1. **Narrative Clarity**: The primary objective of a cinematic scene is to advance the story. Ensure that your audience understands the narrative elements, character motivations, and plot developments through your cinematography.
2. **Composition**: Consider the composition of your shots. Composing your scenes effectively involves framing, camera angles, and the placement of characters and objects within the frame. Rule-of-thirds, leading lines, and balance are compositional techniques that can guide your cinematography.
3. **Emotional Impact**: Use camera movements, lighting, and character performances to evoke emotions in your audience. The choice of camera angle, shot duration, and pacing can significantly impact the emotional resonance of a scene.
4. **Visual Cohesion**: Maintain visual consistency within your cinematic sequences. Ensure that lighting, color grading, and the overall visual style align with the narrative and the established visual language of your game.

Previsualization (Previs)

BEFORE DIVING INTO full production, it's often beneficial to create previsualizations or "previs" of your cinematic scenes. Previs involves creating rough, low-fidelity versions of your scenes to plan camera angles, character movements, and shot sequences. This process allows you to experiment with different ideas and refine your cinematic direction before investing significant resources in production.

In Unreal Engine, you can use Sequencer to create previs sequences quickly. Here's a simplified example:

```
// Create a Camera Actor

CameraActor = SpawnActor<ACameraActor>(CameraClass, CameraLocation, CameraRotation);

// Attach the Camera to a Sequencer Camera Cut Track

SequencerActor->GetCameraCutTrack()->AddCamera(CameraActor, CameraStartFrame, CameraEndFrame);
```

In this code snippet, we spawn a Camera Actor, position it in the scene, and then attach it to a Sequencer Camera Cut Track. This allows you to plan and preview camera shots in real-time.

Shot Planning

SHOT PLANNING IS A critical aspect of cinematic direction. It involves determining the specific camera shots and movements for each scene. Consider the following shot types commonly used in cinematic storytelling:

- **Establishing Shot**: An initial wide-angle shot that sets the scene's location, context, and mood.

- **Master Shot**: A wide shot that captures the entire scene or action, providing an overview of the situation.

- **Close-Up**: A shot that focuses on a character's face or an important object, emphasizing emotions or details.

- **Over-the-Shoulder Shot**: Often used in dialogues, this shot shows the character speaking from behind another character's shoulder.

- **Tracking Shot**: The camera moves along with the action, either following characters or objects.

- **Aerial Shot**: Captured from a high vantage point, this shot provides a bird's-eye view of the scene.

- **Dolly Shot**: The camera moves forward or backward while maintaining its focus on a subject.

- **Pan and Tilt**: Camera movement horizontally (pan) or vertically (tilt) to reveal or emphasize elements within the frame.

When planning shots, consider the purpose of each shot within the scene. Ask yourself how it contributes to the narrative, reveals character emotions, or highlights important details.

Directing Performances

DIRECTING CHARACTER performances is another crucial aspect of cinematic direction. To achieve convincing performances, consider the following:

1. **Character Motivation**: Understand the characters' motivations and emotions within the scene. Provide actors (whether human or digital) with context to deliver authentic performances.
2. **Blocking**: Plan character movements and positions within the scene (blocking) to ensure that their actions align with the narrative and shot composition.

3. **Rehearsals**: Conduct rehearsals to fine-tune character movements, expressions, and interactions before recording.
4. **Camera-Actor Coordination**: Coordinate camera movements with character actions to capture important moments effectively.
5. **Emotionally Charged Moments**: Pay special attention to scenes with heightened emotions, ensuring that characters' expressions and body language convey the intended emotions.

Camera Movement

CAMERA MOVEMENT IS a powerful tool in cinematic direction. It can convey emotions, create visual interest, and guide the audience's attention. Consider the following camera movements:

- **Zoom**: Change the focal length to zoom in or out on a subject, highlighting details or changing the perspective.

- **Pan**: Move the camera horizontally, often used to follow characters or reveal elements within the frame.

- **Tilt**: Tilt the camera vertically to emphasize objects or characters.

- **Dolly**: Move the camera forward or backward, often used for tracking shots or to create a sense of depth.

- **Crane**: Raise or lower the camera on a crane or jib for sweeping, dynamic shots.

- **Steadicam**: Use a Steadicam or handheld camera for fluid, immersive shots that mimic human movement.

- **Static Shots**: Sometimes, static shots can be effective, allowing characters and actions to move within the frame while the camera remains still.

Lighting and Atmosphere

LIGHTING PLAYS A CRUCIAL role in cinematic direction. It sets the mood, highlights characters and objects, and can create a sense of atmosphere. Experiment with different lighting setups and techniques to achieve the desired visual impact. Unreal Engine provides a range of lighting features, including dynamic and baked lighting, real-time global illumination, and post-processing effects, to enhance your cinematic scenes.

In conclusion, directing cinematic scenes in Unreal Engine is a multifaceted process that combines creative storytelling with technical expertise. By applying principles of cinematography, shot planning, character direction, camera movement, and lighting, you can create compelling and immersive cinematic sequences that enhance the storytelling experience in your games.

12.3 Scripting Interactive Story Elements

SCRIPTING INTERACTIVE story elements in Unreal Engine adds depth and engagement to your game's narrative. It allows players to make choices that influence the story's outcome, creating a dynamic and immersive experience. In this section, we'll explore how to script interactive story elements using Blueprints, Sequencer, and Unreal's scripting capabilities.

Blueprint-Based Interactivity

UNREAL ENGINE'S BLUEPRINTS provide a powerful and user-friendly way to create interactive story elements. Here's a step-by-step guide to scripting interactive choices in your game:

1. Define Choices:

START BY DEFINING THE narrative choices you want to include in your story. These choices can range from simple decisions to complex branching narratives.

2. Create Choice Points:

IN YOUR GAME WORLD, designate specific locations or objects as "choice points" where players can make decisions. These choice points trigger interactive events.

3. Create Blueprint Actors:

FOR EACH CHOICE POINT, create a Blueprint Actor that encapsulates the interactive elements. This could include characters, objects, or UI elements representing the choices.

4. Implement Decision Logic:

INSIDE THE BLUEPRINT Actors, implement the decision logic using Blueprints. You can use nodes like "Input Key," "Branch," and "Sequence" to create decision pathways based on player input.

5. Update Variables:

USE BLUEPRINT VARIABLES to track the player's choices and the state of the game. For example, you might have a variable to store the player's alignment or the progression of the story.

6. Trigger Sequencer:

WHEN A PLAYER MAKES a choice, trigger the relevant Sequencer sequence or camera cut that corresponds to that choice. Sequencer allows you to create custom animations, camera movements, and dialogues for each choice.

7. Set Consequences:

DETERMINE THE CONSEQUENCES of each choice. Depending on the player's decisions, these consequences could affect the story's progression, character relationships, or the game's ending.

8. Branching Narratives:

FOR COMPLEX BRANCHING narratives, use Blueprint functions and variables to manage the flow of the story. You can create conditional branches based on variables, such as the player's alignment or previous choices.

9. Player Feedback:

PROVIDE FEEDBACK TO the player to indicate that their choices matter. This can include character reactions, changes in the environment, or on-screen text updates.

10. Save and Load:

IF YOUR GAME INCLUDES saving and loading, ensure that the player's choices are saved and can be loaded later to maintain continuity in the narrative.

Sequencer Integration

UNREAL ENGINE'S SEQUENCER is a valuable tool for creating cinematic sequences, including those related to interactive storytelling. Here's how to integrate Sequencer into your interactive story elements:

1. Create Sequencer Sequences:

DESIGN AND CREATE SEQUENCER sequences for each interactive choice point. These sequences should include character animations, dialogues, camera movements, and any other cinematic elements.

2. Trigger Sequences:

IN YOUR BLUEPRINT-BASED interactivity logic, trigger the appropriate Sequencer sequence when a player makes a choice. You can use Blueprint nodes like "Play" or "Pause" in Sequencer to control the playback.

3. Synchronize with Choices:

ENSURE THAT THE EVENTS in your Sequencer sequences are synchronized with the player's choices. For example, if the player chooses to befriend a character, trigger the corresponding sequence where the friendship develops.

4. Branch Sequences:

FOR BRANCHING NARRATIVES, create multiple Sequencer sequences that correspond to different story branches. Use Blueprint logic to select and play the appropriate sequence based on the player's choices.

5. Seamless Transitions:

TO MAKE THE TRANSITIONS between gameplay and cinematic sequences seamless, consider using techniques like blending or fading between sequences.

Unreal's Scripting Capabilities

UNREAL ENGINE PROVIDES extensive scripting capabilities through Blueprints and C++. Here are some additional scripting tips for interactive storytelling:

1. Dialogue Systems:

IMPLEMENT DIALOGUE systems to manage character interactions and conversations. Use Blueprint nodes to display character dialogues based on player choices.

2. Inventory Systems:

CREATE INVENTORY SYSTEMS that allow players to collect items or clues that can influence the story. Use Blueprint variables to manage the player's inventory and its impact on the narrative.

3. Quest Systems:

IF YOUR GAME INCLUDES quests or missions, design Blueprint-based quest systems that track the player's progress and update the story accordingly.

4. AI Behaviors:

SCRIPT AI BEHAVIORS that respond to the player's choices. For example, if the player chooses to spare an enemy, modify the enemy AI's behavior to reflect this choice.

5. Audio and Music:

USE BLUEPRINT SCRIPTING to trigger audio cues, music changes, and sound effects based on the player's choices and the narrative's progression.

6. UI Feedback:

DESIGN USER INTERFACES that provide feedback on the player's choices, such as displaying a choice log or updating character relationships in a visual format.

7. Data Management:

IMPLEMENT DATA MANAGEMENT systems to handle player choices, including saving and loading game states with different narrative branches.

In conclusion, scripting interactive story elements in Unreal Engine offers endless possibilities for creating engaging and dynamic narratives. By combining Blueprint-based interactivity, Sequencer integration, and Unreal's scripting capabilities, you can craft immersive and player-driven storytelling experiences in your games.

12.4 Integrating Narrative into Gameplay

INTEGRATING NARRATIVE elements seamlessly into gameplay is a fundamental aspect of creating immersive and engaging games. In this section, we'll explore various techniques and best practices for integrating storytelling, character development, and plot progression into your gameplay using Unreal Engine.

Storytelling Techniques

1. **Environmental Storytelling**: Use level design, props, and environmental details to convey narrative information without explicit exposition. For example, a bloodstain and a discarded weapon can suggest a violent altercation without words.
2. **Character Backstories**: Develop rich backstories for your characters, even if these details aren't directly presented in the game. Knowing a character's history can inform their motivations and actions, adding depth to their interactions.
3. **In-Game Books and Documents**: Scatter books, diaries, letters, or documents throughout your game world that players can read to learn more about the lore, history, or character backgrounds.
4. **Non-Player Character (NPC) Dialogue**: Craft meaningful dialogues for NPCs that provide insights into the game world, its factions, and the overall narrative. Allow players to engage in conversations that deepen their understanding.

5. **Hidden Lore**: Reward exploration by hiding narrative clues and lore in out-of-the-way places. This encourages players to explore and discover additional layers of the story.

Dynamic Narrative Events

1. **Player Choices**: Create branching narratives where player choices affect the story's direction. Choices can lead to different outcomes, character reactions, or quest progression. Use Blueprint scripting to manage branching narratives.
2. **Dynamic Dialogue**: Implement dynamic dialogue systems that adapt to the player's choices and actions. Use Unreal's Dialogue System to handle branching dialogues based on player decisions.
3. **Character Arcs**: Develop character arcs that evolve throughout the game. Characters should react to the player's actions and grow or change as the narrative unfolds.

Quest Design and Storytelling

1. **Quest Objectives**: Ensure that quest objectives align with the narrative and character motivations. Quests should feel like a natural part of the story rather than arbitrary tasks.
2. **Quest Dialogue**: Craft quest dialogue that provides context and narrative depth. Use dialogues to immerse players in the story and establish clear objectives.
3. **Pacing**: Balance the pacing of your quests to maintain the narrative's momentum. Mix action-packed sequences with moments of character development and world-building.
4. **Cinematic Quests**: Use Sequencer to create cinematic

quests or story-driven sequences. These can include cutscenes, important character interactions, or dramatic events that advance the plot.

Character Development

1. **Character Growth**: Allow characters to evolve over the course of the game. Use gameplay events and narrative choices to influence character development, making it feel organic and player-driven.
2. **Character Relationships**: Implement systems that track character relationships. Characters' attitudes toward the player and each other can change based on player actions, impacting the narrative.
3. **Reactive AI**: Program AI characters to respond to the player's choices and actions. This can include friendly or hostile reactions, altered dialogue, or even shifting alliances.

Scripting Gameplay Events

UNREAL ENGINE PROVIDES various tools and scripting capabilities for integrating narrative into gameplay:

- **Blueprints**: Use Blueprints to script interactive narrative events, character behaviors, and choice-based dialogues.

- **Sequencer**: Create cinematic sequences that seamlessly blend with gameplay. Use Sequencer for storytelling moments, character introductions, and important events.

- **Event Dispatchers**: Implement event dispatchers to trigger gameplay events based on narrative milestones.

This can include unlocking new areas, changing character behavior, or revealing story details.

- **Level Sequences**: Create level sequences to control scripted events within specific game levels. Level sequences are useful for pacing and storytelling within individual levels or chapters.

Feedback and Testing

ITERATE ON YOUR NARRATIVE integration to ensure it enhances gameplay. Collect player feedback to gauge the effectiveness of storytelling elements and make adjustments as needed. Playtesting is essential to identify any issues with narrative pacing, player comprehension, or the impact of player choices on the story.

In conclusion, integrating narrative into gameplay is a dynamic and creative process that requires careful planning and execution. Unreal Engine provides a range of tools and scripting capabilities to facilitate storytelling, character development, and player-driven narratives. By applying these techniques and continually refining your narrative integration, you can create compelling and immersive gaming experiences.

12.5 Using Camera Techniques for Storytelling

CAMERA TECHNIQUES ARE powerful storytelling tools in game development, enabling you to convey emotions, direct player attention, and immerse players in the narrative. In this section, we'll explore various camera techniques and best practices in Unreal Engine for effective storytelling.

Camera as a Narrative Device

THE CAMERA IS MORE than just a viewpoint in a game; it's a narrative device that can enhance storytelling in several ways:

1. **Framing Emotions**: Use camera angles and framing to capture character emotions and reactions. Close-ups can reveal their expressions, while wide shots can emphasize their surroundings.
2. **Visual Metaphors**: Employ camera techniques like tilts, pans, and zooms to create visual metaphors that symbolize story elements. For example, a camera tilting to show a character's vulnerability.
3. **Point of View (POV)**: Experiment with different character POVs to immerse players in their perspectives. A character's POV can provide unique insights and emotional engagement.
4. **Environmental Storytelling**: Use the camera to highlight important environmental details that contribute to the narrative. Slow camera movements can encourage exploration and discovery.

Dynamic Camera Movement

DYNAMIC CAMERA MOVEMENT adds depth and engagement to your storytelling. Unreal Engine provides tools and techniques to achieve this:

1. **Cinematic Cameras**: Utilize Unreal's Cinematic Cameras to create smooth and controlled camera movements. These cameras are ideal for cinematic sequences and storytelling moments.
2. **Sequencer**: Seamlessly integrate camera movements into your gameplay using Sequencer. You can script camera cuts,

pans, zooms, and transitions to align with the narrative.

3. **Player-Controlled Cameras**: For player-controlled games, implement dynamic camera movement that adapts to the player's actions. This can include following the player character, focusing on points of interest, or offering cinematic views during specific gameplay events.

Camera Transitions

CAMERA TRANSITIONS are essential for maintaining a coherent narrative and gameplay experience. Here are some transition techniques:

1. **Cuts**: Use straightforward cuts between camera angles to switch perspectives or scenes. Cuts are commonly used in cinematic sequences and dialogue exchanges.
2. **Crossfades**: Crossfades can smoothly transition between two shots or scenes, creating a more seamless and less jarring shift.
3. **Wipes and Dissolves**: Employ wipes or dissolves for dream sequences, flashbacks, or transitions that suggest the passage of time.
4. **Pan and Tilt**: Transition the camera by panning or tilting from one viewpoint to another. This technique can be used to reveal hidden elements or emphasize changes in the environment.

Establishing Shots

ESTABLISHING SHOTS are wide-angle views that provide context and set the stage for a scene. They are crucial for storytelling in open-world games, large environments, or when introducing new locations. Unreal Engine's powerful rendering capabilities make it possible to create stunning establishing shots that capture the grandeur of your game world.

Player-Character Connection

FOR GAMES WITH PLAYER-controlled characters, establish a strong connection between the player and their avatar. Ensure that the camera reflects the character's perspective, movements, and actions. Use visual cues, like camera shakes during intense moments or changes in FOV (Field of View), to convey the character's emotions or physical state.

Foreshadowing and Suspense

CAMERA TECHNIQUES CAN be used to build anticipation and suspense in your narrative. Techniques like tracking shots, revealing hidden threats, or foreshadowing important events through camera positioning can keep players engaged and curious about what's to come.

Subverting Expectations

CONSIDER SUBVERTING player expectations with unconventional camera techniques. A sudden change in camera perspective or an unexpected shift in focus can create memorable and impactful storytelling moments.

Testing and Feedback

ITERATE ON YOUR CAMERA techniques and gather player feedback to fine-tune your storytelling. Conduct playtests to ensure that camera movements and transitions enhance the narrative without causing discomfort or disorientation for players.

In conclusion, mastering camera techniques in Unreal Engine is essential for effective storytelling in games. The camera serves as a powerful tool to convey emotions, immerse players in the narrative, and guide their attention. By leveraging Unreal's cinematic tools, dynamic camera movement, and transition techniques, you can create compelling and immersive storytelling experiences that captivate your audience.

Chapter 13: Custom Plugin Development

13.1 Basics of Unreal Plugin Architecture

CUSTOM PLUGIN DEVELOPMENT is a powerful way to extend and customize Unreal Engine's functionality to suit your specific project needs. In this section, we will delve into the basics of Unreal plugin architecture, including the structure of plugins, how to create them, and the essential concepts you need to grasp.

What Is an Unreal Plugin?

AN UNREAL PLUGIN IS a modular package that contains code, assets, and configuration files. It allows you to add new features, functionality, or modifications to the Unreal Engine editor and runtime. Plugins can range from simple additions like custom actors or assets to complex systems such as custom physics engines or rendering pipelines.

Plugin Structure

UNREAL PLUGINS HAVE a specific directory structure. When you create a new plugin, you'll typically find the following directories and files:

- **Binaries**: Compiled plugin binaries for different platforms.
- **Content**: Assets, such as textures, meshes, and materials, that the plugin uses.

- **Source**: The source code for the plugin, organized into folders like "Public" for headers and "Private" for implementation details.
- **Resources**: Additional resources like configuration files or localization data.
- **Intermediate**: Temporary build files generated during compilation.
- ***.uplugin**: The plugin descriptor file that defines the plugin's metadata, dependencies, and module information.

Creating a New Plugin

TO CREATE A NEW PLUGIN in Unreal Engine, follow these steps:

1. Open the Unreal Engine editor.
2. Click on "Edit" in the menu, then select "Plugins."
3. Click on "New Plugin" to create a new plugin project.
4. Provide a name for your plugin, choose its type (Runtime or Editor), and specify the folder where it should be created.
5. Click "Create Plugin" to generate the plugin's directory structure and necessary files.

Plugin Modules

PLUGINS CONSIST OF one or more modules, where each module is a logical unit of code. Modules are defined in the plugin's .uplugin file and can be either "Runtime" or "Editor" modules. Runtime modules are loaded when the game is running, while

Editor modules are loaded when working in the Unreal Engine editor.

Each module has a set of C++ source files (.cpp) and header files (.h) that define its functionality. You can specify module dependencies in the .uplugin file to ensure that they are loaded in the correct order.

Extending Engine Functionality

PLUGINS CAN EXTEND Unreal Engine's functionality in various ways:

1. **Custom Actors and Components**: Create custom actors, components, and classes that can be used in your game or project.
2. **Editor Tools**: Develop custom editor tools and utilities to streamline your workflow or enhance the Unreal Engine editor.
3. **Asset Types**: Define custom asset types with their own properties and behavior.
4. **Third-Party Libraries**: Integrate third-party libraries or SDKs into your Unreal project by encapsulating them in a plugin.

Building and Packaging Plugins

TO BUILD AND PACKAGE your plugin for distribution, follow these steps:

1. Open the plugin's .uplugin file in a text editor and ensure that it includes all necessary information, including module dependencies.
2. Build the plugin by running the "Generate Visual Studio project files" command from the Unreal Editor's "File"

menu.

3. Open the generated Visual Studio solution and build the plugin.
4. After successful compilation, the plugin binaries will be located in the plugin's "Binaries" folder.
5. To package the plugin, you can either distribute the plugin directory as is or create a .zip archive for easy distribution to other users or projects.

Plugin Activation

BEFORE YOU CAN USE a plugin in your project, you need to activate it. In the Unreal Engine editor, navigate to the "Plugins" window and enable the desired plugin from the list. Once activated, you can access and use the plugin's functionality within your project.

Debugging and Testing

DEBUGGING PLUGINS FOLLOWS the same principles as debugging regular Unreal Engine projects. You can set breakpoints in your plugin's code, inspect variables, and use Unreal's debugging tools.

Testing your plugin within the Unreal Engine editor is also straightforward. You can create test maps or scenes that specifically exercise your plugin's features, ensuring that it functions as intended.

In conclusion, understanding the basics of Unreal plugin architecture is essential for customizing and extending Unreal Engine to meet your project's requirements. Plugins offer a modular and organized way to add new features, assets, and functionality, making them a valuable tool for game development and customization.

13.2 Developing Custom Editor Tools

DEVELOPING CUSTOM EDITOR tools is a significant aspect of Unreal Engine plugin development. These tools can streamline your workflow, automate repetitive tasks, and provide a more user-friendly experience for your team. In this section, we'll explore the process of creating custom editor tools within your Unreal Engine plugin.

Why Create Custom Editor Tools?

CUSTOM EDITOR TOOLS offer several advantages:

1. **Workflow Efficiency**: They can automate complex or repetitive tasks, reducing the time required for content creation and level design.
2. **Specialized Features**: Custom tools can add features specific to your project's needs that may not be available in the default Unreal Engine editor.
3. **User Experience**: They can enhance the user experience by providing an intuitive and streamlined interface for performing common tasks.
4. **Data Validation**: Custom tools can validate data, ensuring that assets and levels adhere to project-specific standards and constraints.

Editor Utility Widgets

UNREAL ENGINE PROVIDES a feature called Editor Utility Widgets, which allows you to create custom user interfaces within the editor. These widgets can be used to create tools and panels that interact with the editor's functionality.

Creating an Editor Utility Widget

1. To create an Editor Utility Widget, go to the "File" menu in the Unreal Editor, select "User Interface," and choose "Editor Utility Widget."
2. Give your widget a name and location, then click "Create."
3. The widget will open in the Widget Blueprint Editor, where you can design its user interface and functionality using Blueprint scripting.

Designing the User Interface

IN THE WIDGET BLUEPRINT Editor, you can design the user interface for your custom tool. This can include buttons, input fields, lists, and other widgets that allow users to interact with your tool.

Blueprint Scripting

YOU CAN USE BLUEPRINT scripting to define the functionality of your custom editor tool. This scripting can involve interacting with assets, manipulating level data, or performing any other tasks relevant to your tool's purpose.

Here's a basic example of a custom editor tool that renames selected actors:

Event Construct:

Get Selected Actors -> ForEach Loop (Loop Body)

Rename Actor (New Name)

This simple tool iterates through selected actors and renames them.

Testing and Deployment

YOU CAN TEST YOUR CUSTOM editor tool directly within the Unreal Engine editor by adding it to the Toolbar or by opening it from the "Window" menu.

To share your custom editor tool with your team or distribute it with your project, you can package it within your plugin. When users activate your plugin, they will have access to the custom tools and utilities you've created.

Extending the Editor Interface

IN ADDITION TO EDITOR Utility Widgets, Unreal Engine allows you to extend the editor's interface by creating custom tabs, panels, and property editors. These extensions can provide specialized views or additional functionality within the editor.

Creating Custom Tabs and Panels

1. To create a custom tab, panel, or property editor, you'll need to define a new class that extends the appropriate Unreal Engine editor class, such as FAssetEditorToolkit or FDetailsView.
2. Implement the necessary functionality and user interface elements within your class.
3. Register your custom editor extension with Unreal Engine to ensure it appears in the editor interface.

Example: Creating a Custom Editor Tab

CLASS FMyCustomEditorTab : **public** FAssetEditorToolkit

```
{
public:
// Implement your custom tab's functionality and UI here.
};
```

Integrating with Editor Features

YOUR CUSTOM EDITOR tools can interact with existing Unreal Engine editor features. For example, you can use the Unreal Engine Asset Registry to query and manipulate assets within your tool. Additionally, you can create custom editor modes and controls that integrate seamlessly with the editor's interface.

Debugging and Testing

DEBUGGING CUSTOM EDITOR tools involves standard debugging practices, such as setting breakpoints in your code, inspecting variables, and using Unreal's debugging tools.

Testing your custom tools within the Unreal Engine editor is essential to ensure they function as expected. Thoroughly test the tool's functionality and user interface to identify and fix any issues.

In conclusion, developing custom editor tools within your Unreal Engine plugin empowers you to tailor the editor to your project's specific needs. Whether you're automating tasks, creating specialized features, or enhancing the user experience, custom editor tools can significantly improve your workflow and the efficiency of your game development process.

13.3 Extending Engine Capabilities with Plugins

EXTENDING UNREAL ENGINE'S capabilities through plugins allows you to add new features, modify existing functionality, and integrate third-party libraries or services. In this section, we'll explore how you can extend Unreal Engine using plugins, including examples of common plugin use cases.

Why Extend Unreal Engine with Plugins?

1. **Custom Functionality**: Plugins enable you to add custom functionality to Unreal Engine tailored to your project's needs.
2. **Third-Party Integrations**: You can seamlessly integrate third-party libraries, middleware, or services into your Unreal Engine project.
3. **Project-Specific Modifications**: Plugins allow you to make project-specific modifications without altering the engine's source code, making it easier to maintain engine updates.
4. **Asset Types**: Create custom asset types and editors for your project to manage unique resources efficiently.

Types of Plugins

UNREAL ENGINE SUPPORTS several types of plugins, each serving different purposes:

1. **Editor Plugins**: These extend the Unreal Engine editor's functionality. They can add new tools, panels, or menu items to the editor interface.
2. **Runtime Plugins**: These add functionality to your game

when it's running. For example, you can use runtime plugins to integrate analytics, in-app purchases, or cloud services.

3. **Tool Plugins**: Tool plugins provide utilities and features for content creation, such as mesh editing tools, material editors, or animation tools.
4. **Platform Plugins**: Platform plugins are used for platform-specific implementations, including console SDK integrations or device-specific features.

Plugin Development Workflow

DEVELOPING A PLUGIN for Unreal Engine typically follows these steps:

1. **Plugin Creation**: Create a new plugin using the Unreal Engine editor's plugin wizard or manually set up a plugin folder structure.
2. **Code Implementation**: Write C++ code to implement the desired functionality. This may include adding new classes, functions, or modifying existing ones.
3. **Asset Creation**: If your plugin involves new asset types, create the necessary asset classes and editors using Unreal's asset management system.
4. **Packaging**: Package the plugin with your project or distribute it separately as needed.
5. **Activation**: Activate the plugin within your Unreal Engine project.

Common Plugin Use Cases

HERE ARE SOME COMMON use cases for extending Unreal Engine using plugins:

1. Custom Input Handling

YOU CAN CREATE PLUGINS to handle custom input devices or gestures, allowing your game to support unique control methods.

```
// Custom input plugin example

void UCustomInputPlugin::HandleCustomInput()

{

// Handle custom input logic here

}
```

2. AI Behavior

PLUGINS CAN INTRODUCE custom AI behaviors or integrate external AI libraries to enhance NPC interactions.

```
// Custom AI behavior plugin example

void UCustomAIBehaviorPlugin::CustomNPCBehavior()

{

// Implement custom AI logic here

}
```

3. Analytics and Telemetry

INTEGRATE ANALYTICS and telemetry services to gather insights about player behavior and game performance.

```
// Analytics plugin example
```

```
void UAnalyticsPlugin::TrackEvent(const FString& eventName, const FString& eventData)
{
// Send analytics data to a service
}
```

4. Custom Networking

EXTEND UNREAL ENGINE'S networking capabilities to support specific multiplayer features or integrate with custom server solutions.

```
// Custom networking plugin example
void UNetworkingPlugin::CustomServerLogic()
{
// Implement custom server logic
}
```

5. External Libraries and SDKs

INTEGRATE THIRD-PARTY libraries or SDKs for services like physics simulation, machine learning, or audio processing.

```
// External library integration plugin example
void
UExternalLibraryIntegrationPlugin::UseExternalLibraryFunction()
{
```

```
// Call functions from an external library
}
```

6. UI Customization

CREATE CUSTOM UI ELEMENTS, widgets, or interfaces to tailor the user experience for your project.

```
// Custom UI plugin example
void UCustomUIPlugin::CreateCustomWidget()
{
// Design and display custom UI elements
}
```

7. Asset Pipeline

DEVELOP PLUGINS TO automate asset import/export processes or to introduce custom asset types.

```
// Asset pipeline plugin example
void UAssetPipelinePlugin::CustomAssetImport()
{
// Implement custom asset import logic
}
```

Debugging and Testing

DEBUGGING PLUGINS IN Unreal Engine is similar to debugging regular C++ code. You can set breakpoints, inspect variables, and utilize Unreal's debugging tools to troubleshoot issues.

Testing plugins involves thorough testing within the engine to ensure the plugin functions as expected. Additionally, testing across different project configurations and platforms may be necessary to guarantee compatibility.

In summary, extending Unreal Engine's capabilities through plugins provides flexibility and customization options for your project. Whether you need to add custom functionality, integrate external services, or modify existing features, plugins offer a modular and efficient way to extend the Unreal Engine's capabilities to meet your project's requirements.

13.4 Plugin Distribution and Marketplace Best Practices

DISTRIBUTING YOUR UNREAL Engine plugin effectively and adhering to best practices is crucial for ensuring that your plugin reaches its intended audience and is easy to use. In this section, we'll explore the steps and best practices for distributing your plugin and making it available on the Unreal Engine Marketplace or through other distribution channels.

Preparing Your Plugin for Distribution

BEFORE DISTRIBUTING your plugin, you need to ensure it is well-prepared and meets certain requirements:

1. Documentation:

- Create comprehensive documentation for your plugin. Include installation instructions, usage guides, and any necessary setup steps. Clear and well-structured documentation is crucial for users to understand and utilize your plugin effectively.

2. Licensing:

- Define the licensing terms for your plugin. Specify whether it's free, open-source, or requires a purchase. Ensure that you comply with Unreal Engine's licensing terms.

3. Testing:

- Thoroughly test your plugin to identify and fix any bugs or issues. Ensure it works seamlessly with the intended Unreal Engine versions.

4. Performance:

- Optimize your plugin for performance. Avoid resource-intensive operations or inefficient code that could impact the overall performance of Unreal Engine projects using your plugin.

5. User Interface:

- If your plugin has a user interface, make sure it is intuitive and user-friendly. Consider usability principles and ensure it aligns with Unreal Engine's design conventions.

Distribution Options

YOU HAVE SEVERAL DISTRIBUTION options for your Unreal Engine plugin:

1. Unreal Engine Marketplace:

- The Unreal Engine Marketplace is the official platform for distributing plugins, assets, and content. Submitting your plugin to the Marketplace provides a centralized location for users to discover and download your work.

2. GitHub or GitLab:

- You can host your plugin's source code and assets on platforms like GitHub or GitLab. This allows users to access and contribute to your plugin, making it open-source and fostering a community around it.

3. Personal Website:

- If you prefer full control over distribution, you can create a dedicated website for your plugin. Provide download links, documentation, and support resources on your website.

Marketplace Submission

IF YOU CHOOSE TO DISTRIBUTE your plugin through the Unreal Engine Marketplace, follow these best practices for a successful submission:

1. Marketplace Guidelines:

- Familiarize yourself with the Unreal Engine Marketplace guidelines and requirements. Ensure that your plugin complies with all submission criteria.

2. Submission Process:

- Follow the Marketplace submission process, which typically involves providing detailed information about your plugin, uploading assets, setting pricing and licensing terms, and submitting for review.

3. High-Quality Assets:

- Ensure that any assets included with your plugin are of high quality. Provide clear and detailed previews of these assets.

4. Documentation:

- Upload comprehensive documentation to the Marketplace that users can access when they download your plugin.

5. *Support:*

- Offer prompt and helpful support to users who have questions or encounter issues with your plugin.

Version Compatibility

MAINTAIN COMPATIBILITY with the latest Unreal Engine versions and provide updates as needed. Users rely on up-to-date plugins that work with the most recent engine releases.

User Feedback and Community Engagement

ENCOURAGE USER FEEDBACK and actively engage with the community using your plugin. Respond to questions, address issues promptly, and consider user suggestions for improvements.

Marketing and Promotion

PROMOTE YOUR PLUGIN through various channels, including social media, forums, and developer communities. Highlight its unique features and benefits to attract potential users.

Documentation and Tutorials

IN ADDITION TO DOCUMENTATION, consider creating video tutorials or written guides that demonstrate how to use your plugin effectively. These resources can be invaluable for users who want to learn how to make the most of your plugin.

Continuous Improvement

REGULARLY UPDATE YOUR plugin to fix bugs, add new features, and improve performance based on user feedback and evolving Unreal Engine standards.

User Reviews and Ratings

ENCOURAGE USERS TO provide reviews and ratings for your plugin on the Unreal Engine Marketplace. Positive reviews and high ratings can boost your plugin's visibility and credibility.

Conclusion

DISTRIBUTING YOUR UNREAL Engine plugin effectively and following best practices is essential for its success. Whether you choose to distribute it through the Unreal Engine Marketplace, on version control platforms like GitHub, or through your website, prioritizing user experience, documentation, support, and community engagement will help your plugin gain recognition and serve its intended purpose effectively.

13.5 Maintaining and Updating Plugins

ONCE YOUR UNREAL ENGINE plugin is distributed and in use by developers, it's essential to maintain and update it regularly to ensure compatibility with new engine versions, fix bugs, and improve functionality. In this section, we'll explore the best practices for maintaining and updating your Unreal Engine plugins effectively.

Version Compatibility

ONE OF THE MOST CRITICAL aspects of plugin maintenance is ensuring compatibility with different Unreal Engine versions. As the engine evolves, you need to adapt your plugin to work seamlessly with new releases. Follow these guidelines:

1. Stay Informed:

- Keep yourself informed about Unreal Engine updates, release notes, and roadmap to anticipate changes that may affect your plugin.

2. Testing:

- Test your plugin thoroughly with each new Unreal Engine version. Identify and fix compatibility issues promptly.

3. Update Dependencies:

- Check if any external libraries or dependencies used by your plugin need updates to support the latest engine version.

Bug Fixes

REGULARLY ADDRESS BUG reports and issues reported by users. Promptly fix bugs to provide a stable and reliable experience. Follow these steps:

1. Bug Tracking:

- Use a bug tracking system to keep track of reported issues and their status.

2. Clear Communication:

- Maintain clear communication with users who report bugs. Provide updates on bug fixes and expected release dates.

3. Regression Testing:

- After fixing a bug, perform regression testing to ensure that the issue is resolved without introducing new problems.

Feature Updates

ENHANCE YOUR PLUGIN by adding new features or improving existing ones based on user feedback and changing requirements. Here's how to handle feature updates:

1. User Feedback:

- Solicit user feedback to identify feature requests and areas for improvement.

2. Prioritization:

- Prioritize feature requests based on user demand and the impact on your plugin's functionality.

3. Roadmap:

- Develop a roadmap for feature updates, including timelines and milestones.

4. Testing:

- Thoroughly test new features to ensure they work as intended and do not introduce regressions.

Documentation and User Support

KEEP YOUR DOCUMENTATION up to date. As you introduce new features or modify existing ones, update your documentation to reflect these changes. Maintain robust user support to help users with any questions or issues they encounter.

Version Control

USE VERSION CONTROL systems like Git to manage your plugin's source code. This allows you to track changes, collaborate with others, and easily roll back to previous versions if needed.

Compatibility with Other Plugins

CONSIDER THE COMPATIBILITY of your plugin with other popular plugins or assets that users might use in conjunction with yours. Compatibility issues can lead to user frustration, so it's essential to address them promptly.

Release Notes

WHEN YOU RELEASE UPDATES, provide detailed release notes that outline the changes, bug fixes, and new features introduced in the latest version. This helps users understand what to expect and how the update might impact their projects.

Deprecation and Removal

IF YOU NEED TO DEPRECATE or remove certain features from your plugin, clearly communicate this to users in advance. Provide guidance on how they can migrate to newer alternatives or workarounds.

Backward Compatibility

STRIVE TO MAINTAIN backward compatibility whenever possible. Avoid breaking changes that could disrupt existing projects using your plugin. If you must introduce breaking changes, document them thoroughly and provide migration guides.

User Communication

ESTABLISH CLEAR CHANNELS of communication with your plugin's user community. This includes forums, email lists, or Discord channels. Regularly update users on plugin developments, bug fixes, and upcoming features.

Licensing and Royalties

ENSURE THAT YOUR LICENSING terms and royalty agreements, if applicable, are consistent and well-documented. If you make changes to licensing terms, communicate them clearly to users.

User Data and Privacy

IF YOUR PLUGIN COLLECTS user data, ensure that you comply with privacy regulations and communicate how user data is handled and protected.

In conclusion, maintaining and updating your Unreal Engine plugins is a continuous process that involves adapting to new engine versions, addressing bugs, adding new features, and providing excellent user support. By following these best practices, you can ensure that your plugin remains a valuable asset to the Unreal Engine community and continues to meet the evolving needs of developers.

14. Performance Tuning and Optimization

14.1 Analyzing and Diagnosing Performance Issues

PERFORMANCE TUNING and optimization are critical aspects of game development to ensure that your Unreal Engine project runs smoothly and efficiently on a variety of platforms. In this section, we will focus on the initial steps of performance optimization, which involve analyzing and diagnosing performance issues.

The Importance of Performance Optimization

PERFORMANCE OPTIMIZATION is essential because it directly affects the player's experience. A poorly optimized game can suffer from frame rate drops, long loading times, and other issues that disrupt gameplay and immersion. Whether you're developing for PC, console, or mobile, optimizing your game's performance is crucial for a successful release.

Profiling Tools

PROFILING TOOLS ARE essential for identifying performance bottlenecks and areas that need optimization. Unreal Engine provides a range of profiling tools that help you gather data and insights into your game's performance:

1. Unreal Insights:

- Unreal Insights is a powerful profiling tool that provides in-depth data on CPU, GPU, and memory usage. It allows you to visualize performance data in real-time, making it easier to pinpoint bottlenecks.

2. Stat Commands:

• Unreal Engine includes various stat commands that allow you to measure and display performance data in the editor or console. For example, you can use the "stat Unit" command to check CPU and GPU performance.

3. Frame Rate Profiler:

• The Frame Rate Profiler displays a breakdown of the time taken to render a single frame, helping you identify which parts of your game consume the most processing time.

4. GPU Visualizer:

• The GPU Visualizer provides a visual representation of the GPU workload, allowing you to identify rendering issues that might affect frame rates.

5. Memory Profiler:

• Use the Memory Profiler to track memory usage and identify memory leaks or excessive allocations.

Performance Metrics

TO OPTIMIZE YOUR GAME effectively, you should focus on key performance metrics:

1. Frame Rate (FPS):

- The number of frames rendered per second. A consistent and high frame rate is crucial for smooth gameplay.

2. Frame Time:

- The time taken to render a single frame. Analyzing frame times helps identify performance bottlenecks.

3. CPU Usage:

- Monitoring CPU usage helps you understand how much processing power your game consumes. High CPU usage can lead to frame rate drops.

4. GPU Usage:

- GPU usage indicates how much of the graphics card's processing power is being utilized. High GPU usage may lead to frame rate issues and overheating.

5. Memory Usage:

- Tracking memory usage is essential to avoid excessive allocations and memory leaks, which can impact performance and stability.

Identifying Performance Issues

TO DIAGNOSE PERFORMANCE issues, follow these steps:

1. ***Profiling Sessions:***

- Start profiling sessions using Unreal Insights or other profiling tools while running your game.

2. ***Analyze Data:***

- Examine the collected data to identify performance bottlenecks. Look for spikes in frame times, high CPU or GPU usage, and excessive memory consumption.

3. ***Focus on Hotspots:***

- Prioritize optimization efforts on the most significant performance hotspots. These are the areas that have the most impact on overall performance.

4. ***Iterative Testing:***

- Make incremental changes to your code or assets and continually test performance improvements. Profiling tools will help you measure the impact of each change.

5. ***Optimization Techniques:***

- Implement optimization techniques such as level of detail (LOD), occlusion culling, and efficient asset management to address performance issues.

6. Monitor on Target Platforms:

- Test your game on the target platforms to ensure that performance improvements translate to real-world scenarios.

7. Collaborate and Iterate:

- Work closely with your development team to identify and address performance issues collaboratively. Performance optimization is often an iterative process.

IN CONCLUSION, ANALYZING and diagnosing performance issues is the first step in optimizing your Unreal Engine project. Profiling tools and performance metrics are your allies in identifying bottlenecks and areas that need improvement. Once you've pinpointed the issues, you can proceed with implementing optimization techniques and iteratively testing your game's performance to achieve a smooth and enjoyable player experience.

14.2 Optimizing Game Assets for Performance

OPTIMIZING GAME ASSETS is a crucial part of achieving good performance in your Unreal Engine project. Game assets include 3D models, textures, animations, and sound files. In this section, we'll explore various techniques and best practices for optimizing these assets to ensure your game runs smoothly on a wide range of hardware.

Importance of Asset Optimization

WELL-OPTIMIZED ASSETS not only improve the overall performance of your game but also reduce loading times and memory usage. This is especially important for games targeting mobile devices, consoles, or lower-end PCs, where hardware resources are limited.

3D Model Optimization

1. Level of Detail (LOD):

- Implement LODs for 3D models. LODs reduce the level of detail in a model as it moves away from the camera, decreasing the number of polygons rendered.

2. Mesh Simplification:

- Use mesh simplification tools to reduce the polygon count of complex models while preserving visual quality.

3. Mesh Merging:

- Combine multiple small meshes into a single larger mesh where possible. This reduces draw calls and overhead.

4. Material Instances:

- Utilize material instances to reduce the number of unique materials used on models. Share materials when appropriate.

Texture Optimization

1. Texture Resolutions:

- Choose appropriate texture resolutions based on the asset's importance and visibility. Use lower resolutions for distant objects.

2. Texture Compression:

- Use texture compression formats (e.g., BC7, ASTC, ETC2) to reduce texture file sizes while maintaining quality.

3. Texture Streaming:

- Implement texture streaming to load and unload textures dynamically based on the player's location, reducing memory usage.

4. Texture Atlases:

- Create texture atlases to combine multiple textures into a single texture sheet, reducing draw calls.

Animation Optimization

1. Animation LODs:

- Similar to model LODs, create simplified versions of animations for distant characters to reduce CPU overhead.

2. Animation Culling:

- Implement animation culling to stop updating animations for characters that are not visible or are too far away.

3. Animation Compression:

- Use animation compression techniques to reduce the memory footprint of animations.

Sound Optimization

1. Sound Quality Levels:

- Use different sound quality levels for various audio sources based on their importance. Distant sounds can have lower quality.

2. Sound Occlusion and Attenuation:

- Implement sound occlusion and attenuation to reduce the number of active sounds and their impact on performance.

Asset Streaming

1. Asset Bundles:

- Group assets into bundles and load them on demand to reduce initial loading times.

2. Asynchronous Loading:

- Use asynchronous loading to load assets in the background while the game is running, avoiding frame rate drops during loading.

Testing and Profiling

1. Profiling Tools:

- Use Unreal Engine's profiling tools to identify assets that contribute to performance issues. Focus optimization efforts on these assets.

2. Benchmarking:

- Benchmark your game on target hardware to ensure that assets are optimized for the specific platforms you're targeting.

Collaboration and Iteration

OPTIMIZATION IS OFTEN an iterative process that involves collaboration among artists, designers, and programmers. Regularly communicate with your team to identify assets that need further optimization.

Documentation and Guidelines

CREATE DOCUMENTATION and guidelines for asset optimization to ensure that all team members follow best practices. This documentation should cover topics like LOD creation, texture compression settings, and asset bundling.

In summary, optimizing game assets is essential for achieving good performance in Unreal Engine projects. By implementing techniques such as LODs, texture compression, and animation culling, you can reduce CPU and GPU overhead, decrease loading times, and create a smoother gaming experience for players. Collaboration, testing, and documentation play key roles in the asset optimization process.

14.3 Advanced Rendering Optimization Techniques

ADVANCED RENDERING optimization techniques are crucial for achieving high-quality visuals while maintaining optimal performance in your Unreal Engine project. These techniques go beyond basic asset optimization and involve fine-tuning rendering settings and implementing advanced features. In this section, we'll explore some of these techniques.

Level of Detail (LOD) Hierarchy

WHILE LODS FOR 3D MODELS are common, consider applying LODs to other aspects of your game, such as particle effects and textures. For particle effects, use simpler versions of effects for distant objects. Additionally, use mipmaps for textures to reduce the texture's resolution as it gets farther from the camera, improving performance and reducing aliasing.

Occlusion Culling

IMPLEMENT OCCLUSION culling to reduce the rendering load on the GPU. Occlusion culling involves determining which objects are not visible to the camera and skipping their rendering. Unreal Engine provides built-in support for occlusion culling, which can significantly improve performance, especially in complex scenes.

Screen Space Reflections (SSR)

SCREEN SPACE REFLECTIONS simulate real-time reflections by analyzing what's visible on the screen. While SSR can enhance visual quality, it can be performance-intensive. Use SSR sparingly and consider reducing its intensity or using reflection probes in areas where high-quality reflections are essential.

Static and Stationary Lights

IN UNREAL ENGINE, LIGHTS can be categorized as static, stationary, or dynamic. Static and stationary lights are precomputed and offer better performance compared to dynamic lights. Whenever possible, use static or stationary lights in your scene, especially for non-moving objects or environments.

Distance Field Ambient Occlusion (DFAO)

DISTANCE FIELD AMBIENT Occlusion is a feature that provides high-quality ambient occlusion while being more performance-friendly than traditional screen-space techniques. Enabling DFAO can improve the overall visual quality of your scene without a significant performance hit.

Particle Optimization

PARTICLES ARE OFTEN used for various effects in games, but they can be performance-intensive. Optimize particle systems by using lower-poly meshes for particles, limiting the number of particles spawned, and adjusting particle lifetimes. Additionally, use LODs for particle effects to simplify them at a distance.

Hierarchical Level of Detail (HLOD)

HLOD IS AN ADVANCED optimization technique that combines multiple static mesh actors into a single, simplified mesh when they are viewed from a distance. This reduces draw calls and improves rendering performance. HLOD can be especially beneficial in open-world or large-scale environments.

Procedural Content Generation

CONSIDER USING PROCEDURAL content generation techniques to create parts of your game world. Procedurally generated assets can be optimized for performance and memory usage since they can be generated on the fly, reducing the need for storing large amounts of static data.

Occlusion Queries

OCCLUSION QUERIES ALLOW you to check if an object is visible from a certain viewpoint before rendering it. While this technique can be complex to implement, it can lead to significant performance gains, especially in scenes with many objects.

GPU Particle Simulation

OFFLOAD PARTICLE SIMULATIONS to the GPU whenever possible. Unreal Engine supports GPU particle systems that can run simulations on the graphics card, reducing CPU overhead and improving performance for particle-heavy scenes.

Post-Processing Effects

EVALUATE THE USE OF post-processing effects in your project. Some effects, while visually appealing, can have a significant impact on performance. Adjust the quality and intensity of post-processing effects to strike a balance between visuals and performance.

Shader Optimization

OPTIMIZE YOUR SHADERS to reduce rendering overhead. This includes simplifying complex shaders, eliminating unused code, and using shader permutations efficiently. Unreal Engine provides tools for profiling and optimizing shaders.

In conclusion, advanced rendering optimization techniques are essential for achieving the desired visual quality while maintaining optimal performance in Unreal Engine projects. By carefully selecting and implementing these techniques based on your project's specific requirements, you can create visually stunning games that run smoothly on a wide range of hardware configurations.

14.4 Memory Management and Garbage Collection

EFFICIENT MEMORY MANAGEMENT is vital for maintaining optimal performance and stability in your Unreal Engine project. Unreal Engine uses a garbage collection system to handle memory allocation and deallocation, but it's essential to understand how to manage memory effectively and avoid common pitfalls. In this section, we'll delve into memory management and garbage collection techniques.

Understanding Memory in Unreal Engine

UNREAL ENGINE USES a combination of static and dynamic memory allocation to manage game assets, objects, and resources. Here's a brief overview of memory types:

1. Static Memory:

- Static memory is used for objects that persist throughout the entire game's lifetime. Examples include level geometry, static meshes, and textures.

2. Dynamic Memory:

- Dynamic memory is allocated and deallocated during runtime as needed. This includes memory for game objects, particle systems, and temporary data structures.

3. Garbage Collection:

- Unreal Engine employs a garbage collection system to reclaim memory occupied by objects that are no longer in use. Garbage collection periodically scans the memory for unreferenced objects and frees up their memory.

Avoiding Memory Leaks

MEMORY LEAKS OCCUR when allocated memory is not properly deallocated, leading to a gradual increase in memory usage over time. To avoid memory leaks:

1. Use Smart Pointers:

- Unreal Engine provides smart pointers like TSharedPtr and TWeakPtr to manage object references automatically. Use them to ensure objects are deallocated when they are no longer needed.

2. Clean Up Event Handlers:

- Remove event handlers and delegates when they are no longer necessary. Failure to do so can prevent objects from being garbage collected.

3. Avoid Circular References:

- Be cautious of circular references where two objects reference each other. Use TWeakPtr or break the reference cycle when possible.

4. Handle Assets Properly:

- Unload unused assets and textures to free up memory. Unreal Engine provides asset management tools for this purpose.

Object Lifetimes

UNDERSTANDING OBJECT lifetimes is crucial for memory management:

1. Transient Objects:

- Transient objects have a short lifespan and are usually used for temporary calculations or gameplay logic. Unreal Engine automatically manages memory for transient objects.

2. UObject Lifetimes:

- UObject-derived objects are managed by Unreal Engine's garbage collector. Ensure that you don't keep references to objects longer than necessary, as this can impact performance.

3. Resource Management:

- Resources such as textures, materials, and meshes should be managed efficiently. Load them when needed and unload them when they are no longer in use.

Memory Profiling

USE UNREAL ENGINE'S memory profiling tools to identify memory usage patterns and potential issues:

1. Memory Profiler:

- The Memory Profiler provides insights into memory allocations, allowing you to track memory usage in real-time and analyze memory leaks.

2. Memory Snapshots:

- Take memory snapshots at key points in your game to identify memory spikes or patterns of memory growth.

Custom Memory Allocation

IN SOME CASES, CUSTOM memory allocation strategies can be beneficial. Unreal Engine allows you to implement custom memory allocators tailored to your specific needs, such as optimizing memory for a specific platform or usage pattern.

Streaming and Unloading

IMPLEMENT ASSET STREAMING and unloading strategies to load assets on demand and unload them when no longer needed. This approach minimizes the memory footprint and loading times of your game.

Memory Budgeting

SET MEMORY BUDGETS for your game to ensure that it runs smoothly on target hardware. Monitor memory usage during development and adjust assets and content accordingly to stay within the budget.

Documentation and Best Practices

DOCUMENT MEMORY MANAGEMENT guidelines and best practices for your development team. Ensure that all team members follow these guidelines to maintain consistency and avoid memory-related issues.

In conclusion, effective memory management and garbage collection are essential for maintaining optimal performance and stability in Unreal Engine projects. By understanding memory types, avoiding memory leaks, and using memory profiling tools, you can create games that run efficiently and provide a smooth player experience. Additionally, consider custom memory allocation strategies, asset streaming, and memory budgeting to fine-tune memory usage for your specific project requirements.

14.5 Scalability Settings and Platform-

Specific Tuning

SCALABILITY SETTINGS and platform-specific tuning are crucial aspects of optimizing your Unreal Engine project to run efficiently across a variety of hardware configurations and platforms. By adjusting scalability settings and making platform-specific optimizations, you can ensure that your game provides the best possible experience to players. In this section, we'll explore these techniques in detail.

Scalability Settings

UNREAL ENGINE OFFERS scalability settings that allow players to adjust graphics quality based on their hardware capabilities. These settings ensure that your game remains accessible to a wide range of players, from those with high-end gaming rigs to those with more modest setups.

1. Scalability Levels:

- Unreal Engine provides different scalability levels, such as Low, Medium, High, and Epic. Each level adjusts various graphical features, including texture quality, shadows, and post-processing effects.

2. Auto-Adjustment:

- Implement automatic scalability adjustment based on the player's hardware. If the game detects low performance, it can lower the scalability level to maintain a stable frame rate.

3. User Customization:

- Allow players to customize scalability settings within the game's options menu. This provides flexibility and caters to individual preferences.

Platform-Specific Optimization

OPTIMIZING YOUR GAME for specific platforms, such as PC, consoles, and mobile devices, is essential for maximizing performance and taking advantage of platform-specific features.

1. PC Optimization:

- For PC gaming, offer options for higher resolutions, advanced graphical features, and support for a wide range of input devices. Ensure that the game runs smoothly on various PC configurations.

2. Console Optimization:

- Consoles have specific hardware constraints and capabilities. Optimize your game to leverage the console's strengths while maintaining a stable frame rate and performance.

3. Mobile Optimization:

- Mobile devices vary in terms of processing power and screen size. Optimize your game for mobile by reducing texture sizes, simplifying shaders, and implementing touch controls.

4. Cross-Platform Development:

- If targeting multiple platforms, design your game with cross-platform development in mind. Use platform-agnostic features whenever possible and implement platform-specific optimizations as needed.

Performance Profiling for Each Platform

TO ACHIEVE OPTIMAL performance on each platform, use performance profiling tools specific to the target platform:

1. Platform Profilers:

- Platforms like PlayStation, Xbox, and Nintendo Switch offer profiling tools and SDKs that provide insights into performance bottlenecks and optimizations.

2. Mobile Profilers:

- Mobile development environments, including Android Studio and Xcode, provide profilers for identifying performance issues on mobile devices.

3. PC Profilers:

- PC gaming platforms offer a range of performance profiling tools, including GPU profilers and CPU analyzers.

Platform-Specific Features

LEVERAGE PLATFORM-SPECIFIC features to enhance your game's performance and functionality:

1. Console-Specific APIs:

- Consoles often provide APIs for features like controller input, online multiplayer, and cloud saves. Utilize these APIs to enhance the player experience.

2. Mobile Device Features:

- Mobile devices have unique features such as gyroscopes and touchscreens. Implement these features creatively to enhance gameplay and immersion.

3. PC-Specific Features:

- On PC, take advantage of features like multi-monitor support, custom keybindings, and mod support to cater to the preferences of PC gamers.

Continuous Testing and Optimization

OPTIMIZING FOR VARIOUS platforms is an ongoing process. Continuously test your game on target hardware, gather performance data, and make iterative improvements to ensure that your game runs smoothly on each platform.

Documentation and Guidelines

DOCUMENT PLATFORM-SPECIFIC optimization guidelines and best practices for your development team. Clear documentation ensures that everyone understands the requirements and constraints of each platform.

In summary, scalability settings and platform-specific tuning are vital components of optimizing your Unreal Engine project for a wide audience. By offering adjustable graphics settings and making platform-specific optimizations, you can provide an enjoyable gaming experience on various devices and hardware configurations. Continuous testing and documentation are essential for maintaining a high level of performance across platforms.

Chapter 15: Building for Different Platforms

15.1 Cross-Platform Development Strategies

CROSS-PLATFORM DEVELOPMENT is the practice of creating a single game that can run on multiple platforms, such as PC, consoles, mobile devices, and more. It offers several advantages, including wider reach and potential for higher revenue. However, developing for multiple platforms presents unique challenges that require careful planning and execution. In this section, we'll explore cross-platform development strategies in Unreal Engine.

1. Platform-Agnostic Design:

- Start with a platform-agnostic design approach. Identify core gameplay mechanics, art styles, and features that can work seamlessly across all platforms.

2. Input Handling:

- Implement a flexible input handling system that can adapt to various input devices, including keyboards, game controllers, touchscreens, and more. Unreal Engine provides input abstraction layers for this purpose.

3. Resolution and Aspect Ratio:

• Design your user interface and gameplay to adapt to different screen resolutions and aspect ratios. Consider using responsive UI techniques to ensure elements scale correctly.

4. Performance Optimization:

• Optimize your game's performance to run smoothly on lower-end devices without sacrificing visual quality. Use scalability settings and platform-specific optimizations to achieve this.

5. Platform-Specific Features:

• Identify and utilize platform-specific features to enhance the player experience. For example, on consoles, you can leverage unique controller capabilities, while on mobile, you can incorporate touch and gyroscopic inputs.

6. Testing on Target Platforms:

• Regularly test your game on target platforms to ensure that it performs as expected. Identify and address platform-specific issues promptly.

7. Cross-Platform Play:

- If applicable, consider implementing cross-platform multiplayer to allow players on different devices to play together. Be mindful of balancing gameplay for different input methods and hardware capabilities.

8. Content Localization:

- Plan for content localization from the beginning. Make sure your game's text and audio can be easily translated to cater to a global audience.

9. Submission and Certification:

- Understand the submission and certification requirements of each platform, whether it's a console manufacturer, an app store, or a PC gaming platform. Prepare your game accordingly to pass certification.

10. Version Control and Branching:

- **Use** version control systems **like** Git **to manage** different versions **of** your game **for** various platforms. **Create** branches **for** platform-specific development **and** bug fixing.

11. Community Engagement:

- ENGAGE WITH THE COMMUNITIES of each platform you target. Gather feedback, address concerns, and build a player **base** on different platforms.

12. Post-Launch Support:

- AFTER LAUNCHING YOUR game, continue to provide updates and support for all platforms. This includes bug fixes, content updates, and optimization patches.

13. Monetization Strategies:

- TAILOR YOUR MONETIZATION strategy to the specific platforms you target. Consider in-app purchases, advertising, or premium pricing, depending on the platform's audience and expectations.

14. Analytics and User Data:

- IMPLEMENT ANALYTICS to track user behavior and performance on different platforms. Use **this data** to make informed decisions **for** ongoing development and updates.

15. Documentation and Knowledge Sharing:

- MAINTAIN CLEAR DOCUMENTATION on platform-specific requirements, guidelines, and best practices. Share **this** knowledge with your development team to ensure consistent implementation.

Cross-platform development can be complex, but it offers the potential for a broader player base and increased revenue. By following these strategies and adapting your development process to the specific needs of each platform, you can successfully create and release your game on multiple platforms while providing a consistent and enjoyable experience for players.

15.2 Adapting to Console-Specific Limitations and Features

WHEN DEVELOPING GAMES for consoles, it's crucial to adapt to the specific limitations and features of each platform. Consoles have their unique hardware constraints, performance characteristics, and capabilities, and understanding and optimizing for these differences is essential. In this section, we'll explore strategies for adapting your game to console-specific limitations and leveraging console-specific features in Unreal Engine.

Console Hardware Constraints

1. CPU and GPU Limitations:

- Consoles often have fixed CPU and GPU specifications. Ensure that your game's performance is optimized to run smoothly within these constraints.

2. Memory Limitations:

- Console memory is finite and shared between various game components. Manage memory efficiently, optimize assets, and use Unreal Engine's memory profiling tools to avoid memory-related issues.

3. Load Times:

- Consoles may have slower storage devices compared to high-end PCs. Implement efficient streaming and loading techniques to minimize load times.

4. Input Devices:

• Consoles come with specific input devices, such as game controllers. Design your game's controls and user interface to work seamlessly with these input methods.

Leveraging Console-Specific Features

1. Controller Integration:

• Take advantage of the unique features of console controllers. Implement haptic feedback, motion controls, and adaptive triggers to enhance gameplay and immersion.

2. Console APIs:

• Each console provides a set of APIs and SDKs for various features like achievements, leaderboards, and multiplayer. Integrate these features to enhance the player experience.

3. Console-Specific Rendering Techniques:

• Consoles often support rendering techniques and features not available on other platforms. Utilize these capabilities to enhance graphical fidelity.

4. Performance Modes:

• Some consoles offer different performance modes, such as "Performance" and "Quality" modes. Allow players to choose between these modes to prioritize frame rate or visual quality.

Platform Certification and Guidelines

1. Submission Requirements:

- Understand the submission requirements of console manufacturers. Each console has specific certification processes that your game must pass before release.

2. Guidelines and Restrictions:

- Follow the guidelines and restrictions provided by console manufacturers. These guidelines cover various aspects of game development, from UI design to performance optimization.

3. Security and Anti-Cheat:

- Implement security measures and anti-cheat systems as required by console platforms to maintain a fair and secure gaming environment.

Cross-Platform Play and Multiplayer

1. Cross-Platform Play:

- If feasible, enable cross-platform play to allow console players to interact with players on other platforms. Ensure gameplay balance and fairness.

2. Multiplayer Features:

- Leverage console-specific multiplayer features, such as party systems and voice chat, to enhance the social aspects of your game.

Post-Launch Support

1. Patches and Updates:

- Continue to support your game after launch by releasing patches and updates to address issues and improve performance on consoles.

2. Downloadable Content (DLC):

- Consider developing console-specific DLC or content updates to engage the console player base and generate additional revenue.

IN CONCLUSION, ADAPTING your game to console-specific limitations and features is essential for a successful console release. By optimizing performance, leveraging unique console capabilities, adhering to platform certification requirements, and providing ongoing post-launch support, you can create a seamless and enjoyable gaming experience for console players while maximizing the potential of your game on these platforms.

15.3 Mobile Game Development Challenges

DEVELOPING GAMES FOR mobile devices presents a unique set of challenges due to the diversity of hardware, software, and user expectations. While mobile gaming offers a vast audience and revenue potential, developers must address several specific challenges to succeed in this competitive market. In this section, we'll explore some of the key challenges faced in mobile game development and strategies to overcome them in Unreal Engine.

Fragmented Hardware Landscape

1. Diverse Hardware Specifications:

- The mobile market comprises a wide range of devices with varying CPU, GPU, RAM, and screen resolutions. Ensuring your game performs well across this hardware spectrum is a significant challenge.

2. Optimization for Low-End Devices:

- To reach a broader audience, your game should run smoothly on lower-end devices. Implement performance optimizations, scalability settings, and asset management techniques to achieve this.

User Interface (UI) and Controls

1. Screen Size and Touch Controls:

- Mobile devices have limited screen real estate, making UI design a critical consideration. Create responsive and user-friendly interfaces that work well on smaller screens and accommodate touch controls.

2. Virtual Joysticks and Buttons:

• Implement virtual joysticks and buttons for games that require precise input. Ensure these on-screen controls are customizable and adapt to different play styles.

Monetization Models

1. In-App Purchases (IAP):

• Design effective IAP systems that offer value to players without feeling intrusive. Balance the progression curve and ensure a fair free-to-play experience.

2. Ad Integration:

• If using ads as a monetization strategy, integrate them seamlessly into the gameplay. Avoid disruptive ads that negatively impact the player experience.

Performance and Battery Life

1. Performance Optimization:

• Mobile devices have limited computational resources compared to PCs and consoles. Use Unreal Engine's profiling tools to identify performance bottlenecks and optimize accordingly.

2. Battery Consumption:

- High-performance games can drain a device's battery quickly. Optimize your game to minimize power consumption, especially for long play sessions.

App Store Policies and Guidelines

1. App Store Submission:

- Understand the submission and review processes for app stores like the Apple App Store and Google Play Store. Comply with their guidelines to avoid rejections or removals.

2. App Store Fees:

- Be aware of the fees associated with distributing your game on app stores. Budget for these expenses when planning your monetization strategy.

Testing on Multiple Devices

1. Device Fragmentation:

- Testing your game on a variety of devices is essential to ensure compatibility and performance. Consider using cloud-based testing services to cover a broader range of hardware.

Competition and Visibility

1. Market Saturation:

- The mobile app market is highly saturated, making it challenging to stand out. Invest in marketing, user acquisition, and ASO (App Store Optimization) to improve visibility.

2. User Reviews and Ratings:

- User reviews and ratings can significantly impact your game's success. Provide excellent customer support, address issues promptly, and encourage satisfied players to leave positive reviews.

Cross-Platform Development

1. Cross-Platform Considerations:

- If planning to release your game on multiple platforms, consider how cross-platform development affects gameplay, controls, and performance.

2. Code Portability:

- Unreal Engine offers code portability between platforms, but you may still need to address platform-specific code and optimizations for mobile.

IN CONCLUSION, MOBILE game development comes with its set of challenges, but it also offers significant opportunities for success. By addressing hardware fragmentation, optimizing performance, designing user-friendly UIs, choosing effective monetization models, adhering to app store guidelines, and implementing a robust testing and marketing strategy, you can navigate the challenges and create a successful mobile game using Unreal Engine.

15.4 Best Practices for PC and Console Ports

PORTING YOUR GAME FROM one platform to another, such as from PC to consoles or vice versa, requires careful consideration of hardware differences, user expectations, and performance optimization. In this section, we'll explore best practices for successfully porting your game to PC and consoles using Unreal Engine.

Understand Target Platform Differences

1. Hardware Variations:

- Recognize that PC and console hardware differ significantly in terms of CPU, GPU, memory, and storage. Ensure your game can adapt to these hardware variations.

2. Input Methods:

- Consoles typically use game controllers, while PCs have various input options, including keyboard, mouse, and gamepad. Design and test your game's controls for both platforms.

Performance Optimization

1. Target Frame Rate:

• Determine the target frame rate for each platform. While consoles often aim for a steady 30 or 60 FPS, PC gamers expect more flexibility to maximize their hardware capabilities.

2. Scalability Settings:

• Implement scalability settings for PC to allow players to adjust graphics quality based on their hardware. For consoles, optimize performance to maintain a consistent frame rate.

3. Asset Optimization:

• Optimize game assets for each platform. Reduce texture sizes, simplify materials, and utilize LODs (Level of Detail) to manage asset quality efficiently.

4. Load Times:

• Address differences in storage speed by optimizing loading screens and streaming assets efficiently, especially for consoles with slower storage devices.

User Interface (UI) and Controls

1. Responsive UI:

- Ensure that your game's UI scales and adapts effectively to different screen resolutions and aspect ratios, providing an excellent experience on both PCs and consoles.

2. Input Mapping:

- Create customizable input mapping options for PC players, allowing them to remap controls to their preference. On consoles, adhere to platform-specific input standards.

Certification and Guidelines

1. Certification Requirements:

- Familiarize yourself with the certification requirements of each console manufacturer or PC gaming platform. Comply with their guidelines to pass certification smoothly.

2. App Store and Marketplace Policies:

- When porting to PC, understand the policies and requirements of digital distribution platforms like Steam or Epic Games Store.

Testing and Debugging

1. Diverse Testing:

- Test your game on a range of PC configurations and console models to ensure compatibility and performance. Use Unreal Engine's console development kits for console testing.

2. Performance Profiling:

- Utilize profiling tools and performance analyzers provided by Unreal Engine to identify and resolve platform-specific performance bottlenecks.

Multiplayer and Cross-Platform Play

1. Multiplayer Considerations:

- When porting a multiplayer game, ensure that cross-platform play is balanced and fair. Address any gameplay differences between PC and console players.

2. Server Infrastructure:

- Plan for server infrastructure that can handle cross-platform play if applicable, and ensure that it maintains fairness and connectivity for all players.

Post-Launch Support

1. Patch and Update Synchronization:

- Coordinate patch and update releases across platforms to avoid fragmentation and ensure all players have access to the latest content and improvements.

2. Community Engagement:

- Engage with the communities of both PC and console players. Gather feedback, address concerns, and build a player base on each platform.

Marketing and Monetization

1. Platform-Specific Marketing:

- Tailor your marketing efforts to the specific preferences and demographics of PC and console gamers.

2. Monetization Strategies:

- Adjust your monetization strategy to match the expectations and behaviors of players on each platform. Consider platform-specific DLC or in-game purchases.

BY FOLLOWING THESE best practices, you can successfully port your game to both PC and consoles while providing a high-quality gaming experience tailored to each platform's unique characteristics and player expectations. Careful planning and optimization are key to a successful multi-platform release using Unreal Engine.

15.5 Testing and Quality Assurance Across Platforms

ENSURING THE QUALITY and stability of your game across multiple platforms is a critical aspect of successful multi-platform development. Testing and quality assurance (QA) are essential to identify and address platform-specific issues, performance variations, and compatibility challenges. In this section, we'll explore best practices for testing and QA across various platforms in Unreal Engine.

Platform Coverage

1. Comprehensive Testing:

- Test your game on all target platforms, including PC, consoles, and mobile devices. Cover different hardware configurations and versions, including older models if applicable.

2. Emulators and Simulators:

- Utilize platform-specific emulators and simulators to expand your testing coverage, especially for mobile devices where acquiring multiple physical devices may be challenging.

Functional Testing

1. Platform-Specific Functionality:

- Ensure that platform-specific features, such as achievements, leaderboards, and cloud saves, work correctly on each platform.

2. Cross-Platform Play:

- Test cross-platform multiplayer functionality to confirm that players on different devices can interact seamlessly and fairly.

3. User Interface (UI):

- Verify that the UI adapts appropriately to different screen sizes, resolutions, and aspect ratios across all platforms. Ensure that UI elements are functional and easy to navigate.

Performance Testing

1. Frame Rate Analysis:

- Monitor and analyze frame rates on each platform to ensure they meet the target frame rate. Address performance issues promptly, optimizing as needed.

2. Load Time Testing:

- Measure and compare load times between platforms. Optimize loading processes to provide a consistent and efficient experience for players.

3. Memory Usage:

- Track memory usage on different platforms to identify potential memory leaks or excessive resource consumption. Address memory-related issues to prevent crashes or performance degradation.

Compatibility Testing

1. Platform-Specific Bugs:

- Document and prioritize platform-specific bugs and issues. Ensure that fixes are applied to the correct platform without introducing new problems on others.

2. Input and Controls:

- Test input responsiveness and controls on each platform to confirm that they work as intended. Verify that control schemes are optimized for different input methods, including gamepads, touchscreens, and keyboards.

Regression Testing

1. Post-Update Regression:

- After releasing updates or patches, perform regression testing on all platforms to ensure that new changes do not introduce unintended issues or break existing functionality.

Localization and Language Testing

1. Localized Content:

- Verify that localized content, including text, audio, and subtitles, is correctly displayed and functional on all platforms. Ensure translations are accurate and contextually appropriate.

Network and Multiplayer Testing

1. Network Performance:

- Test network performance and latency on each platform to ensure a consistent online experience. Address issues related to lag, synchronization, and disconnections.

2. Cross-Platform Multiplayer:

- Thoroughly test cross-platform multiplayer functionality to confirm that players on different devices can play together without issues or imbalances.

Certification Testing

1. Platform-Specific Certification:

- Follow the certification processes for each platform diligently. Ensure that your game meets all platform-specific requirements and guidelines.

Documentation and Bug Tracking

1. Bug Tracking System:

- Implement a bug tracking system to record and prioritize issues across platforms. Communicate effectively with your development team and QA testers to address these issues promptly.

2. Documentation and Checklists:

- Maintain detailed documentation and checklists for each platform's testing procedures and requirements. This helps ensure consistency and thoroughness in testing efforts.

IN SUMMARY, TESTING and quality assurance across multiple platforms are crucial to delivering a polished and enjoyable gaming experience. By adopting a comprehensive testing approach, addressing platform-specific challenges, and documenting your testing processes, you can successfully release your game on various platforms with confidence in its quality and performance.

Chapter 16: Advanced UI and UX Design

16.1. Designing Complex User Interfaces

WHEN IT COMES TO DESIGNING complex user interfaces (UI) in Unreal Engine, the focus is on creating an interactive and intuitive experience that seamlessly integrates with the gameplay. This process involves a deep understanding of both technical and aesthetic aspects, as well as a keen insight into user behavior and preferences.

Understanding User Needs and Gameplay Requirements

THE FIRST STEP IN DESIGNING a complex UI is to thoroughly understand the needs of the user and how these needs intersect with the gameplay requirements. This involves researching user demographics, playing styles, and preferences. It's crucial to balance functionality with aesthetics, ensuring that the UI enhances the overall gaming experience without overwhelming or confusing the player.

Leveraging Unreal Engine's UMG (Unreal Motion Graphics)

UNREAL ENGINE'S UMG is a powerful tool for UI design. It allows developers to create interactive and dynamic user interfaces with ease. UMG works in tandem with Blueprints, Unreal's visual scripting language, enabling designers to craft intricate UI elements without extensive coding knowledge.

Implementing Adaptive UI Layouts

ADAPTIVE UI LAYOUTS are essential for games that are played on multiple platforms. This involves designing UI elements that can adjust dynamically to different screen sizes and resolutions. Responsive design principles are key here, ensuring that UI elements are legible and accessible regardless of the device used.

Utilizing Widget Blueprints for Interactivity

WIDGET BLUEPRINTS ARE a crucial component of UI design in Unreal Engine. They allow designers to create custom widgets that can interact with game logic and player inputs. This could range from simple buttons and sliders to more complex interactive maps and inventory systems.

Customizing Visuals with Styles and Themes

CREATING A UNIQUE VISUAL style for your UI is important for game branding and player immersion. This can be achieved by customizing the colors, fonts, and overall themes of the UI elements. Consistency in visual style helps in maintaining an intuitive and cohesive user experience.

Implementing HUD (Heads-Up Display)

THE HUD IS A CRITICAL aspect of any game's UI, providing players with essential information like health stats, maps, and inventory. Designing an effective HUD requires a balance between providing necessary information and avoiding screen clutter. It should be easily accessible but not disruptive to the gaming experience.

Accessibility Features

INCORPORATING ACCESSIBILITY features in UI design is vital. This includes options for colorblind modes, text-to-speech for visually impaired players, and customizable control settings. Ensuring that your game is accessible to a wider audience not only broadens your market but also adheres to inclusive design principles.

Animation and Dynamic Elements

USING ANIMATION IN UI elements can enhance the user experience significantly. Subtle animations for button clicks, transitions, and notifications add a layer of polish to the game. However, it's important to use animations judiciously to avoid distractions.

Integrating In-Game and Menu UI

THE TRANSITION BETWEEN in-game UI and menu screens should be seamless. Players should be able to navigate through menus and return to gameplay without confusion or interruption. This requires thoughtful layout and design consistency.

Advanced Techniques: Scripting UI Elements

FOR MORE COMPLEX UI elements, scripting might be necessary. Using Unreal's scripting languages, C++ or Blueprints, developers can create highly interactive and dynamic UI components. This could include custom scripts for inventory management, skill trees, or interactive story elements.

Testing and Iteration

USER INTERFACE DESIGN is an iterative process. It involves continuous testing and feedback to refine the UI. This could be achieved through user testing sessions, A/B testing, or gathering feedback from early access releases.

Performance Optimization

UI ELEMENTS, ESPECIALLY those with animations and dynamic changes, can impact game performance. It's crucial to optimize these elements, ensuring they are not resource-intensive. This might involve optimizing textures, reducing the complexity of animations, and ensuring efficient script execution.

Scalability and Multi-Language Support

SCALABILITY IN UI DESIGN refers to the UI's ability to handle different languages and regional settings. This includes not only translation of text but also considerations for text length, font support, and cultural differences in UI layout.

Integrating with Game Mechanics

THE UI SHOULD BE TIGHTLY integrated with the game mechanics. This means that UI changes should reflect gameplay changes in real-time, like updating health bars, ammo counts, or experience points.

Custom Cursors and Interactive Feedback

CUSTOM CURSORS AND interactive feedback mechanisms can significantly enhance the user experience. This includes changing cursor designs based on context and providing tactile or auditory feedback during interactions.

Creating Intuitive Navigation Systems

FOR GAMES WITH COMPLEX menus and options, creating an intuitive navigation system is key. This might involve implementing breadcrumb trails, clear back and home buttons, and logical grouping of menu items.

Balancing Aesthetics and Functionality

WHILE AESTHETICS ARE important, they should not overshadow functionality. The UI should be pleasing to the eye but, more importantly, it should be functional and easy to navigate. A well-designed UI blends both these aspects seamlessly.

Advanced Input

16.2. UX Principles for Game Design

UNDERSTANDING AND IMPLEMENTING user experience (UX) principles in game design is crucial for creating engaging and user-friendly games. This section delves into various aspects of UX design, offering insights and strategies to enhance the player's experience in Unreal Engine-based games.

Player-Centric Design Approach

THE CORNERSTONE OF good UX is a player-centric design approach. This means prioritizing the needs, preferences, and expectations of the player at every stage of game development. It's about understanding who your players are, what they want, and how they interact with your game.

Conducting User Research

EFFECTIVE UX DESIGN begins with thorough user research. This involves gathering data about your target audience, their gaming habits, preferences, and feedback on similar games. Surveys, interviews, and usability testing are key methods to gather this information.

Creating User Personas

BASED ON THE RESEARCH, create user personas that represent different segments of your target audience. Personas help in visualizing the typical users of your game, guiding design decisions to cater to their preferences and needs.

Designing for Usability

USABILITY IS A FUNDAMENTAL aspect of UX design. It refers to how easy and intuitive it is for players to navigate and interact with your game. This involves clear instructions, intuitive controls, and an easy-to-navigate interface.

Streamlining Onboarding Processes

THE ONBOARDING PROCESS is the player's first interaction with your game. It should be smooth and engaging, teaching the basic controls and gameplay mechanics without overwhelming the player. Interactive tutorials and gradual difficulty progression are effective strategies.

Balancing Challenge and Accessibility

FINDING THE RIGHT BALANCE between challenge and accessibility is key to retaining players. Games should be challenging enough to be engaging but not so difficult that they become frustrating. Difficulty settings and adaptive difficulty mechanisms can help achieve this balance.

Integrating Feedback Loops

FEEDBACK LOOPS ARE essential in UX design. They provide players with immediate and clear feedback on their actions, which is crucial for learning and engagement. This includes visual, auditory, and tactile feedback.

Consistent Game World Design

CONSISTENCY IN GAME world design enhances the user experience by providing a coherent and immersive environment. This includes consistent art styles, physics, and interactions within the game world.

Optimizing Load Times and Performance

LONG LOAD TIMES AND poor performance can significantly detract from the user experience. Optimizing game performance, including efficient asset loading and rendering, is crucial for maintaining player engagement.

Adaptive UI for Different Player Types

NOT ALL PLAYERS INTERACT with games in the same way. Designing an adaptive UI that can cater to different types of players, such as casual vs. hardcore gamers, enhances the overall UX.

Implementing Accessibility Features

ACCESSIBILITY FEATURES such as colorblind modes, subtitles, and customizable control schemes make your game more inclusive and reachable to a wider audience, which is a crucial aspect of UX design.

Leveraging Analytics for Continuous Improvement

USING ANALYTICS TOOLS to gather data on player behavior and preferences is vital for continuous UX improvement. This data can guide updates and adjustments to enhance the player experience over time.

Creating Engaging Narrative Elements

AN ENGAGING NARRATIVE can significantly enhance the UX. This involves crafting compelling stories, characters, and worlds that resonate with the player and add depth to the gameplay.

Designing Reward Systems

EFFECTIVE REWARD SYSTEMS motivate and engage players. This includes achievements, progress tracking, and rewards for skill development and exploration.

Ensuring Player Autonomy

PLAYER AUTONOMY, THE ability to make meaningful choices that impact the game, is a key element of good UX. This includes options in gameplay, paths, and customization.

Cognitive Load Management

MANAGING THE COGNITIVE load, or the amount of mental effort required to play the game, is essential. This means avoiding information overload and designing interfaces and gameplay that are easy to understand and interact with.

Emotional Design Elements

EMOTIONAL DESIGN ELEMENTS like character empathy, narrative arcs, and aesthetic choices can profoundly impact the player's experience, making the game more memorable and engaging.

Integrating Social Features

FOR MANY PLAYERS, SOCIAL interaction is a key part of the gaming experience. Integrating features like multiplayer modes, leaderboards, and social sharing can enhance UX.

Iterative Design and Player Feedback

UX DESIGN IS AN ITERATIVE process. Regularly updating the game based on player feedback and changing trends ensures that the game remains relevant and enjoyable.

Fostering Community Engagement

BUILDING A COMMUNITY around your game can greatly enhance the UX. This includes forums, social media interaction, and events that encourage player engagement and feedback.

In summary, applying these UX principles in game design is about creating an experience that is engaging, intuitive, and enjoyable for the player. It's a continuous process of learning, adapting, and innovating to meet and exceed player expectations.

16.3. Implementing Adaptive UI Systems

ADAPTIVE UI SYSTEMS are designed to dynamically adjust to different user needs, contexts, and device specifications. In the realm of Unreal Engine game development, creating such systems involves a combination of design innovation and technical implementation.

Understanding the Need for Adaptive UI

ADAPTIVE UI IS CRUCIAL in modern game design due to the variety of devices and user preferences. It ensures that the game interface provides an optimal experience across various screen sizes, resolutions, and user settings.

Analyzing User Context

THE FIRST STEP IN CREATING an adaptive UI is understanding the user context. This includes analyzing the devices used, player preferences, and environmental factors that might influence how players interact with the game.

Responsive Design Principles

RESPONSIVE DESIGN IS a key concept in adaptive UI. It involves creating UI layouts that automatically adjust to the size and orientation of the screen. This can be achieved through fluid grids and flexible images.

Scalable Vector Graphics (SVGs)

USING SVGS FOR UI ELEMENTS ensures that graphics remain sharp and clear at any resolution. Unlike raster images, SVGs scale without losing quality, making them ideal for high-resolution displays and varying screen sizes.

Dynamic Layouts with UMG

UNREAL ENGINE'S UMG (Unreal Motion Graphics) provides tools for designing dynamic UIs. You can use anchors, constraints, and size rules to create layouts that adapt to different screen sizes and aspect ratios.

Utilizing Blueprints for Adaptive Logic

BLUEPRINTS, UNREAL Engine's visual scripting system, can be used to add logic to UI elements. This can include changing sizes, positions, and visibility of UI components based on certain conditions, like screen size or user settings.

Implementing User Preferences

ADAPTIVE UI SYSTEMS should account for user preferences. This includes settings for font size, color schemes, and control layouts that can be modified by the player for a personalized experience.

Accessibility Considerations

ADAPTIVE UI MUST ALSO be accessible. This involves designing UI elements that are easy to read and navigate for players with disabilities. Features like screen readers, high contrast modes, and button remapping are essential.

Device-Specific UI Adaptations

WHEN DEVELOPING FOR multiple platforms, consider device-specific UI adaptations. For example, touch controls for mobile devices and simplified UI for VR headsets.

Adaptive Input Handling

ADAPTING TO DIFFERENT input methods (like touch, gamepad, or keyboard and mouse) is crucial. This can involve changing UI elements' size and interactivity based on the input device.

Testing Across Devices and Conditions

THOROUGH TESTING ACROSS various devices and under different conditions is vital to ensure that the adaptive UI works seamlessly. This includes testing on different hardware, operating systems, and screen sizes.

Performance Optimization

ADAPTIVE UIS CAN BE more demanding on system resources. Optimize performance by minimizing the use of heavy assets, using efficient scripting, and leveraging Unreal Engine's built-in optimization tools.

Localization and Cultural Adaptation

ADAPT YOUR UI TO DIFFERENT languages and cultures. This includes not just translating text but also adapting graphics, layout, and content to suit different cultural norms and preferences.

Dynamic Content Loading

IMPLEMENT DYNAMIC CONTENT loading to adapt to user progression and choices. This can include loading different UI elements based on the game's state or player achievements.

Custom Widgets for Specialized Functions

DEVELOP CUSTOM WIDGETS for specialized functions. This can include interactive maps, dynamic inventories, or custom control panels that adapt to the game context.

Feedback Mechanisms

IMPLEMENT FEEDBACK mechanisms in the UI to guide and inform the player. This includes visual cues, sound effects, and haptic feedback that adapt based on the player's actions and the game state.

Continuous User Feedback and Iteration

GATHER CONTINUOUS FEEDBACK from users to refine the adaptive UI. This involves monitoring how players interact with the UI and making iterative improvements based on this data.

Integrating AI for Personalization

CONSIDER INTEGRATING AI to personalize the UI experience. AI can analyze player behavior and automatically adjust UI elements for a more personalized and engaging experience.

Documentation and Best Practices

MAINTAIN THOROUGH DOCUMENTATION of your adaptive UI systems and establish best practices for future development. This ensures consistency and facilitates easier updates and maintenance.

Incorporating these elements into an adaptive UI system in Unreal Engine will not only enhance the player's experience but also ensure that the game remains accessible and enjoyable across a wide range of devices and user preferences.

16.4. Accessibility Features and Considerations

INCORPORATING ACCESSIBILITY features in game design is crucial to ensure that your game is playable and enjoyable for a wide range of players, including those with disabilities. This section explores various strategies and considerations for implementing accessibility features in Unreal Engine games.

Understanding the Importance of Accessibility

ACCESSIBILITY IN GAMING means making games playable for people with various disabilities, including visual, auditory, motor, and cognitive impairments. It's about inclusivity and ensuring that everyone can enjoy your game.

Conducting Accessibility Research

START BY RESEARCHING the common barriers faced by players with disabilities. This includes understanding the types of disabilities and how they affect gaming experiences. Resources like the Web Content Accessibility Guidelines (WCAG) can provide valuable insights.

Customizable Control Schemes

OFFERING CUSTOMIZABLE control schemes is essential for players with motor disabilities. Allow players to remap keyboard, mouse, and gamepad inputs to suit their needs.

Visual Accessibility Features

FOR PLAYERS WITH VISUAL impairments, include features like high contrast modes, scalable fonts, and screen reader support. These features can be implemented using Unreal Engine's UMG system.

Auditory Accessibility Options

FOR AUDITORY ACCESSIBILITY, provide subtitles and visual indicators for important audio cues. Ensure that subtitles are clear, readable, and accurately represent the audio content.

Simplified UI Modes

CREATE SIMPLIFIED UI modes that reduce cognitive load and are easier to navigate. This includes decluttering the screen, using simple menus, and providing clear navigation paths.

Assisted Gameplay Modes

IMPLEMENT ASSISTED gameplay modes for players who might find the standard gameplay too challenging. This can include features like aim assist, easier difficulty levels, or the ability to skip challenging sections.

Colorblind Modes

INCORPORATE COLORBLIND modes to accommodate different types of color vision deficiencies. Ensure that color is not the sole method of conveying important information.

Haptic Feedback for Tactile Cues

UTILIZE HAPTIC FEEDBACK to provide tactile cues for players who might have auditory or visual impairments. This can be an effective way to convey game information through vibration patterns.

Testing with Diverse User Groups

CONDUCT TESTING WITH a diverse group of users, including those with disabilities. This helps identify any issues and areas for improvement in your accessibility features.

Providing Accessibility Documentation

OFFER DETAILED DOCUMENTATION and tutorials on how to use the accessibility features in your game. This helps players understand and make full use of these features.

Adjustable Game Speed

ALLOW PLAYERS TO ADJUST the game speed to accommodate different reaction times and play styles. This can be particularly helpful for players with cognitive and motor disabilities.

Scalable Difficulty Levels

IMPLEMENT SCALABLE difficulty levels that can be adjusted to suit the player's abilities. This ensures that the game remains challenging but not frustrating.

Voice Command Support

FOR PLAYERS WITH LIMITED mobility, voice command support can be a game-changer. Integrating voice recognition can allow players to control the game and navigate menus using voice commands.

Alternative Input Devices

SUPPORT ALTERNATIVE input devices such as adaptive controllers, eye-tracking systems, and single-switch devices. This broadens the range of players who can comfortably play your game.

Co-Pilot Mode

CONSIDER A CO-PILOT mode where two players can control a single character. This allows players with disabilities to enjoy the game with the help of a friend or caregiver.

Clear Interface and Feedback

ENSURE THAT YOUR GAME interface is clear and provides immediate feedback. This is essential for players with cognitive disabilities who might find complex interfaces overwhelming.

Continuous Improvement and Updates

ACCESSIBILITY SHOULD be an ongoing commitment. Continuously seek feedback and make updates to improve the accessibility features in your game.

Community Engagement

ENGAGE WITH THE GAMING community, especially with groups advocating for accessibility in gaming. This can provide valuable insights and help you stay informed about best practices in accessibility.

Leveraging Unreal Engine's Capabilities

UTILIZE UNREAL ENGINE'S capabilities to implement these features effectively. The engine's flexibility and tools can be leveraged to create a more inclusive gaming experience.

By considering these accessibility features and integrating them into your game development process, you can ensure that your Unreal Engine game is more inclusive and accessible to a wider audience.

16.5. UI Animation and Dynamic Elements

INCORPORATING ANIMATIONS and dynamic elements into the user interface (UI) can significantly enhance the user experience in Unreal Engine games. This section explores how to effectively use UI animations and dynamic elements to create a more engaging and interactive interface.

The Role of Animation in UI

ANIMATION IN UI SERVES multiple purposes: it can guide the player's attention, provide feedback on actions, and enhance the aesthetic appeal of the game. When used effectively, animations can make the UI feel more responsive and alive.

Principles of UI Animation

BEFORE IMPLEMENTING animations, it's important to understand the basic principles of UI animation. These include timing, easing, and purpose. Animations should be quick enough to be responsive but not so fast that they are jarring. Easing functions can be used to make animations feel more natural.

Using Unreal Engine's UMG for Animation

UNREAL ENGINE'S UMG (Unreal Motion Graphics) system includes tools for creating animations within the UI. UMG animations can be triggered by events in the game, such as a button press or a change in game state.

Animating UI Elements

SIMPLE ANIMATIONS, like fading, scaling, or moving UI elements, can be easily implemented in UMG. These animations can be used to highlight important elements, indicate changes, or simply add visual interest.

Feedback Animations

ANIMATIONS CAN PROVIDE valuable feedback to the player. For instance, a button could animate when hovered over or pressed, giving immediate feedback that an action has been recognized.

Dynamic UI Elements

DYNAMIC UI ELEMENTS are those that change based on game conditions. For example, a health bar that changes color or shape depending on the player's health status. These elements can be created using UMG's binding system, which allows UI elements to react to changes in game variables.

Creating Interactive Widgets

INTERACTIVE WIDGETS, such as sliders, toggles, and custom controls, can be enhanced with animations. For instance, a slider could expand or change color when interacted with, providing a more engaging experience.

Particle Effects in UI

UNREAL ENGINE'S PARTICLE system can be used to create dynamic and visually appealing effects in the UI. These effects can be used for emphasizing rewards, indicating status changes, or just adding visual flair.

Transition Animations

TRANSITION ANIMATIONS can smooth the change between different UI screens or states. For example, when opening a menu or switching between tabs, transition animations can make these changes feel more fluid.

Performance Considerations

WHILE ANIMATIONS CAN enhance the UI, it's important to consider their impact on performance. Keep animations efficient and test their performance impact, especially on lower-end devices.

Responsiveness and Interactivity

ENSURE THAT ANIMATIONS do not hinder the responsiveness of the UI. Interactive elements should remain responsive even when animations are playing.

Adaptive Animations for Different Devices

ANIMATIONS MAY NEED to be adapted for different devices. For example, subtler animations might be necessary for smaller mobile screens, while more elaborate animations can be used on larger PC monitors.

Using Blueprints for Animation Logic

BLUEPRINTS, UNREAL'S visual scripting language, can be used to add logic to UI animations. This allows for more complex and responsive animations that can react to player actions or game events.

Timeline Animations for Complex Sequences

FOR MORE COMPLEX ANIMATION sequences, Unreal Engine's timeline feature can be used. Timelines allow for precise control over the timing and sequencing of animations.

Animation Loops for Continuous Effects

ANIMATION LOOPS CAN be used for continuous effects, such as a pulsating glow or a spinning icon. These loops can add a dynamic element to the UI without requiring constant updates.

Incorporating Sound with UI Animations

ADDING SOUND EFFECTS to UI animations can enhance the overall impact. For example, a click sound when a button is pressed or a swoosh when a menu opens can make the UI feel more interactive.

Testing and Iteration

AS WITH ANY ASPECT of game design, testing and iteration are key. Gather feedback on the UI animations and make adjustments as necessary to ensure they enhance the user experience.

By effectively integrating UI animations and dynamic elements, you can create a more engaging and intuitive interface for your Unreal Engine game, enriching the overall player experience.

Chapter 17: Source Control and Collaboration

17.1. Advanced Source Control Techniques

SOURCE CONTROL IS A fundamental aspect of any software development project, including game development with Unreal Engine. Advanced source control techniques are crucial for maintaining code integrity, facilitating collaboration, and streamlining the development process.

Understanding Source Control Systems

THE FIRST STEP IS TO understand the different source control systems available, such as Git, Perforce, and SVN. Each system has its own strengths and is suited for different types of projects and team sizes.

Choosing the Right Source Control for Your Project

THE CHOICE OF SOURCE control system can depend on various factors, such as the size of your team, the complexity of your project, and your specific workflow requirements. For Unreal Engine projects, Perforce and Git are commonly used due to their robustness and integration with the engine.

Setting Up a Source Control Repository

SETTING UP A REPOSITORY involves initializing the source control system, setting up server and client environments, and establishing initial directories and branches. This setup is crucial for ensuring that all team members can access and contribute to the project efficiently.

Branching Strategies

IMPLEMENTING EFFECTIVE branching strategies is key to maintaining a clean and organized codebase. This includes deciding on a branching model, such as Git Flow or feature branching, and adhering to it throughout the development process.

Commit Best Practices

ESTABLISHING BEST PRACTICES for commits helps in maintaining a readable and useful commit history. This includes writing clear commit messages, making small and logical commits, and ensuring that each commit represents a functional state of the project.

Handling Merge Conflicts

MERGE CONFLICTS ARE an inevitable part of collaborative development. Understanding how to effectively resolve these conflicts is essential. This includes using tools like diff and merge tools, and establishing protocols for conflict resolution.

Code Reviews and Pull Requests

CODE REVIEWS AND PULL requests are essential for maintaining code quality and ensuring that new additions meet the project's standards. They provide an opportunity for team members to give feedback on code changes before they are integrated into the main codebase.

Continuous Integration (CI) Systems

INTEGRATING A CI SYSTEM can automate various aspects of the development process, such as building, testing, and deploying.

This ensures that the codebase is always in a deployable state and reduces the chances of integration issues.

Automated Testing with Source Control

AUTOMATED TESTING FRAMEWORKS can be integrated with source control to run tests automatically on each commit or pull request. This ensures that new changes do not break existing functionality.

Version Tagging and Release Management

VERSION TAGGING IS important for tracking different releases of the project. This involves assigning version numbers to specific states of the codebase, which is especially useful for release management and hotfixes.

Handling Large Assets in Source Control

IN GAME DEVELOPMENT, handling large assets can be challenging. Techniques like Git LFS (Large File Storage) or Perforce's file management capabilities are essential for managing large game assets within source control.

Source Control for Blueprints in Unreal Engine

UNREAL ENGINE'S BLUEPRINTS can be source-controlled just like any other code. However, due to their binary nature, special considerations are needed, such as avoiding concurrent editing and using Blueprint diff tools.

Documentation and Source Control

KEEPING DOCUMENTATION in sync with code changes is important. Integrating documentation within the source control system ensures that it is always up-to-date and versioned alongside the code.

Access Control and Security

MANAGING ACCESS CONTROL and ensuring the security of the source control system is crucial, especially for larger teams. This involves setting up user permissions, using secure communication protocols, and regularly backing up the repository.

Training and Onboarding

TRAINING TEAM MEMBERS on the source control system and established protocols is important for a smooth workflow. This includes providing resources and guidelines on how to use the system effectively.

Scalability and Performance

AS THE PROJECT GROWS, the source control system must be able to scale and perform efficiently. This may involve optimizing repository structure, pruning old branches, and using server-side hooks for automation.

Regular Maintenance and Audits

REGULAR MAINTENANCE of the source control system is necessary to ensure its ongoing efficiency and reliability. This includes tasks like repository compaction, verifying backups, and conducting periodic audits of the system.

By implementing advanced source control techniques, teams can work more effectively on Unreal Engine projects, ensuring that the development process is streamlined, collaborative, and efficient.

17.2. Collaborating Effectively in Large Teams

EFFECTIVE COLLABORATION in large teams is crucial for the successful development of Unreal Engine projects. This section explores various strategies and best practices for enhancing teamwork and communication in large-scale game development environments.

Establishing Clear Communication Channels

IN A LARGE TEAM, ESTABLISHING clear and effective communication channels is vital. This includes choosing the right tools for team communication, such as Slack, Microsoft Teams, or Discord, and setting guidelines for their use.

Structuring the Team for Efficiency

ORGANIZING THE TEAM into smaller, specialized groups can enhance efficiency. This structure allows for focused development within disciplines like programming, art, design, and QA, while still maintaining overall coordination.

Defining Roles and Responsibilities

CLEARLY DEFINING EACH team member's role and responsibilities helps in reducing overlaps and gaps in the development process. This clarity ensures that everyone understands their contributions and how they fit into the larger project.

Implementing Agile Methodologies

AGILE METHODOLOGIES, such as Scrum or Kanban, can be particularly effective in managing large team projects. These frameworks promote flexibility, regular feedback, and iterative progress, which are crucial in game development.

Regular Team Meetings and Stand-Ups

REGULAR MEETINGS, SUCH as daily stand-ups or weekly team updates, keep everyone aligned and informed. These meetings should be concise and focused on progress updates, blockers, and upcoming tasks.

Collaborative Tools and Platforms

UTILIZING COLLABORATIVE tools like JIRA, Trello, or Asana for task tracking and project management helps in keeping the team organized and on schedule. These tools provide visibility into the project's progress and individual responsibilities.

Source Control for Team Coordination

EFFECTIVE USE OF SOURCE control is critical in a large team. It facilitates code sharing, version tracking, and prevents conflicts in the codebase. Regular commits, code reviews, and branch management are essential practices.

Documentation and Knowledge Sharing

MAINTAINING COMPREHENSIVE documentation is key to successful collaboration. This includes technical documentation, design docs, and project guidelines. A central knowledge repository, like Confluence or a shared Wiki, can be very effective.

Encouraging Cross-Discipline Collaboration

ENCOURAGING INTERACTION and collaboration between different disciplines (such as designers working with developers or artists) fosters a more cohesive and innovative development environment.

Conflict Resolution Mechanisms

ESTABLISHING MECHANISMS for conflict resolution is important in large teams. This can include designated mediators, clear escalation paths, and open forums for discussion and resolution.

Regular Feedback and Performance Reviews

IMPLEMENTING REGULAR feedback sessions and performance reviews helps in identifying areas for improvement, both at an individual and team level. Constructive feedback fosters personal and professional growth.

Training and Skill Development

PROVIDING OPPORTUNITIES for training and skill development can greatly enhance team performance. This includes workshops, webinars, and access to learning resources.

Fostering a Positive Team Culture

CREATING A POSITIVE and inclusive team culture is essential for collaboration. This involves recognizing achievements, encouraging open communication, and creating an environment where all team members feel valued.

Managing Remote Teams and Time Zones

FOR TEAMS SPREAD ACROSS different locations and time zones, special considerations are needed. This includes flexible meeting times, asynchronous communication practices, and tools that facilitate remote collaboration.

Balancing Autonomy with Coordination

WHILE IT'S IMPORTANT to give team members autonomy in their work, it's equally important to ensure that their efforts are coordinated and aligned with the project goals. Regular check-ins and clear project roadmaps can help balance these aspects.

Utilizing Internal Playtests and Feedback

CONDUCTING REGULAR internal playtests within the team allows for early feedback and identification of issues. Encouraging team members to provide feedback on different aspects of the game can lead to valuable insights.

Change Management in Large Projects

EFFECTIVELY MANAGING changes, whether they are in project scope, team composition, or technology, is crucial in large projects. This involves clear communication, adjustment of plans, and ensuring that everyone is on board with the changes.

Celebrating Milestones and Successes

ACKNOWLEDGING AND CELEBRATING milestones and successes helps in keeping the team motivated. Recognizing the hard work and achievements of team members can boost morale and foster a sense of accomplishment.

Continuous Improvement

ENCOURAGE A CULTURE of continuous improvement where team members are always looking for ways to enhance processes, communication, and collaboration. Regular retrospectives and feedback sessions can aid in this continuous improvement.

By implementing these strategies, large teams can collaborate more effectively, leading to a more efficient, enjoyable, and productive game development process.

17.3. Versioning and Branching Strategies

EFFECTIVE VERSIONING and branching strategies are vital in managing the development of Unreal Engine projects, especially when working with large teams. This section outlines best practices for utilizing version control systems to streamline development processes.

Understanding Version Control in Game Development

VERSION CONTROL IS the practice of tracking and managing changes to software code. In game development, this not only includes source code but also assets, scripts, and other project files. It's essential for coordinating work among team members and maintaining a history of changes.

Choosing a Version Control System

SELECT A VERSION CONTROL system that suits your project's scale and team size. Popular options include Git, Perforce, and SVN. Each has its strengths, with Git being widely used for its flexibility and Perforce being favored in scenarios requiring handling of large binary files, common in game development.

Semantic Versioning

ADOPT SEMANTIC VERSIONING (SemVer) for your project. This system uses a three-part version number (MAJOR.MINOR.PATCH), where you increment the:

- MAJOR version when you make incompatible API changes,
- MINOR version when you add functionality in a backward-compatible manner, and
- PATCH version when you make backward-compatible bug fixes.

Developing a Branching Model

DEVELOP A BRANCHING model that fits your development workflow. Common models include:

- Feature branching: Creating a new branch for each feature.
- Git Flow: A robust model with specific branches for features, development, releases, and hotfixes.
- Trunk-based development: Everyone commits to the main branch, with short-lived feature branches.

Feature Branching Best Practices

WHEN USING FEATURE branching, create a new branch for each feature or bug fix. This keeps the main branch stable and allows for parallel development of features.

Managing Release Branches

CREATE RELEASE BRANCHES for preparing and polishing a new release. This allows you to freeze the feature set for a release while continuing new development on the main branch.

Hotfix Branches

FOR URGENT BUG FIXES, use hotfix branches branched from the necessary release tag. Once fixed, merge these changes back into the main branch and update any affected release branches.

Regular Merges to Main Branch

REGULARLY MERGE FEATURE branches back into the main branch to avoid long-running branches that can create integration nightmares. This also ensures regular testing of the integrated codebase.

Tagging Releases

USE TAGS TO MARK RELEASE points in your version control system. This provides a snapshot of the code at the point of each release, which is crucial for bug fixes and understanding changes over time.

Binary Files and Large Assets

FOR BINARY FILES AND large assets common in game development, consider using tools like Git LFS (Large File Storage) or Perforce's Helix Core, which are designed to handle large files more efficiently.

Pull Requests and Code Reviews

UTILIZE PULL REQUESTS (PRs) for merging branches. This facilitates code review, ensuring that new changes meet quality standards and conform to project guidelines before being merged into the main branch.

Automated Builds and Continuous Integration

IMPLEMENT CONTINUOUS integration (CI) to automate building and testing your project. CI systems can be configured to trigger builds and tests whenever changes are pushed to specific branches, ensuring that issues are caught early.

Conflict Resolution

DEVELOP A CLEAR PROCESS for resolving merge conflicts. This often involves the developer responsible for the branch resolving the conflicts, possibly with input from other team members.

Documentation and Communication

DOCUMENT YOUR VERSIONING and branching strategy and ensure it is communicated to all team members. This includes guidelines on when and how to branch, commit, merge, and tag.

Training and Onboarding

PROVIDE TRAINING AND onboarding for new team members to ensure they understand and can effectively use the version control system and adhere to the project's branching strategy.

Regular Audits and Cleanup

REGULARLY AUDIT YOUR branches and remove obsolete ones. This keeps the repository clean and reduces clutter, making it easier for the team to navigate and manage.

Adapting Strategies as Needed

BE PREPARED TO ADAPT your versioning and branching strategies as your project evolves. What works at the start of a project may need adjustment as the team, codebase, or objectives change.

By following these practices, teams can ensure a smooth, efficient, and error-minimized development process, vital for the complex and dynamic nature of Unreal Engine game development.

17.4. Continuous Integration and Deployment

CONTINUOUS INTEGRATION (CI) and Deployment (CD) are critical practices in modern game development with Unreal Engine, especially for larger teams and complex projects. This section explores how to effectively implement CI/CD pipelines to streamline development, testing, and deployment processes.

Understanding CI/CD in Game Development

CI/CD REFERS TO THE automation of integrating code changes and deploying them to production. In game development, this includes not just code, but also assets, levels, and other game components. CI ensures that new changes integrate smoothly, while CD automates the deployment process.

Setting Up a CI Server

CHOOSE AND SET UP A CI server that integrates with your version control system. Popular choices include Jenkins, TeamCity, and GitLab CI. The CI server should be capable of handling the specific requirements of Unreal Engine projects.

Automated Builds

CONFIGURE THE CI PIPELINE to automatically build the game project whenever changes are pushed to the repository. This ensures that every change is immediately tested for build integrity.

Automated Testing

INCORPORATE AUTOMATED testing into the CI pipeline. This can include unit tests, integration tests, and UI tests. Unreal Engine provides tools for automated testing, which can be integrated into the CI pipeline.

Static Code Analysis

INTEGRATE STATIC CODE analysis tools into the CI process. These tools analyze the code for potential issues, such as memory leaks or performance bottlenecks, without having to run the game.

Artifact Management

SET UP ARTIFACT MANAGEMENT within the CI pipeline. This involves storing build artifacts, like executables and asset bundles, in a way that they can be easily accessed and deployed.

Deployment Strategies

DEVELOP DEPLOYMENT strategies suitable for your project. This might involve deploying to different environments (like staging and production) or using techniques like blue-green deployment to reduce downtime and risk.

Environment Configuration

ENSURE THAT THE CI/CD pipeline can handle different configuration settings for various environments. This includes different database settings, API keys, and other environment-specific configurations.

Versioning and Release Management

AUTOMATE VERSIONING and release management through the CI/CD pipeline. This can include tagging releases, generating changelogs, and managing release branches.

Handling Large Assets

INCORPORATE STRATEGIES to handle large assets common in Unreal Engine projects. Tools like Git LFS or Perforce's Helix Core can be integrated into the CI/CD pipeline to manage these large assets efficiently.

Automated Notifications

SET UP AUTOMATED NOTIFICATIONS for the team. This includes notifications for successful builds, failed tests, or deployment statuses. These can be sent via email, Slack, or other communication tools.

Rollback Mechanisms

IMPLEMENT ROLLBACK mechanisms in the CD process. This allows you to quickly revert to a previous version if a new deployment causes issues, reducing downtime and negative impact on players.

Performance Monitoring

INTEGRATE PERFORMANCE monitoring into the deployment process. This involves tracking key performance metrics post-deployment to ensure that the new changes do not negatively impact game performance.

Security Checks

INCLUDE SECURITY CHECKS in the CI/CD pipeline. Automated security scanning can identify vulnerabilities before they are deployed to production.

Documentation and Training

DOCUMENT THE CI/CD process and provide training for team members. This ensures that everyone understands how to work with the CI/CD pipeline and what actions to take in case of failures or issues.

Continuous Feedback Loop

ESTABLISH A CONTINUOUS feedback loop where the results from CI/CD processes are used to improve development practices. This involves analyzing build failures, test results, and deployment issues to identify areas for improvement.

Scalability of CI/CD Infrastructure

ENSURE THAT YOUR CI/CD infrastructure can scale with your project. As the project grows, the demands on the CI/CD system will increase, requiring more resources and possibly more complex configurations.

Regular Maintenance and Updates

REGULARLY MAINTAIN and update your CI/CD pipeline. This includes updating tools and scripts, optimizing performance, and ensuring compatibility with the latest versions of Unreal Engine.

Integrating with Third-Party Services

CONSIDER INTEGRATING with third-party services that can enhance your CI/CD pipeline, such as cloud services, testing platforms, or analytics tools.

By implementing a robust CI/CD pipeline, teams can significantly reduce integration issues, streamline testing and deployment processes, and maintain a high level of code quality throughout the development lifecycle of Unreal Engine projects.

17.5. Documentation and Knowledge Sharing

IN THE REALM OF GAME development with Unreal Engine, documentation and knowledge sharing are pivotal for maintaining project clarity, continuity, and efficiency, especially in larger teams or complex projects. This section delves into strategies and best practices for effective documentation and knowledge dissemination.

The Importance of Comprehensive Documentation

EFFECTIVE DOCUMENTATION serves as the backbone for any project, providing a reference point for current and future team members. It covers coding standards, project architecture, feature documentation, and more, ensuring everyone is on the same page.

Documenting Code and Blueprints

DOCUMENTING CODE AND Blueprints is essential. This includes comments in the code, explaining complex logic or why certain decisions were made, and annotating Blueprints for clarity. Use a consistent style for comments to maintain readability.

Creating a Project Wiki

SET UP A PROJECT WIKI or knowledge base. This centralized repository can house all project-related information, from design documents to technical guidelines, making it easy for team members to find and access the information they need.

Standardizing Documentation Formats

STANDARDIZE THE FORMATS and templates for documentation. Consistent formats make it easier to read and understand the documents and ensure that all necessary information is included.

Regularly Updating Documentation

DOCUMENTATION SHOULD be a living entity in the project lifecycle. Regularly update it to reflect changes in the project, new practices, or tools. This ensures that the documentation remains relevant and useful.

Using Version Control for Documentation

KEEP DOCUMENTATION under version control. This allows you to track changes over time, revert to previous versions if necessary, and ensure that everyone has access to the latest information.

Documenting APIs and Interfaces

FOR PROJECTS WITH APIS or interfaces, comprehensive documentation is crucial. This includes clear explanations of the API endpoints, expected inputs and outputs, and examples of use.

Onboarding Documentation for New Team Members

CREATE SPECIFIC ONBOARDING documentation to help new team members get up to speed quickly. This can include project overviews, setup guides, and key contacts.

Encouraging Team Contribution to Documentation

FOSTER A CULTURE WHERE all team members contribute to documentation. Everyone has unique insights and knowledge, and contributing to the documentation can help share this knowledge across the team.

Creating Technical and Design Documents

TECHNICAL AND DESIGN documents are essential for detailing the architecture of the game, its features, and the design philosophy. These documents should be detailed enough to guide development but flexible enough to allow for changes.

Best Practices and Coding Standards

DOCUMENT BEST PRACTICES and coding standards. This helps maintain a high code quality and ensures that the codebase is consistent and maintainable.

Tool and Workflow Documentation

DOCUMENT THE TOOLS and workflows used in the project. This includes instructions on using version control, project management tools, and any custom tools or scripts developed for the project.

Keeping Track of Decisions

DOCUMENT KEY DECISIONS made during the project. This can be helpful in understanding the rationale behind certain choices and can be invaluable for future projects or when revisiting past decisions.

Sharing Knowledge through Meetings and Reviews

USE MEETINGS, CODE reviews, and team discussions as opportunities for knowledge sharing. Encourage team members to share tips, tricks, and insights they have gained.

Creating Video Tutorials and Demos

CONSIDER CREATING VIDEO tutorials or demos for complex features or workflows. Videos can be an effective way to demonstrate processes and provide a visual reference.

Establishing a Feedback Loop for Documentation

ESTABLISH A FEEDBACK loop for documentation. Encourage team members to suggest improvements, point out outdated information, and contribute their own insights.

Leveraging Documentation in Issue Tracking

INTEGRATE DOCUMENTATION references in issue tracking. When logging bugs or features, link to relevant documentation for context and further information.

Regular Audits of Documentation

CONDUCT REGULAR AUDITS of the documentation to ensure it's up-to-date and meets the team's needs. This might involve reviewing, restructuring, or even rewriting parts of the documentation.

Rewarding Contributions to Documentation

RECOGNIZE AND REWARD contributions to documentation. Acknowledging the effort put into maintaining and improving documentation can motivate team members to contribute.

Cross-Training Sessions

HOLD CROSS-TRAINING sessions where team members share knowledge about different aspects of the project. This not only helps in knowledge dissemination but also fosters team bonding.

By prioritizing documentation and knowledge sharing, teams can enhance collaboration, minimize misunderstandings, and maintain a high standard of development throughout the lifecycle of Unreal Engine projects.

Chapter 18: Legal and Ethical Considerations

18.1. Intellectual Property Rights in Game Development

NAVIGATING INTELLECTUAL property (IP) rights is a critical aspect of game development, ensuring that creative works are protected and legal liabilities are minimized. This section explores the key facets of IP rights within the context of Unreal Engine game development.

Understanding Intellectual Property in Games

INTELLECTUAL PROPERTY in games encompasses a wide range of elements, from game code and art assets to music, storylines, and characters. It's essential to understand what constitutes IP and how it is protected under law.

Copyright Laws and Game Content

COPYRIGHT LAW IS THE primary form of protection for game content. It automatically protects original works of authorship, including games, from the moment of their creation. Understanding copyright laws helps in protecting your work and respecting others' rights.

Licensing Agreements

WHEN USING THIRD-PARTY assets or tools, it's crucial to understand the terms of licensing agreements. This includes the rights granted, any restrictions, and the obligations of both parties.

Trademarks in Gaming

TRADEMARKS PROTECT brand names, logos, and other identifiers that distinguish your game. If you plan to build a brand around your game, consider registering a trademark to protect your brand identity.

Patents in Game Development

WHILE PATENTS IN GAME development are less common, they can apply to unique game mechanics or technology. Be aware of existing patents to avoid infringement and consider patenting truly innovative technologies.

Protecting Your Game's IP

TAKE PROACTIVE STEPS to protect your game's IP. This can include copyright registration, trademark registration, and ensuring confidentiality through NDAs (Non-Disclosure Agreements) with team members and partners.

Dealing with IP Infringement

IF YOU FACE IP INFRINGEMENT, either as an enforcer or defender, it's important to understand your legal rights and options. This may involve cease and desist letters, negotiations, or legal action.

Fair Use and Parody in Games

THE CONCEPT OF FAIR use allows limited use of copyrighted material without permission for purposes such as criticism, comment, news reporting, teaching, scholarship, or research. Understand how fair use might apply to game development, particularly in parody or homage.

Open Source Software in Game Development

USING OPEN-SOURCE SOFTWARE in your game requires adherence to specific licenses, like GPL, MIT, or Apache. Ensure you understand and comply with these licenses, particularly regarding distribution and derivative works.

User-Generated Content and IP

IF YOUR GAME INCLUDES user-generated content, establish clear guidelines and policies regarding IP rights. This includes who owns the content and how it can be used.

Contracts and Work for Hire

WHEN HIRING CONTRACTORS or employees, use clear contracts that specify the ownership of any created IP. Work-for-hire agreements can ensure that IP rights are transferred to the company.

Protecting Game Code

PROTECTING YOUR GAME code is crucial. This includes both source code and any proprietary algorithms or systems developed for the game. Use version control and access restrictions to safeguard your code.

Music and Sound Effects

MUSIC AND SOUND EFFECTS are often subject to copyright. When using music, either compose original tracks, use royalty-free music, or obtain proper licenses for copyrighted music.

Art Assets and Visual Design

ART ASSETS, INCLUDING character designs, environments, and UI elements, are protected by copyright. Ensure that all art is original or properly licensed.

Avoiding Plagiarism and Idea Theft

WHILE IDEAS THEMSELVES are not copyrighted, the expression of those ideas is. Be mindful to avoid plagiarism and respect the creative works of others.

Legal Consultation and Advice

FOR COMPLEX IP MATTERS, seek legal advice. Consulting with a lawyer specializing in intellectual property law can provide clarity and help avoid legal pitfalls.

International IP Law Considerations

BE AWARE OF INTERNATIONAL differences in IP law, especially if you plan to release your game globally. IP protection and enforcement can vary significantly between countries.

Continuous Learning and Awareness

STAY INFORMED ABOUT changes and developments in IP law as they pertain to game development. This includes following industry news and participating in developer communities.

By understanding and effectively managing intellectual property rights, game developers can protect their creative works, respect the rights of others, and navigate the legal landscape of the gaming industry confidently.

18.2. Navigating Licenses and Royalties with Unreal

NAVIGATING THE COMPLEX landscape of licenses and royalties is essential for game developers using Unreal Engine. Understanding these legal aspects helps in ensuring compliance and making informed decisions about your project's development and distribution.

Understanding Unreal Engine's Licensing Model

UNREAL ENGINE OPERATES under a licensing model that allows free access to the engine but imposes certain royalty requirements. Familiarize yourself with the specifics of this model, including when and how royalties are applied.

Royalty Rates and Exemptions

AS OF MY LAST UPDATE, Unreal Engine requires a royalty payment for commercial products after a certain revenue threshold is reached. Stay updated on the current rates and any exemptions or special conditions that might apply to your project.

Revenue Reporting Requirements

IF YOUR GAME GENERATES revenue above the specified threshold, you are required to report your earnings to Epic Games and pay the applicable royalties. Understand the process for reporting and the timelines involved.

License Agreements for Marketplace Assets

WHEN USING ASSETS FROM the Unreal Marketplace, it's crucial to understand the license agreements associated with each asset. These agreements outline how you can use the assets and any restrictions or obligations.

Custom Licensing Agreements

IF YOUR PROJECT HAS specific needs or you're negotiating a deal with a publisher, you may need to consider custom licensing agreements. This might involve discussing terms directly with Epic Games or other third parties.

Incorporating Third-Party Software

IF YOUR GAME INCORPORATES third-party software, plugins, or tools, understand the licensing terms of these components. This includes open-source software, which may have its own set of requirements and restrictions.

Distributing Games Built with Unreal

WHEN DISTRIBUTING YOUR game, be aware of the licensing implications. This includes platforms like Steam, console marketplaces, and mobile app stores, each with its own set of rules and requirements.

Handling Updates and DLC

UNDERSTAND HOW UPDATES, downloadable content (DLC), and in-game transactions affect your royalty obligations. Often, these are treated as part of the game's revenue and are subject to royalties.

Legal Considerations for Crowdfunding

IF YOU ARE USING CROWDFUNDING platforms like Kickstarter to fund your game, understand how this impacts your licensing and royalty obligations. Revenue from crowdfunding can sometimes count towards your royalty calculations.

Educational and Non-Profit Projects

UNREAL ENGINE OFFERS different terms for educational and non-profit projects. If your project falls into these categories, research the specific licensing terms and any exemptions that may apply.

Collaborations and Revenue Sharing

IN COLLABORATIVE PROJECTS or when revenue sharing with other creators, outline how royalties and licensing responsibilities are handled. This should be part of your contractual agreements with collaborators.

Consulting with Legal Professionals

FOR COMPLEX LICENSING scenarios or if you have specific legal questions, consult with legal professionals. They can provide advice tailored to your project's specifics.

Keeping Records and Financial Transparency

MAINTAIN THOROUGH RECORDS of your game's revenue and expenses. This is important not only for royalty calculations but also for general business practices and potential audits.

Protecting Intellectual Property

WHILE NAVIGATING LICENSES and royalties, also consider how you protect your own intellectual property. This includes trademarks, copyrights, and patents where applicable.

Monitoring Changes in Licensing Policies

STAY INFORMED ABOUT any changes in Unreal Engine's licensing policies or royalty rates. Epic Games occasionally updates these policies, and staying current is crucial for compliance.

Preparing for Audits

BE PREPARED FOR POTENTIAL audits from Epic Games or other licensors. This involves having clear, accessible records of revenue, expenses, and compliance with licensing terms.

Negotiating Terms for Large Projects

FOR LARGE-SCALE PROJECTS or those with significant funding, consider negotiating terms directly with Epic Games or other licensors. This can sometimes result in more favorable terms for your specific situation.

Understanding Global Licensing Implications

CONSIDER THE GLOBAL implications of licensing, especially if you plan to release your game in multiple countries. Licensing laws and royalty requirements can vary internationally.

By carefully navigating the landscape of licenses and royalties associated with Unreal Engine, developers can ensure legal compliance, optimize their financial obligations, and focus on the creative and technical aspects of game development.

18.3. Ethical Considerations in Game Design

ETHICAL CONSIDERATIONS in game design are increasingly important in today's gaming landscape. This section explores the various ethical aspects that Unreal Engine developers should consider during the game development process.

Understanding Ethics in Game Design

ETHICS IN GAME DESIGN refers to the moral principles guiding the creation and distribution of games. It encompasses issues like representation, content sensitivity, player impact, and business practices.

Player Impact and Responsibility

CONSIDER THE IMPACT your game may have on players. This includes potential addiction, the portrayal of violence, and the effects on mental health. Design games responsibly to minimize negative impacts.

Representation and Diversity

ETHICAL GAME DESIGN involves inclusive representation and diversity. This means creating characters and narratives that reflect a diverse range of backgrounds, cultures, and experiences.

Content Sensitivity and Ratings

BE AWARE OF CONTENT sensitivity. Design your game's content keeping in mind the appropriate age ratings and cultural sensitivities, ensuring that it aligns with the standards of the regions you are targeting.

Ethical Monetization Strategies

IMPLEMENT ETHICAL MONETIZATION strategies. This includes being transparent about costs, avoiding predatory practices like hidden fees or manipulative loot boxes, and respecting player spending limits.

Handling User Data Ethically

IF YOUR GAME COLLECTS user data, handle it ethically and responsibly. Follow data protection laws, be transparent about data usage, and provide adequate security to protect user information.

Accessibility and Inclusivity

MAKE YOUR GAME ACCESSIBLE to a wider audience, including players with disabilities. This is not only a legal requirement in some cases but also an ethical obligation to make gaming inclusive for all.

Addressing Social and Political Issues

IF YOUR GAME ADDRESSES social or political issues, do so with sensitivity and awareness. Be mindful of different perspectives and ensure that your game does not perpetuate harmful stereotypes or misinformation.

Environmental Impact

CONSIDER THE ENVIRONMENTAL impact of game development and distribution. This includes digital distribution practices, energy-efficient game design, and sustainable practices in the workplace.

Fair Labor Practices

ENSURE FAIR LABOR PRACTICES in game development. This includes reasonable working hours, fair compensation, and a healthy work environment, especially in the context of 'crunch culture' in the gaming industry.

Ethical Marketing Practices

ADOPT ETHICAL MARKETING practices. Be honest and transparent in your advertising, avoid misleading claims, and respect privacy in marketing campaigns.

Community Standards and Moderation

FOR GAMES WITH ONLINE communities, establish and enforce community standards. This includes moderation policies to prevent harassment, hate speech, and other harmful behaviors.

Dealing with Sensitive Themes

WHEN DEALING WITH SENSITIVE themes like war, tragedy, or personal struggles, approach them with respect and care. Avoid trivializing serious issues and consider the potential impact on players.

Balancing Creativity and Responsibility

STRIVE TO BALANCE CREATIVITY with responsibility. While pushing creative boundaries is important, it should not come at the expense of ethical considerations and the well-being of players.

Continuous Learning and Adaptation

STAY INFORMED ABOUT ethical issues in the gaming industry and be ready to adapt your practices as norms and standards evolve.

Player Feedback and Ethical Adjustments

LISTEN TO PLAYER FEEDBACK regarding ethical concerns and be willing to make adjustments. Player communities can provide valuable insights into how your game is perceived and experienced.

Collaborating with Experts

COLLABORATE WITH CULTURAL consultants, psychologists, and other experts when dealing with complex ethical issues. Their insights can help you navigate sensitive topics more effectively.

Reflecting on Personal Ethics

REFLECT ON YOUR OWN ethics and values and how they influence your game design. Personal ethics play a significant role in the decisions you make as a developer.

Advocating for Ethical Practices

ADVOCATE FOR ETHICAL practices within your team and the broader game development community. Encouraging discussions and awareness about ethics can lead to a more responsible gaming industry.

By considering these ethical aspects, game developers can create games that are not only engaging and entertaining but also responsible, inclusive, and respectful of their audience and society at large.

18.4. Privacy and Data Security in Games

IN THE ERA OF DIGITAL gaming, privacy and data security are paramount concerns for game developers. This section focuses on best practices and considerations for ensuring privacy and securing data in Unreal Engine games.

Understanding Data Privacy in Gaming

DATA PRIVACY IN GAMING involves the responsible handling of player data, including personal information and gameplay statistics. It's essential to understand the legal and ethical implications of data collection and storage.

Compliance with Data Protection Laws

FAMILIARIZE YOURSELF with data protection laws like GDPR in Europe, CCPA in California, and other regional regulations. These laws dictate how you should handle user data, including collection, storage, and user rights.

Transparent Data Collection Policies

BE TRANSPARENT ABOUT your data collection policies. Clearly inform players what data you collect, how it's used, and who has access to it. Obtain explicit consent where required by law.

Secure Data Storage and Transmission

IMPLEMENT ROBUST SECURITY measures for storing and transmitting data. Use encryption for data in transit and at rest, and ensure that your servers and databases are secure against unauthorized access.

Handling User Accounts and Authentication

WHEN HANDLING USER accounts and authentication, employ strong security practices. This includes secure password handling, two-factor authentication, and protection against common vulnerabilities like SQL injection.

Minimizing Data Collection

ADOPT A POLICY OF COLLECTING only the data necessary for the intended purpose. Avoid collecting excessive or irrelevant data, as this increases liability and the risk of privacy breaches.

Regular Security Audits and Updates

CONDUCT REGULAR SECURITY audits of your game and related systems. Stay updated with the latest security patches and updates for any third-party services or libraries you use.

Player-Controlled Privacy Settings

PROVIDE PLAYERS WITH privacy settings that allow them to control their data. This includes options to opt-out of data collection, delete accounts, and access the data you hold about them.

Responding to Data Breaches

HAVE A PLAN IN PLACE for responding to data breaches. This includes timely notification to affected users and regulatory authorities, as required by law, and measures to mitigate the impact.

Training Team Members on Data Security

EDUCATE YOUR TEAM MEMBERS about the importance of data security and privacy. Ensure they understand the best practices and legal requirements for handling user data.

Secure Payment Processing

IF YOUR GAME INCLUDES in-app purchases, ensure that payment processing is secure. Use trusted payment gateways and comply with PCI DSS standards to protect financial data.

Protecting Children's Privacy

IF YOUR GAME IS AIMED at or accessible to children, pay special attention to children's privacy laws, like COPPA in the United States. Implement additional safeguards and obtain parental consent where necessary.

Anonymizing and Aggregating Data

CONSIDER ANONYMIZING and aggregating data where possible. This reduces the risk of individual data being compromised and can still provide valuable insights for game development.

Privacy by Design

INCORPORATE PRIVACY by design principles in your game development process. This means considering privacy and data security at every stage of development, from design to deployment.

Reviewing Third-Party Service Providers

IF YOU USE THIRD-PARTY services, review their privacy and security practices. Ensure they comply with relevant laws and meet your standards for data protection.

Implementing Secure Chat and Communication Features

FOR GAMES WITH CHAT or communication features, ensure these systems are secure and respect user privacy. Implement moderation tools and filters to prevent the sharing of sensitive information.

Data Retention Policies

ESTABLISH CLEAR DATA retention policies. Only keep user data for as long as necessary and have procedures for securely deleting data that is no longer needed.

Privacy Impact Assessments

CONDUCT PRIVACY IMPACT assessments for new features or changes in your game. Assess how these changes might affect user privacy and what measures are needed to mitigate risks.

User Education and Awareness

EDUCATE USERS ABOUT privacy and security within your game. This can include tips on creating strong passwords, awareness about phishing, and information on how to protect their personal data.

By prioritizing privacy and data security, game developers not only comply with legal requirements but also build trust with their player base, creating a safer and more secure gaming environment.

18.5. Community Standards and Player Behavior

MANAGING COMMUNITY standards and player behavior is a crucial aspect of online gaming and game development. This section discusses the strategies and considerations for creating a positive and respectful gaming community for Unreal Engine-based games.

The Importance of Community Standards

ESTABLISHING COMMUNITY standards helps set expectations for player behavior. These standards should promote respect, inclusivity, and a positive gaming experience for all players.

Developing a Code of Conduct

CREATE A CLEAR AND concise code of conduct that outlines acceptable and unacceptable behaviors. This code should be easily accessible to all players and enforced consistently.

Implementing Moderation Tools

DEVELOP AND IMPLEMENT effective moderation tools to help enforce community standards. This can include chat filters, reporting systems, and tools for moderators to manage player interactions.

Training Community Moderators

SELECT AND TRAIN COMMUNITY moderators who understand the importance of maintaining a positive gaming environment. They should be equipped to handle disputes, enforce rules, and support players.

Encouraging Positive Player Interactions

DESIGN GAME MECHANICS and features that encourage positive player interactions. Reward collaborative and respectful behavior to promote a healthy community.

Handling Toxic Behavior

HAVE CLEAR POLICIES and procedures for handling toxic behavior. This includes a process for warnings, suspensions, and bans, depending on the severity of the behavior.

Transparency in Moderation Decisions

MAINTAIN TRANSPARENCY in moderation decisions. Players should understand why actions were taken and have a process to appeal decisions if they feel they were unjust.

Protecting Player Privacy

ENSURE THAT PLAYER privacy is respected in all community interactions. Personal information should never be shared, and players should feel safe participating in the community.

Regularly Reviewing and Updating Policies

REGULARLY REVIEW AND update community standards and moderation policies to reflect the evolving nature of the game and its community.

Providing Resources for Player Support

PROVIDE RESOURCES AND support for players who may be affected by negative behavior. This can include links to external support services or in-game tools for player well-being.

Building an Inclusive Community

STRIVE TO BUILD AN inclusive community that welcomes players from diverse backgrounds. This can involve celebrating different cultures and promoting understanding and respect among players.

Addressing Cheating and Exploits

DEVELOP STRATEGIES to address cheating and the use of exploits. This undermines the gaming experience and should be addressed swiftly and effectively.

Creating Safe Spaces

CONSIDER CREATING SAFE spaces within the game where players can engage without fear of harassment or negative behavior. This can include moderated forums or chat rooms.

Engaging with the Community

ENGAGE WITH THE COMMUNITY through forums, social media, and in-game events. Open communication helps build trust and a sense of belonging among players.

Leveraging Player Feedback

LEVERAGE PLAYER FEEDBACK to improve community standards and moderation practices. Players can provide valuable insights into community dynamics and areas for improvement.

Collaborating with Industry Partners

COLLABORATE WITH INDUSTRY partners and other game developers to share best practices and resources for community management.

Promoting Mental Health Awareness

PROMOTE MENTAL HEALTH awareness within the community. Gaming can have both positive and negative impacts on mental health, and awareness can help mitigate risks.

Crisis Management and Response

PREPARE FOR CRISIS management and response, especially in situations of widespread negative behavior or external threats to the community.

Celebrating Community Achievements

CELEBRATE COMMUNITY achievements and contributions. Recognizing positive community members can reinforce good behavior and encourage others to follow suit.

Learning and Adapting

BE OPEN TO LEARNING and adapting your approach to community management. Communities are dynamic, and strategies may need to evolve to meet changing needs and challenges.

By fostering a respectful and inclusive community, game developers can enhance the gaming experience for all players, encouraging engagement, loyalty, and a positive reputation for their game.

Chapter 19: Marketing and Monetization

19.1. Advanced Marketing Strategies for Games

DEVELOPING AN EFFECTIVE marketing strategy is crucial for the success of any game, especially in the competitive landscape of Unreal Engine-based games. This section covers advanced marketing strategies to maximize the visibility and appeal of your game.

Understanding Your Target Audience

BEGIN BY THOROUGHLY understanding your target audience. Identify their preferences, gaming habits, and where they spend their time online. Tailor your marketing strategy to resonate with this audience.

Building a Strong Brand Identity

DEVELOP A STRONG BRAND identity for your game. This includes a memorable name, an eye-catching logo, and a unique visual style. A strong brand helps your game stand out in a crowded market.

Creating a Compelling Game Trailer

CREATE A COMPELLING trailer that showcases the best aspects of your game. The trailer should be engaging, visually appealing, and give players a taste of what to expect.

Leveraging Social Media Platforms

UTILIZE SOCIAL MEDIA platforms effectively. Each platform has its own strengths and audience, so tailor your content accordingly. Regular updates, behind-the-scenes looks, and interactive posts can engage the community.

Engaging with Influencers and Streamers

PARTNER WITH INFLUENCERS and streamers who align with your target audience. Their endorsements can reach a wide audience and add credibility to your game.

Building a Community Around Your Game

FOCUS ON BUILDING A community around your game. Engage with players through forums, social media, and in-game events. A strong community can provide valuable feedback and word-of-mouth promotion.

Utilizing Email Marketing

IMPLEMENT AN EMAIL marketing campaign to keep potential players informed and engaged. Share updates, exclusive content, and special offers to keep your game top of mind.

Search Engine Optimization (SEO)

OPTIMIZE YOUR GAME'S website and online content for search engines. Effective SEO can increase your website's visibility and attract more organic traffic.

Content Marketing

DEVELOP A CONTENT MARKETING strategy. This can include blog posts, articles, and videos that provide value to your audience while promoting your game.

Paid Advertising Campaigns

CONSIDER PAID ADVERTISING campaigns on platforms like Google Ads, Facebook, or Instagram. Target your ads to reach the most relevant audience for your game.

Cross-Promotion and Partnerships

EXPLORE OPPORTUNITIES for cross-promotion and partnerships with other games or brands. This can help you reach a wider audience and gain additional exposure.

Attending and Showcasing at Gaming Events

ATTEND GAMING EVENTS and conventions to showcase your game. This provides opportunities for networking, media coverage, and direct player feedback.

Offering Demos and Beta Testing

OFFER DEMOS OR BETA testing opportunities to give players a hands-on experience. This can generate excitement and valuable feedback before the full release.

Tracking and Analyzing Marketing Data

TRACK AND ANALYZE YOUR marketing data. Use analytics to understand what strategies are working and where you need to adjust your approach.

Implementing Referral Programs

IMPLEMENT REFERRAL programs to encourage players to invite friends. Incentives like in-game rewards can motivate players to spread the word about your game.

Creative and Interactive Marketing Campaigns

GET CREATIVE WITH YOUR marketing campaigns. Interactive campaigns, online contests, and unique storytelling can capture the interest of potential players.

Regular Updates and Communication

KEEP YOUR AUDIENCE informed with regular updates. Share progress, upcoming features, and any changes to keep players engaged and looking forward to the game's release.

Effective Use of Press Releases

WRITE AND DISTRIBUTE effective press releases. Target gaming news outlets and journalists who might be interested in your game.

Post-Launch Marketing

DON'T NEGLECT POST-launch marketing. Continue your marketing efforts after the game's release to maintain interest and attract new players.

Adapting to Market Changes

STAY ADAPTABLE AND be ready to change your marketing strategy in response to market trends, player feedback, and the evolving gaming landscape.

By implementing these advanced marketing strategies, you can enhance the visibility and appeal of your Unreal Engine game, attract a larger audience, and increase your chances of commercial success.

19.2. Crafting Effective Monetization Models

DEVELOPING EFFECTIVE monetization models is critical for the financial success of any game. This section delves into various monetization strategies suitable for Unreal Engine games, ensuring a balance between profitability and player satisfaction.

Understanding Different Monetization Models

FAMILIARIZE YOURSELF with the different monetization models available for games, such as premium, freemium, subscriptions, in-app purchases, and ad-supported models. Each has its own advantages and challenges.

Premium Pricing Model

IN THE PREMIUM MODEL, players pay a one-time fee to purchase your game. This model is straightforward but requires your game to offer sufficient value to justify the upfront cost.

Freemium and In-App Purchases

THE FREEMIUM MODEL allows players to download and play the game for free, with revenue generated through in-app purchases. This model can attract a large player base, but in-app purchases must be balanced to avoid pay-to-win scenarios.

Subscription-Based Model

CONSIDER A SUBSCRIPTION-based model for games that offer ongoing content or services. This model provides a steady revenue stream but requires regular updates and new content to retain subscribers.

Advertising-Based Revenue

INCORPORATE ADVERTISING as a revenue source. This can include banner ads, video ads, or sponsored content. Ensure that ads are not intrusive and do not detract from the player experience.

Season Passes and DLC

OFFER SEASON PASSES and downloadable content (DLC) as additional revenue streams. This allows players to pay for new content, features, or experiences post-launch.

Virtual Goods and Microtransactions

SELLING VIRTUAL GOODS and microtransactions can be profitable. Offer cosmetic items, special abilities, or other enhancements that do not disrupt game balance.

Ethical Considerations in Monetization

ETHICALLY IMPLEMENT monetization strategies. Avoid exploitative practices and ensure that your monetization model respects the player's time and investment.

Balancing Monetization with Gameplay

BALANCE MONETIZATION with gameplay. The monetization model should complement the game experience, not detract from it.

Player Feedback and Adjustments

GATHER AND CONSIDER player feedback regarding your monetization strategies. Be willing to make adjustments based on player preferences and behaviors.

Market Research and Competitor Analysis

CONDUCT MARKET RESEARCH and competitor analysis to understand current trends and what monetization models are effective in similar games.

Testing Different Monetization Strategies

TEST DIFFERENT MONETIZATION strategies to see what works best for your game. A/B testing can provide insights into player preferences and spending behaviors.

Transparency with Players

BE TRANSPARENT WITH players about your monetization model. Clearly communicate what players are paying for and any terms associated with purchases.

Regional Pricing Strategies

IMPLEMENT REGIONAL pricing strategies to accommodate players in different economic regions. This can help make your game more accessible to a wider audience.

Loyalty Programs and Rewards

IMPLEMENT LOYALTY PROGRAMS and rewards to encourage players to spend more. This can include bonuses, exclusive content, or discounts for frequent spenders.

Integrating Monetization into Game Design

INTEGRATE MONETIZATION into the game design from the beginning. Monetization should feel like a natural part of the game, not an afterthought.

Analyzing and Optimizing Revenue Streams

REGULARLY ANALYZE AND optimize your revenue streams. Track metrics like average revenue per user (ARPU) and lifetime value (LTV) to understand your monetization's effectiveness.

Legal Compliance in Monetization

ENSURE LEGAL COMPLIANCE in your monetization model, particularly regarding in-app purchases and advertising. Adhere to regulations like COPPA and GDPR where applicable.

Continuous Evolution of Monetization Strategy

STAY FLEXIBLE AND BE prepared to evolve your monetization strategy over time. As the market and player expectations change, so should your approach to monetization.

By carefully crafting and implementing an effective monetization model, you can ensure a steady revenue stream while providing a fair and enjoyable experience for your players.

19.3. Community Engagement and Social Media

IN THE WORLD OF GAME development, engaging with your community and effectively utilizing social media are key factors in building a loyal fan base and promoting your game. This section explores strategies to enhance community engagement and make the most out of social media platforms for Unreal Engine games.

Building a Strong Online Presence

CREATE A STRONG ONLINE presence for your game across various social media platforms. Each platform has its own strengths and audience, so tailor your approach accordingly.

Developing a Social Media Strategy

DEVELOP A COMPREHENSIVE social media strategy that outlines your goals, target audience, content types, and posting schedule. Consistency and relevance are key to keeping your audience engaged.

Engaging Content Creation

CREATE ENGAGING CONTENT that resonates with your audience. This can include behind-the-scenes looks, developer diaries, sneak peeks, and user-generated content.

Interactive and Regular Communication

ENCOURAGE INTERACTION by regularly communicating with your audience. Respond to comments, participate in discussions, and create posts that encourage user engagement.

Utilizing Hashtags and Trends

MAKE USE OF RELEVANT hashtags and trends to increase the visibility of your posts. However, ensure that your use of trends and hashtags aligns with your game's identity and audience.

Hosting Live Streams and Q&A Sessions

HOST LIVE STREAMS, Q&A sessions, and virtual events to directly engage with your community. These sessions can provide valuable insights into your audience's thoughts and preferences.

Leveraging Influencer Partnerships

PARTNER WITH INFLUENCERS and content creators who align with your game's genre and style. Influencers can help you reach a broader audience and add credibility to your game.

Creating a Community Platform

CONSIDER CREATING A dedicated platform for your community, such as a forum or Discord server. This allows for deeper engagement and a sense of belonging among your players.

Encouraging User-Generated Content

ENCOURAGE USER-GENERATED content such as fan art, stories, or mods. Showcasing user content not only engages the community but also provides free marketing material.

Community Contests and Giveaways

ORGANIZE CONTESTS, giveaways, and in-game events to keep the community engaged and excited. This can increase player retention and attract new players.

Gathering Community Feedback

ACTIVELY GATHER AND acknowledge community feedback. Use social media platforms and community forums to understand what players like and what they want improved.

Addressing Negative Feedback Constructively

ADDRESS NEGATIVE FEEDBACK constructively. Responding to criticism in a positive and professional manner can turn dissatisfied players into loyal fans.

Showcasing Reviews and Testimonials

SHOWCASE POSITIVE REVIEWS and testimonials on your social media channels. Highlighting positive player experiences can attract new players.

Analyzing Social Media Metrics

REGULARLY ANALYZE YOUR social media metrics to understand what content performs well. Use these insights to refine your social media strategy.

Balancing Promotional and Interactive Content

MAINTAIN A BALANCE between promotional content and content that fosters interaction. Too much promotion can turn off players, while interactive content can build a stronger community.

Highlighting Milestones and Successes

CELEBRATE MILESTONES and successes with your community. Sharing achievements like awards, major updates, or download numbers can build excitement and a sense of shared accomplishment.

Staying Active and Consistent

STAY ACTIVE AND CONSISTENT on social media. Regular updates keep your game in the minds of your audience and show that the project is active and evolving.

Encouraging Community Advocacy

ENCOURAGE YOUR COMMUNITY to advocate for your game. Word-of-mouth recommendations from loyal fans can be more effective than traditional advertising.

Responsiveness to Current Events

BE RESPONSIVE TO CURRENT events and trends, but stay true to your game's identity and values. Timely and relevant content can increase engagement.

Building a Brand Voice

DEVELOP A UNIQUE BRAND voice for your social media presence. Whether it's humorous, informative, or inspirational, a consistent voice can make your posts more recognizable and relatable.

By actively engaging with your community and utilizing social media effectively, you can build a strong, loyal fan base that will support your game long after its initial release.

19.4. Launch Strategies and Post-Launch Support

EFFECTIVE LAUNCH STRATEGIES and post-launch support are crucial for the success of any game. This section covers key considerations and approaches for launching Unreal Engine games and maintaining momentum post-launch.

Planning the Launch Strategy

DEVELOP A COMPREHENSIVE launch strategy that outlines key milestones, marketing efforts, and target audience. A well-planned launch can create significant initial traction for your game.

Timing the Launch

CONSIDER THE TIMING of your game's launch. Avoid launching alongside major titles and consider seasonal trends in gaming. The right timing can maximize visibility and player interest.

Creating a Launch Roadmap

CREATE A DETAILED LAUNCH roadmap outlining all the steps leading up to and following the launch. This should include marketing campaigns, final testing phases, and post-launch content plans.

Beta Testing and Feedback

CONDUCT BETA TESTING phases to gather feedback and make final adjustments. This not only helps in polishing the game but also builds anticipation and a sense of involvement among players.

Building Hype Before Launch

UTILIZE SOCIAL MEDIA, trailers, live streams, and influencer partnerships to build hype leading up to the launch. Excitement and anticipation can drive initial sales and player engagement.

Coordinating with Platform Requirements

COORDINATE WITH GAMING platforms to ensure compliance with their requirements. This includes store page optimization, meeting technical standards, and understanding revenue-sharing models.

Leveraging Pre-Order Campaigns

CONSIDER OFFERING PRE-orders with incentives like early access or exclusive content. Pre-orders can provide early revenue and an indication of the game's potential success.

Launch Day Readiness

ENSURE THAT YOUR TEAM is ready for launch day. This includes having support staff available to handle technical issues, community management, and real-time monitoring of the game's performance.

Post-Launch Content and Updates

PLAN FOR POST-LAUNCH content and updates to keep the game fresh and retain players. Regular updates, new features, and additional content can maintain player interest and extend the game's lifespan.

Community Engagement Post-Launch

MAINTAIN ACTIVE COMMUNITY engagement after the launch. Regular communication, responding to feedback, and involving players in the game's evolution can build a loyal player base.

Monitoring and Responding to Feedback

MONITOR PLAYER FEEDBACK closely post-launch. Addressing issues, bugs, and player concerns promptly can improve player satisfaction and the game's reputation.

Utilizing Analytics for Improvement

USE ANALYTICS TO TRACK player behavior and game performance post-launch. Insights from data can guide improvements, marketing efforts, and future content development.

Managing Reviews and Ratings

ACTIVELY MANAGE REVIEWS and ratings on various platforms. Positive reviews can be highlighted, and constructive responses to negative reviews can mitigate their impact.

Implementing a Marketing Refresh

CONSIDER IMPLEMENTING a marketing refresh post-launch. New campaigns can reinvigorate interest in your game and attract new players.

Hosting Events and Promotions

HOST IN-GAME EVENTS, promotions, or competitions to keep players engaged. These can increase player retention and attract new players.

Offering DLCs and Expansions

DEVELOP DLCS AND EXPANSIONS to expand the game world and offer new experiences. This not only generates additional revenue but also keeps the game relevant.

Continuous Quality Assurance

MAINTAIN CONTINUOUS quality assurance post-launch. Regularly test and fix bugs to ensure the game remains stable and enjoyable.

Managing Player Expectations

MANAGE PLAYER EXPECTATIONS regarding future updates and content. Clear communication can prevent disappointment and maintain a positive community sentiment.

Adapting to Market Changes

BE ADAPTABLE TO CHANGES in the market. Player preferences and industry trends can shift, and being flexible can help you stay relevant.

Celebrating Milestones

CELEBRATE POST-LAUNCH milestones with your community. Acknowledging the game's achievements, such as download numbers or awards, can enhance community ties and promote positive word-of-mouth.

By executing a strategic launch and maintaining strong post-launch support, you can maximize the success of your Unreal Engine game, ensuring it remains compelling and relevant to players over time.

19.5. Analyzing Player Data for Marketing Insights

ANALYZING PLAYER DATA is a powerful tool for gaining marketing insights and making informed decisions about the development and promotion of your game. This section explores how to effectively utilize player data in the context of Unreal Engine game development.

Importance of Player Data Analysis

UNDERSTAND THE IMPORTANCE of player data analysis in shaping marketing strategies. Data can reveal player preferences, behaviors, and patterns that are crucial for targeted marketing and game improvements.

Collecting Player Data Ethically

ENSURE ETHICAL PRACTICES in collecting player data. Be transparent about what data is collected and how it will be used, and always obtain player consent where necessary.

Adhering to Data Protection Regulations

ADHERE TO DATA PROTECTION regulations such as GDPR and CCPA. This includes providing players with the option to opt-out of data collection and ensuring the security of the data collected.

Utilizing Analytics Tools

USE ANALYTICS TOOLS to gather and analyze player data. Tools like Google Analytics, Mixpanel, or custom analytics integrated into your game can provide valuable insights.

Identifying Key Performance Indicators (KPIs)

IDENTIFY KEY PERFORMANCE indicators (KPIs) relevant to your game. KPIs can include daily active users (DAU), retention rates, average revenue per user (ARPU), and session length.

Segmenting the Player Base

SEGMENT YOUR PLAYER base to target specific groups effectively. Segmentation can be based on player behavior, spending habits, geographic location, or game progression.

Analyzing Player Feedback

COMBINE QUANTITATIVE data with qualitative player feedback. Analyze reviews, forum posts, and social media comments to gain a deeper understanding of player sentiments.

Understanding Player Behaviors

DIVE INTO PLAYER BEHAVIOR analytics to understand how players interact with your game. Look for patterns in gameplay, feature usage, and drop-off points.

A/B Testing for Marketing Strategies

EMPLOY A/B TESTING to evaluate different marketing strategies. Test different versions of advertisements, email campaigns, or in-game promotions to see what resonates best with your audience.

Tracking Marketing Campaign Effectiveness

TRACK THE EFFECTIVENESS of marketing campaigns using player data. Analyze changes in player acquisition, engagement, and revenue following marketing initiatives.

Personalizing Player Experiences

USE DATA TO PERSONALIZE player experiences. Tailored recommendations, personalized in-game offers, and customized communications can enhance player engagement.

Predictive Analytics for Future Trends

UTILIZE PREDICTIVE analytics to anticipate future trends and player behaviors. This can inform content updates, marketing campaigns, and feature development.

Optimizing Monetization Strategies

ANALYZE PLAYER SPENDING patterns to optimize monetization strategies. Identify the most popular in-game purchases and adjust pricing or offers accordingly.

Enhancing Player Retention

USE DATA TO IDENTIFY factors that contribute to player retention. Tailor your game's development and marketing efforts to enhance these factors and keep players engaged.

In-Game Behavior and Level Design

ANALYZE IN-GAME BEHAVIOR to inform level and game design. Identify levels or features where players struggle or disengage, and make necessary adjustments.

Dynamic Content Adjustment

IMPLEMENT DYNAMIC CONTENT adjustment based on player data. This can include changing difficulty levels, offering targeted in-game items, or unlocking personalized content.

Feedback Loop with Development Team

ESTABLISH A FEEDBACK loop with the development team. Share insights from player data analysis to guide game updates and improvements.

Privacy-First Data Approach

ADOPT A PRIVACY-FIRST approach in data analysis. Ensure that player data is anonymized and used responsibly, respecting player privacy at all times.

Continuous Learning from Data

CONTINUOUSLY LEARN from player data. The gaming market is dynamic, and ongoing data analysis is key to staying relevant and competitive.

By effectively analyzing player data, game developers can gain valuable insights to guide marketing strategies, enhance player experiences, and ultimately drive the success of their Unreal Engine games.

Chapter 20: Future-Proofing Your Unreal Skills

20.1. Staying Updated with Unreal Engine's Evolution

IN THE RAPIDLY EVOLVING field of game development, staying updated with the latest advancements in Unreal Engine is crucial for maintaining relevant skills and knowledge. This section offers strategies for keeping up with Unreal Engine's ongoing evolution.

Regularly Checking Unreal Engine Updates

REGULARLY CHECK FOR updates and new releases of Unreal Engine. Each update can bring new features, improvements, and bug fixes that can significantly impact your development process.

Participating in Unreal Engine Communities

PARTICIPATE IN UNREAL Engine communities, such as forums, social media groups, and online platforms. These communities are valuable resources for learning about updates, sharing knowledge, and staying connected with industry trends.

Attending Webinars and Workshops

ATTEND WEBINARS, WORKSHOPS, and training sessions focused on Unreal Engine. These events are often led by experts and provide in-depth insights into new features and best practices.

Following Industry Blogs and Newsletters

SUBSCRIBE TO INDUSTRY blogs and newsletters that cover Unreal Engine and game development. Staying informed about industry news can help you anticipate and adapt to changes in the engine.

Engaging with Beta Releases

ENGAGE WITH BETA RELEASES of Unreal Engine when available. Testing beta versions allows you to familiarize yourself with new features before they are officially released.

Experimenting with New Features

REGULARLY EXPERIMENT with new features in Unreal Engine. Hands-on experience is one of the best ways to understand and master new functionalities.

Updating Personal and Professional Projects

UPDATE YOUR PERSONAL and professional projects to the latest version of Unreal Engine. This practice ensures compatibility and helps you stay adept with current engine capabilities.

Leveraging Online Tutorials and Courses

UTILIZE ONLINE TUTORIALS and courses to learn about new updates and features in Unreal Engine. Many online platforms offer courses specifically tailored to different aspects of the engine.

Networking with Other Developers

NETWORK WITH OTHER Unreal Engine developers. Sharing experiences and insights can provide practical knowledge and tips on handling the challenges of new updates.

Contributing to Open Source Projects

CONTRIBUTE TO OPEN-source projects using Unreal Engine. This experience can provide a deeper understanding of the engine and its capabilities in different scenarios.

Attending Industry Conferences

ATTEND INDUSTRY CONFERENCES and events that focus on game development and Unreal Engine. These events are opportunities for learning, networking, and discovering the latest industry trends.

Reading Official Documentation

REGULARLY READ UNREAL Engine's official documentation. The documentation is a comprehensive resource for understanding the functionalities and features of the engine.

Participating in Beta Testing Programs

IF POSSIBLE, PARTICIPATE in Unreal Engine's beta testing programs. Beta testers often get early access to new features and can provide feedback that shapes the final release.

Exploring Advanced Features

DON'T SHY AWAY FROM exploring advanced features and experimental tools in Unreal Engine. These features can open up new possibilities for game development.

Staying Flexible and Adaptable

MAINTAIN A FLEXIBLE and adaptable mindset. The technology landscape is constantly changing, and being open to learning and adapting is key to staying relevant.

Sharing Knowledge and Experiences

SHARE YOUR KNOWLEDGE and experiences with the community. Teaching others can reinforce your own understanding and keep you engaged with the latest developments.

Monitoring Performance Improvements

KEEP AN EYE ON PERFORMANCE improvements in each new Unreal Engine update. Understanding these improvements can help you optimize your projects more effectively.

Keeping an Eye on Emerging Technologies

STAY INFORMED ABOUT emerging technologies that can integrate with or affect Unreal Engine. Technologies like VR, AR, and AI are constantly evolving and can significantly impact game development.

Continuous Learning and Practice

COMMIT TO CONTINUOUS learning and regular practice. The field of game development is one where ongoing education and hands-on experience are vital for success.

By actively staying updated with Unreal Engine's evolution, developers can ensure their skills remain sharp, their projects are optimized, and they are well-prepared for the future of game development.

20.2. Exploring Emerging Technologies in Gaming

THE GAMING INDUSTRY is continuously influenced by emerging technologies. Understanding and integrating these technologies can provide innovative opportunities for Unreal Engine developers. This section explores various emerging technologies and their potential impact on gaming.

Virtual Reality (VR) and Its Advancements

STAY INFORMED ABOUT advancements in Virtual Reality (VR). VR technology is rapidly evolving, offering new ways to create immersive gaming experiences. Explore how Unreal Engine supports VR development.

Augmented Reality (AR) Integration

AUGMENTED REALITY (AR) is another area of rapid growth. Investigate how AR can be integrated into your games to create unique, interactive experiences that blend the real world with digital elements.

Artificial Intelligence (AI) in Game Design

ARTIFICIAL INTELLIGENCE (AI) is revolutionizing game design and player interaction. Explore how AI can be used for creating dynamic game environments, realistic NPC behaviors, and personalized player experiences.

Machine Learning and Analytics

MACHINE LEARNING AND analytics are powerful tools for understanding player behavior and improving game design. Learn how to utilize these technologies to gather insights and tailor your games to player preferences.

Blockchain and Gaming

UNDERSTAND THE IMPACT of blockchain technology on gaming. This includes areas like secure and transparent in-game transactions, digital ownership, and the integration of cryptocurrencies.

Cloud Gaming and Its Implications

STAY ABREAST OF DEVELOPMENTS in cloud gaming. Cloud technology allows games to be streamed directly to devices, which can change the way games are distributed and played.

The Internet of Things (IoT) and Gaming

EXPLORE THE POTENTIAL of the Internet of Things (IoT) in gaming. IoT devices could open new avenues for game interactions and create more connected and immersive gaming experiences.

5G Technology and Mobile Gaming

WITH THE ROLLOUT OF 5G technology, mobile gaming is expected to see significant advancements. Faster and more reliable internet can lead to more complex and engaging mobile games.

Cross-Platform Play and Development

CROSS-PLATFORM PLAY is becoming increasingly popular. Understanding how to develop games that offer seamless experiences across multiple platforms can be a significant advantage.

Wearable Gaming Technology

INVESTIGATE WEARABLE gaming technology, such as haptic feedback suits and motion tracking accessories. These devices can enhance the immersive experience of games.

Advanced Graphics and Rendering Techniques

STAY UPDATED WITH ADVANCED graphics and rendering techniques. Techniques like ray tracing are becoming more accessible and can dramatically improve the visual quality of games.

Voice Recognition and Control

EXPLORE THE INTEGRATION of voice recognition and control in games. This technology can offer new ways for players to interact with games, making them more accessible and intuitive.

Biometric Feedback in Gaming

CONSIDER THE USE OF biometric feedback in games, which can include heart rate or motion sensors to create responsive gaming experiences that adapt to the player's physical state.

Interactive Storytelling Techniques

INTERACTIVE STORYTELLING continues to evolve with technology. Look into new ways of narrative delivery that can make game stories more engaging and personalized.

Environmental and Social Impact of Gaming

UNDERSTAND THE ENVIRONMENTAL and social impact of emerging technologies in gaming. Consider sustainable practices and the ethical implications of new technologies.

Procedural Content Generation

PROCEDURAL CONTENT generation can create vast, dynamic worlds with minimal input. Learn how this technology can be utilized in Unreal Engine to enhance game development.

Photorealistic Graphics and Real-time Rendering

PHOTOREALISTIC GRAPHICS and real-time rendering are pushing the boundaries of what's visually possible in games. Explore how Unreal Engine supports these advancements.

Integration with Non-Gaming Technologies

LOOK INTO THE INTEGRATION of non-gaming technologies into gaming. This includes educational tools, fitness apps, and more, expanding the utility and appeal of games.

Continuous Learning and Experimentation

EMPHASIZE CONTINUOUS learning and experimentation with these technologies. Staying hands-on and experimenting with new tools and techniques is essential for innovation.

By exploring and integrating these emerging technologies, Unreal Engine developers can stay ahead in the competitive gaming industry, creating groundbreaking and captivating gaming experiences.

20.3. Preparing for Next-Gen Gaming Developments

AS THE GAMING INDUSTRY rapidly evolves, staying prepared for next-gen gaming developments is essential for Unreal Engine developers. This section discusses strategies to adapt to and leverage upcoming trends and advancements in gaming.

Understanding Next-Gen Hardware Capabilities

STAY INFORMED ABOUT the capabilities of next-gen gaming consoles and high-end PCs. Understanding their hardware specifications, such as processing power, graphics capabilities, and storage, can help you optimize your games for these platforms.

Leveraging Increased Computing Power

UTILIZE THE INCREASED computing power of next-gen hardware. This includes creating more detailed game worlds, enhancing AI complexity, and improving overall game performance.

Adapting to New Storage Solutions

ADAPT TO THE NEW STORAGE solutions, like SSDs, being used in next-gen systems. These can significantly reduce load times and offer new possibilities for game design and structure.

Exploring Advanced Graphics and Rendering Techniques

EXPLORE ADVANCED GRAPHICS and rendering techniques that next-gen hardware enables. Techniques like ray tracing and 4K resolutions can significantly enhance visual fidelity.

Developing for Enhanced Connectivity

TAKE ADVANTAGE OF ENHANCED connectivity features in next-gen consoles. Consider incorporating features that leverage fast internet connections, such as seamless multiplayer experiences and cloud-based gaming elements.

Integrating Next-Gen Controller Features

INTEGRATE NEXT-GEN controller features, such as haptic feedback and adaptive triggers, into your game design. These features can create more immersive and interactive gaming experiences.

Preparing for Virtual Reality (VR) Advancements

PREPARE FOR ADVANCEMENTS in VR technology. Next-gen VR is likely to offer improved visuals, better tracking, and more immersive experiences, which can open up new possibilities in VR game development.

Adapting to Changing Player Expectations

UNDERSTAND AND ADAPT to changing player expectations. Next-gen gamers may expect more immersive, realistic, and interactive gaming experiences.

Emphasizing Cross-Platform Compatibility

FOCUS ON CROSS-PLATFORM compatibility. As the gaming ecosystem becomes more interconnected, the ability to offer cross-platform play and progression can be a significant advantage.

Utilizing Cloud Gaming Technologies

UTILIZE CLOUD GAMING technologies. Cloud gaming can change the way games are distributed and played, offering opportunities for new gaming experiences.

Incorporating AI and Machine Learning

INCORPORATE ADVANCEMENTS in AI and machine learning into your games. These technologies can be used for dynamic game world creation, intelligent NPC behavior, and personalized player experiences.

Enhancing Audio Experience

PAY ATTENTION TO THE audio experience in next-gen gaming. Advances in spatial audio and 3D sound can significantly enhance immersion in games.

Implementing Efficient Resource Management

IMPLEMENT EFFICIENT resource management in your game development. Next-gen developments will require more efficient use of resources like memory and processing power.

Staying Informed About Industry Trends

REGULARLY FOLLOW INDUSTRY news and trends. Being informed about the direction in which the industry is heading can help you anticipate changes and adapt your development strategies accordingly.

Continuous Learning and Skill Upgradation

ENGAGE IN CONTINUOUS learning and skill upgradation. As new technologies and methodologies emerge, updating your skills and knowledge is essential to stay relevant.

Experimenting with New Gameplay Mechanics

EXPERIMENT WITH NEW gameplay mechanics that next-gen technologies enable. This can help you create unique gaming experiences that set your games apart.

Engaging with Developer Communities

ENGAGE WITH DEVELOPER communities focused on next-gen gaming. Community discussions and collaborations can provide insights and opportunities for learning.

Preparing for Higher Development Costs

BE PREPARED FOR POTENTIALLY higher development costs associated with next-gen games. This includes considerations for larger teams, more detailed assets, and longer development times.

Balancing Innovation with Feasibility

BALANCE INNOVATION with feasibility. While it's important to leverage next-gen capabilities, it's also crucial to consider the practical aspects of game development, such as budgets and timelines.

Exploring New Distribution Platforms

EXPLORE NEW DISTRIBUTION platforms and opportunities. Next-gen gaming may see shifts in how games are distributed and monetized.

By preparing for next-gen gaming developments, Unreal Engine developers can stay at the forefront of the industry, leveraging new technologies and trends to create groundbreaking and successful games.

20.4. Continuous Learning and Skill Development

IN THE EVER-EVOLVING field of game development, continuous learning and skill development are vital for keeping pace with new technologies and methodologies. This section provides insights into maintaining and enhancing your skills as an Unreal Engine developer.

Embracing a Mindset of Lifelong Learning

ADOPT A MINDSET OF lifelong learning. The technology and gaming industry are constantly evolving, and staying curious and open to new knowledge is key to your growth as a developer.

Regularly Updating Unreal Engine Skills

REGULARLY UPDATE YOUR Unreal Engine skills. Stay informed about the latest versions, features, and best practices in Unreal Engine development.

Expanding Knowledge Beyond Unreal Engine

EXPAND YOUR KNOWLEDGE beyond Unreal Engine. Understanding related areas like 3D modeling, animation, and audio design can enhance your game development skills.

Participating in Online Courses and Tutorials

PARTICIPATE IN ONLINE courses, tutorials, and workshops. There are numerous resources available that cover various aspects of game development and Unreal Engine.

Attending Industry Conferences and Events

ATTEND INDUSTRY CONFERENCES and events. These gatherings are great opportunities for learning from experts, networking, and staying updated with industry trends.

Engaging with Developer Communities

ENGAGE WITH DEVELOPER communities, both online and offline. Communities can be valuable resources for advice, feedback, and staying connected with industry peers.

Reading Industry Publications and Books

READ INDUSTRY PUBLICATIONS, books, and research papers. They can provide deeper insights into game development techniques, emerging technologies, and industry best practices.

Learning from Postmortems and Case Studies

LEARN FROM POSTMORTEMS and case studies of other games. Understanding the successes and failures of other projects can provide valuable lessons for your own development work.

Experimenting with New Technologies and Techniques

EXPERIMENT WITH NEW technologies and techniques in your projects. Hands-on experience is one of the best ways to understand and master new skills.

Developing Personal Projects

WORK ON PERSONAL PROJECTS. They provide a platform for experimentation, creativity, and applying new skills in a practical context.

Collaborating on Open Source Projects

CONTRIBUTE TO OPEN source projects related to game development. This can enhance your skills, expand your portfolio, and connect you with a community of developers.

Seeking Feedback and Mentoring

SEEK FEEDBACK ON YOUR work and consider finding a mentor. Constructive feedback and guidance from experienced professionals can accelerate your learning and development.

Sharing Knowledge with Others

SHARE YOUR KNOWLEDGE with others. Teaching and mentoring can reinforce your own understanding and provide a different perspective on what you know.

Staying Informed About Industry Trends

STAY INFORMED ABOUT industry trends and market demands. Understanding the current market can help you align your skill development with industry needs.

Balancing Specialization and Generalization

BALANCE SPECIALIZATION with a broad understanding of game development. While specializing in a particular area is valuable, a broad skill set can make you more versatile.

Practicing Problem-Solving and Critical Thinking

REGULARLY PRACTICE problem-solving and critical thinking. These skills are crucial in game development, where creative and technical challenges are common.

Attending Training and Certification Programs

CONSIDER ATTENDING formal training and certification programs. Certifications can add credibility to your skills and open up new professional opportunities.

Leveraging Online Resources and Forums

MAKE USE OF ONLINE resources and forums. Websites like Stack Overflow, GitHub, and Unreal Engine forums are excellent places to find information and ask questions.

Engaging in Continuous Portfolio Development

CONTINUOUSLY DEVELOP your portfolio. Keep it updated with your latest work, showcasing a range of skills and projects.

Reflecting on Personal Growth and Goals

REGULARLY REFLECT ON your personal growth and set goals for your skill development. This helps in maintaining focus and direction in your learning journey.

By committing to continuous learning and skill development, you can ensure that your abilities as an Unreal Engine developer remain sharp, relevant, and in demand in the dynamic field of game development.

20.5. Participating in the Unreal Developer Community

ACTIVE PARTICIPATION in the Unreal Developer Community is not just about staying informed; it's a crucial part of professional growth and contribution. This section highlights the importance and methods of engaging with the Unreal community.

Understanding the Value of Community Engagement

RECOGNIZE THE VALUE of engaging with the Unreal Developer Community. This engagement provides support, fosters learning, and helps in staying updated with the latest trends and best practices.

Joining Unreal Engine Forums

JOIN AND PARTICIPATE in Unreal Engine forums. These platforms are rich resources for asking questions, sharing knowledge, and connecting with other developers.

Contributing to Online Discussions

ACTIVELY CONTRIBUTE to online discussions related to Unreal Engine. Share your insights, answer questions, and engage in constructive debates to enrich the community knowledge base.

Attending Meetups and User Groups

ATTEND LOCAL MEETUPS and user groups focused on Unreal Engine. These gatherings are excellent opportunities for networking, learning from peers, and sharing your experiences.

Engaging in Social Media Groups and Channels

BE ACTIVE IN SOCIAL media groups and channels dedicated to Unreal Engine. Platforms like LinkedIn, Twitter, and Facebook host vibrant communities where news, ideas, and resources are shared.

Collaborating on Community Projects

COLLABORATE ON COMMUNITY projects or game jams. These collaborative efforts can improve your skills, expand your portfolio, and foster meaningful connections within the community.

Offering Help and Mentorship

OFFER HELP AND MENTORSHIP to others in the community. Assisting beginners or fellow developers not only contributes to the community but also enhances your own understanding of Unreal Engine.

Staying Informed About Community Events

STAY INFORMED ABOUT community events, both online and offline. Participating in workshops, webinars, and conferences can provide insights and inspiration for your own work.

Sharing Your Development Experiences

SHARE YOUR DEVELOPMENT experiences, whether they are successes or failures. Documenting and discussing your journey can help others and open up avenues for feedback and improvement.

Creating and Sharing Tutorials and Guides

CREATE AND SHARE TUTORIALS and guides. Educational content contributes significantly to the community and can establish you as a knowledgeable source in the field.

Participating in Beta Testing and Feedback Programs

PARTICIPATE IN BETA testing and feedback programs for Unreal Engine. Your contributions can help shape the future of the engine and its tools.

Writing Blogs or Articles

WRITE BLOGS OR ARTICLES about your experiences and learnings with Unreal Engine. Sharing your expertise can benefit others and enhance your professional profile.

Keeping an Open Mind to Feedback

BE OPEN TO RECEIVING and acting on feedback from the community. Constructive criticism can be invaluable for personal and professional growth.

Engaging with Epic Games' Initiatives

ENGAGE WITH INITIATIVES and contests hosted by Epic Games. These activities can challenge your skills and provide opportunities to showcase your work.

Leveraging Community Resources for Learning

MAKE USE OF COMMUNITY-generated resources for learning and problem-solving. The community offers a wealth of knowledge and innovative solutions.

Following Influential Community Members

FOLLOW INFLUENTIAL members of the Unreal community. Influencers often share valuable insights, tips, and industry news.

Volunteering for Community Activities

VOLUNTEER FOR COMMUNITY activities and events. This can include organizing meetups, moderating forums, or helping with community projects.

Contributing to Open Source Unreal Projects

CONTRIBUTE TO OPEN source projects related to Unreal Engine. Open source contributions can improve your skills and give back to the community.

Networking and Building Professional Relationships

USE COMMUNITY ENGAGEMENT as an opportunity to network and build professional relationships. Connections made through the community can lead to collaborative projects and career opportunities.

Respecting Diversity and Inclusiveness

PROMOTE AND RESPECT diversity and inclusiveness within the community. A diverse community brings different perspectives and ideas, enriching the overall experience for everyone.

By actively participating in the Unreal Developer Community, you not only gain access to a wealth of knowledge and resources but also contribute to the growth and vibrancy of the Unreal ecosystem.

www.ingramcontent.com/pod-product-compliance
Lightning Source LLC
LaVergne TN
LVHW090258210926
848480LV00001B/64